NEVER MISS A
BEAT

Also by Michael Atherton:

The ABC Book of Musical Instruments

Musical Instruments and Sound-Producing Objects of Oceania: The collections of the Australian Museum

Australian Made… Australian Played…. Handcrafted musical instruments from didjeridu to synthesizer

A Coveted Possession: The rise and fall of the piano in Australia

In Exile From St Petersburg: The life and times of Abram Saulovich Kagan, Book Publisher (with Anatol Kagan)

Poems of a Single Breath

NEVER MISS A BEAT

Michael Atherton

ASHWOOD
PUBLISHING
Tasmania

Copyright © Michael J. Atherton 2025

All rights reserved. Apart from as permitted by Australian copyright law, no part of this work may be reproduced by any means without the permission of the author. Contact the publisher for information.

ISBN-paperback: 978-1-7636921-0-7

ISBN-epub: 978-1-7636921-1-4

Published by Ashwood Publishing, Cradoc, Tasmania.
ashwoodpublishing.com.au
info@ashwoodpublishing.com.au

The verse from David Campbell's poem 'Lyrebird' is used by kind permission of the Campbell family.
The Henry Lawson verses quoted in Chapter 5 are from 'The Unknown Patient', first published in *The Bulletin*, 1915.
The quote from Ravi Shankar in Chapter 7 is from 'My Music, My Life', Simon and Schuster, 1968, p. 20.
'Synchronous Sounds: the film composer' appeared in *Sounds Australian* 25, Australian Music Centre, 1990, p. 8.

Cover design: Susan Young
Cover photo of Michael Atherton by Tod Clarke

The work of Ashwood Publishing is nurtured by the beautiful country of the Melukerdee people in the Huon Valley in southern Lutruwita / Tasmania. We acknowledge and pay respect to the traditional owners and continuing custodians of this place.

A catalogue record for this work is available from the National Library of Australia

I thank my parents, John and Gisela, for having the courage to migrate to this wonderful country. I thank the First Nations friends, colleagues, and elders who welcomed me to this country. I thank the Commonwealth for my citizenship. It is a privilege to live in multicultural Australia.

This is a true account as I remember it, but I have changed some of the names of friends and acquaintances from my earlier years to protect their privacy. Aboriginal and Torres Strait Islander people should be aware that this book mentions the names of deceased persons.

M.A.

CONTENTS

Prelude ix

1 AN ENGLISH LAD 1
   Anfield 5
   Cheshire 13
   Sir John Deane's Grammar School 27
   Father 32
   Music at school 39

2 THE POMMIE TEENAGER 45
   A new life in Australia 51
   New connections: football and music 56
   Julie 71

3 WHITE-COLLARED, SELF-SCHOOLED 79
   University 87
   Final undergraduate years, 1971–1972 100

4 MUSIC, POETRY AND MARRIAGE 105
   The Renaissance Players 106
   The Kathy Kanga Fun Show 110
   Touring with the Renaissance Players 112
   Life & relationships 117
   Performing, recording, touring 123
   Heart, Head and Hand 129
   Beginning a teaching career 130

5 HEALING MUSIC 133
   Music as therapy 137
   My practice at Rivendell 139
   Redirection 143

6 GOING FREELANCE 145
   Sirocco 145
   Composing and writing 150
   More performing opportunities 158
   China and Hong Kong 180

7 RIDICULOUSLY BUSY 187
    Atherton Tableband 188
    Winds of Solstice 190
    Marionette Theatre 195
    Composing for film and television 196
    Music for children 199
    Touring again 202
    Southern Crossings tours 208

8 CONSOLIDATION: WRITING AND RECORDING 231
    Recording 232
    Film 237
    Studies into sound and space 246
    Australian Made, Australian Played 251
    The Australian Museum and the sounds of Oceania 256
    The Mahogany Ship 258

9 MOVING INTO THE ACADEMY 263
    Music at UWS 268
    Practice and research 285

10 COLLABORATING AND DISCOVERING 295
    CD recordings: Abundance and Aurora 308
    Change at UWS 310

11 THE SCHOOL OF CONTEMPORARY ARTS 313
    Study leave, January 2001 316
    Winter of discontent 318

12 DEAN'S UNIT 321
    Sync: experiments in music technology 324
    Melismos 327
    Songs of Stone and Silence 328
    Community music 330

Coda 341

Acknowledgements 343

Glossary of Musical Instruments 345

PRELUDE

I changed my surname in 1973, informally, from Jones to Atherton. It was a big decision for me, not taken lightly but out of necessity, after several years of pondering the need to reinvent myself. I needed a new identity other than Jones.

There was nothing inherently wrong with the surname. After all, everyone tries to keep up with the Joneses, but for me, there was a need not to be identified with a student activist called Michael Jones, who was often making headlines and under the gaze of the police. Further, I wanted a new Australian identity, something that inspired me to create a personal story, shape my journey as a future Australian citizen, and, at the same time, maintain a connection with England, the country I left behind.

My change of name was also a means of distancing myself from a father with whom I had long had a turbulent relationship since puberty. The nature of the family's migration, what we left unfinished behind us, and my sense of loss and feelings of shame were palpable. I formalised the change by deed poll at the Public Solicitor's Office on 18 November 1975. It symbolised a reset and the prospect of new horizons. However, my name change was never intended to mask my now quantifiably dominant north Welsh DNA, of which I am very proud. Perhaps this explains my passion for music and poetry.

1

AN ENGLISH LAD

*Musical because we're human;
human because we're musical.*

My memories of childhood have a soundtrack. The squeak of the letterbox in the front door when the postman opened its polished flap and pushed the letters through, the paper-flop as they fell into the hallway, the clank as the shiny brass flap pinged back into place. I loved hearing my grandmother slide shillings into the slot of the gas meter under the stairs and turn the handle, sending the coins rattling into the meter's metal collection box.

There were different doorknocks at the front door, and I'm certain that my ear for music was being attuned in my early childhood. The rent collector's short, sharp knock travelled throughout the house. He came once a fortnight, sporting a leather bag strapped to his waist. His only words were 'Hello' and 'Good day now'. The coalman's arrival was different: one rat-tat, and he called out, 'Cooaal, need any cooaal?' My grandmother would scurry to the door with her purse to pay cash for a large bag of coal. He went back to his truck and heaved a heavy bag onto his back. It rested on a thick leather backplate, like armour. He panted as he carried the bag through the hallway to the kitchen and into the small coal locker. I loved hearing the shiny black lumps clunking and clacking as they tumbled out of the hessian sack, dust rising as a pile formed in the locker.

Occasionally the Anfield soundscape would include the clip-clop of a horse and cart, still operated by some milkmen or 'rag and bone men'. I recall the anarchy of horse droppings in the middle of the road, the dull thud of straw parcels of poo, sweetly pungent. My father told me that when he was ten years old, he made his pocket money following horses to collect their droppings. He walked the Anfield streets, calling out 'Horse manure for your garden, sixpence a bucket.'

The letterbox lid would also squeak when my grandfather's *Liverpool Echo* arrived. The paperboy pushed this folded tabloid icon only half into the door. I could see the blood-red Liver Bird logo visible on the top. My grandfather would sit quietly in the living room, picking his teams for a bet in the Saturday football pools while the clock ticked loudly on the mantelpiece. Hearing the paper arrive in the letterbox, he would rise from his worn leather armchair and shuffle into the hall in the dwindling light of a wintry afternoon. He might cough a few times as he stooped to collect the paper before going back to the living room, where he drew the faded mesh curtains. Sliding back into his chair to read the *Echo*, he would lick his thumb to help turn through the pages to the racehorse form guide. I remember him as a passive and benign person, sipping tea and occasionally fumbling for a packet of large white tablets which he called 'pikes' after the large predatory freshwater fish, because they were big and nasty. My grandmother told me he took them because he had succumbed to tuberculosis.

Meanwhile, sausages sizzled in the kitchen, and the pungent aroma of the burning onions would waft into the living room. My grandmother prepared the evening meals, which mostly included baked beans, eggs, sausages, fried potatoes, and toasted slices of bread and dripping. She seemed to spend most of her time in the kitchen, with its chipped, red-tiled floor, faded glossy eggshell walls and green-painted skirting boards.

By the age of five, I was both fascinated and frightened when the winter winds sang mysteriously in the downpipe of the empty bath. The enamel around the plughole was stained brown from years of dripping copper taps. The sound was eerie, otherworldly, like the wind in telegraph wires. Also, the water pipes shuddered and hammered when the taps were turned on and water coursed through them. After my bath, the water swirled before being sucked down a devouring plughole while I watched, wrapped in a towel, waiting to be carried downstairs to dry off in front of the coal fire in the living room.

A typical winter sound of my Liverpool childhood was the busy scraping of shovels on footpaths to clear snow and ice. There was also a magical silence in the frosty creatures hanging on the clothesline. Clothes left out froze overnight to become starkly beautiful shapes against a backdrop of leafless trees etched out of the snow-sky background. The short winter days brought the discontent of driving sleet, with the occasional falls of soot down the smoky chimney and the static crackle of Grandpa's wireless. Around 5 pm on weekdays, there was a growing number of footsteps on the footpath. Weary blue-collar workers were tramping home to their council houses and the streetlamps would flicker and snap on.

I drew my first breath on 17 February 1950 in a Liverpool maternity hospital at 147a Mill Road, Everton: the same hospital where, on 3 May 1941, German bombs had rained down, killing 78 nurses, mothers, and babies. The Luftwaffe wanted to obliterate Liverpool because it was the second major city in England and a strategic port serving Atlantic shipping. I have a sister, Jennifer (b.1951) and three brothers: Anthony (b.1958), Christopher (b.1959), and Andrew (b.1961).

My father, John Frederick Jones (1920–2006), was born in Liverpool, the second of six children. During World War II he was a gunner on merchant ships in the North Atlantic; he served with the Liverpool Regiment at the Normandy landing in 1944. After the war, my father worked with the occupying allied forces in Germany, where he met my mother, Gisela Olinda Marga Oppermann (1926–2009), born in Sebexen, Saxony. They married on 10 July 1948 in Goslar, a hamlet in the picturesque Harz Mountains. They wore splendid clothes made by her uncle Wilhelm, a successful tailor in Hanover. My parents were young, thankful to be alive, and relaxed in post-war peacetime, drawn together as people were – singing and dancing again, and enjoying summers free from the hell of war.

My parents, John and Gisela Jones, were married in Goslar, Germany, in 1948.

Photos taken in 1947 show my mother was a beautiful woman. She had grown up in a Germany gripped by National Socialism and was thirteen years old at the beginning of the war. Her father Hermann, a tall, bespectacled railways inspector, wanted her to do well in life. During the war, she went to a private school in Göttingen, where she studied English, book-keeping, shorthand, and business. At seventeen, she had to work in a military office, including fingerprinting in Göttingen town hall, to check who was coming in and out of town. They also sent her to Prague to do book-keeping. She said she lived in a chateau which 'when covered in snow, looked like Camelot'. Towards the end of the war, she saw her two conscripted brothers, Hermann and Günter, return emaciated from the Russian front. Both had been prisoners of war. All her family survived, and a new chapter began for Gisela.

In 1949, as the young German wife of a returned English soldier, it would have been difficult for Gisela to leave her parents and siblings and move into a small council house in war-ravaged Liverpool. She was a brave woman to accompany my father into a community that was so strongly anti-German.

Anfield

While I can't remember the hour I was born, my mother told me it was a hard labour that lasted thirty-six hours. I was a whopping lad delivered with the aid of forceps. My father, as per the standard routine, was neither seen nor heard throughout the ordeal. He waited in the wings. Eventually, I arrived with ten fingers, ten toes, hair and instantly hungry. My parents swaddled me and took me by taxi to my grandparents' council house in Anfield, a modest semi-detached 3-up and 2-downer at the end of a row.

They gave me a fanfare as I entered the front door, the firstborn of John and Gisela. I'm certain that my Catholic grandmother was already planning my baptism and enrolment at All Saints Primary. My arrival increased the population at 4 Westcombe Road to seven: my grandparents, my uncles Arthur and Frank, my parents, and myself. Photos show me lovingly cuddled by my tired-looking and perplexed mother, adjusting to life in a sombre Liverpool still piled with rubble from World War II. I smiled a lot, even when I was left outside in a posh pram on the snow-covered patch of grass between the front door and the privet hedge. My mother said I would listen to the chirruping sparrows.

Thirteen months later we increased to eight when my sister, Jenny, was born. As toddlers, we worked out that men's deeper voices dominated the household. My mother spoke good English with a German accent but always deferred to my father, who, like his own father and brothers, spoke in a Scouse accent.

As soon as I could walk, I wanted to visit the air-raid shelter dug into the small garden. Looking over hedges and fences, one saw shelters in most gardens, hastily constructed during the war. I called ours the cubby house, but when told of its real purpose, I was afraid that air-raid sirens might sound again, and we would be sardined into a shelter. It was satisfying for my uncles when they eventually demolished the shelter and filled in the hole before planting lawn seeds into the soil.

I wear my Uncle Arthur's Territorial Army beret and backpack, Liverpool, United Kingdom, 1953. The leather shorts and braces were a gift from German grandparents.
Photo: Arthur Jones

Grandma: Mass and Piano

Like Stephen Daedalus in James Joyce's *Portrait of the Artist as a Young Man*, I experienced epiphanies, especially sonic ones. They would later influence my life in music. The roar of the ocean, a steam loco racing out of a tunnel, the sound of a new cricket ball rushing past my ear and the chanting of football crowds were all deeply meaningful, emotional, and memorable in my world. Some were synaesthetic, such as my first experience of the Catholic mass. The context included the choice of my first school and a sectarian tussle.

My grandmother, Mary Ann Brunton, was of Liverpool-Irish stock. She was a staunch Catholic who attended church every Sunday, crossed herself several times a day, said Hail Marys, never swore, never drank, and often mentioned Purgatory. She was a full-time carer and a true battler, washing, cleaning, ironing, cooking, and praying for her family with unreserved motherly love and affection. She must have had concerns about the souls of the men at Westcombe Road. But she was loving and always had a gentle smile despite the years of hard work coping with so many males around her – my grandfather, my father, and my uncles, Frank and Arthur. Her life was struggling with bags of shopping, loading the copper to wash the sheets, making food and tea. I never saw her sitting down watching TV, or reading the newspaper, going to the football, or putting on a bet.

According to my grandmother, God intended that my first school would be All Saints Catholic Primary. However, my German mother, used as she was to mountains, forest light and village life, found All Saints Anfield to be a depressing clump of drab buildings. She took me instead to Pinehurst Avenue School, a little primary school around the corner from where we lived. It was modest and newly painted and not openly sectarian. I liked the school, its warm classrooms, smelling of paper, glue, and chalk, with classes sitting on little chairs doing things.

Grandma was disappointed and probably worried that I could

become a Protestant. I continued to go to Pinehurst Avenue, but on the condition that Grandma could wake me early for Sunday Mass, to ensure I wouldn't lapse. After all, my mother was a non-practising Evangelical Lutheran and my paternal grandfather a Welsh Methodist whose true religion was gambling. Notwithstanding such perils, I discovered the theatre of the Catholic Mass in Latin.

The priest wore a starched white smock, with gold braiding around the red and green velvet cloth. There were polished candelabra. There was chanting, kneeling, the ringing of a bell and the sound of feet shuffling across the marble floor as communicants went forward for the transubstantiation. During the silences, I heard pigeons in the rafters and the sound of the windchest pumps and the 'chiff' of organ pipes, noting the delay between the organist's playing and the congregation's singing. The murmur of prayers followed the cadential *Amen* which filled the church. I smelled the incense wafting near me.

Throughout the Mass, my grandmother instructed when to kneel, how to cross myself, and when to say amen. Things happened in threes: Hail Mary three times; *Sanctus Sanctus Sanctus*; the Trinity; heaven, purgatory, and hell; and three points on the cross. All Saints School was never mentioned again. My grandmother was happy that I went to church while the men at Westcombe Road slept off their hangovers.

My grandmother had an upright piano in the living room of our minuscule terrace house, although I never heard my parents or relatives play it. I taught myself a scale and played a few tunes, one finger at a time. It was immediately satisfying because a piano is so forgiving to the beginner. Soon I was sitting at the piano improvising and switched to playing and humming the hymn 'All People That on Earth Do Dwell'. Within a few seconds my overly pious grandmother came running into the room in a flour-covered apron and with sausages in her hand, presumably destined for a lard-filled frying pan in the kitchen. 'That's Protestant music, you shouldn't be playing that!' Bewildered, I stopped, not wishing to upset her, and told her we sang it often in school. *Mea culpa*, I was playing Protestant hymns on a Catholic piano!

Grandma's piano (2012)

Grandma's piano –
That musty, woody smell
born of dust,
humidity and rising damp.

Old furniture with ambience and character.
Evidence of mice living inside,
borers, too, voracious feeders
that can topple a piano
into a pile of wood.

Keys yellowing, ivory imbued
with the touch of fingers,
young and old,
chasing myriad scales and arpeggios.

Grandma's gone, and the piano is silent in the corner
A choice beckons: take it to the tip
or cherish a dust-gathering heirloom?

My uncles, Frank and Arthur, were generous with their time for Jenny and me. They gave us pocket money – a tanner (sixpence), a bob (shilling), a florin (two shillings), even half a crown (two shillings and sixpence). At Christmas, they gave us lovely presents and filled our stockings with sweeties (lollies) and shiny coppers (pennies). They would shine the pennies by pushing them into raw potatoes and leaving them for a week or two, or enough time for the oxalic acid in the potato to react with copper and remove its greenish-brown patina, making them look shiny and new. I loved impersonating my uncles by dressing up in their Mackintosh raincoats (macs) and trilby hats. Their garments had a distinctive smell of cigarettes, mixed with Brylcreem hair oil and suffused with a musty smell of perspiration – all significant scents.

Frank worked in the public service and spoke slowly in measured tones; he never raised his voice. His favourite activity was reading the *Oxford English Dictionary* for hours at a time. He never married but took holidays with his mates to places in Italy, Spain, and Greece. His best friend was Billy Meffin, a jovial, outgoing, ruddy-faced Liverpool-Welshman. Billy complemented Frank, who sometimes carried an air of sadness behind his smile. His *melancholia* (a more common term for depression in the 1950s) saw him in and out of hospital care at different stages of his life. I remember Arthur told me that my father carried Frank everywhere when he was a young boy and fought his playground battles for him.

Arthur worked for Hornby-Meccano as a joiner. As a five-year-old, I waited for him every day at the gate at 4:30 pm. Even if tired, he always gave me a crossbar ride around the block; I remember feeling secure with him balancing the two of us. And the same moment we got in the door, I would pester him to open his bag, to see what he had inside. He brought home little offcuts from his sawing at work and taught me to make simple objects with a fretsaw, a hammer, wood glue, and a handful of nails. I spent more time with Arthur than with my father.

Arthur made us toy tanks from bobbins (wooden cotton reels). He would cut notches in the rims of a bobbin to make serrated edges like those on a tank. An elastic band was passed through the bobbin hole and secured at one end to a piece of old pencil that exceeded the diameter of the bobbin. The elastic was secured at the other end with a matchstick positioned over a small piece of candle. To make the tank move, we wound the pencil, tightening the elastic. We placed the tank on the table and watched the elastic untwist, the pencil moving with the help of the wax. It turned the bobbin reel, and the tank moved. We delighted in watching our machines tortoise their way across the kitchen table. Arthur could make anything. He knew so much about engines and tools.

On summer Saturdays, I would hear the clanking rhythms of the push lawnmower as Arthur mowed our little patch of lawn, and I watched the metal, tank-like wheels sinking into the lush grass. Meanwhile, Frank attended to the flower beds and the privet hedges, the snapping of his shears a counterpoint to Arthur's mowing. I remember the glorious flowerbeds in summer, all grown from seeds. There were sweet peas, night-scented stock, marigolds, pansies, and nasturtiums. Arthur and Frank were such practical men, with a gift for solving problems, and I wanted to be like them.

Arthur was intelligent and self-educated. His knowledge of politics and world affairs was formidable. When I was eleven years old, he took me on my first holiday away from my immediate family. This was a fabulous experience. He hired a Morris Mini-Minor, and he and my Aunt Tilly took me to Cornwall. I sat in the back like a king as we drove south, passing through towns and villages, just the three of us. It was an epic journey from the northwest to the tip of the southwest of England.

We stayed in a caravan at Praa Sands, a lovely white sand beach in Cornwall. The weather was beautiful; paddling in the sea was bracing, and ice cream never tasted so good. We'd meet up with my Aunt Margaret, her husband, Jack Gilbert, and their twins, my cousins Michael and Brian. Jack was Cornish, olive-skinned and always smiling. There were many accents in my life then: Arthur and Margaret with their Scouse accents, Tilly with her Belfast-Irish intonation, Jack with his Cornish lilt, and my mother's German accent.

It was on this Cornwall holiday that I first heard talk about Australia. It came while Australian cricketers were thrashing England in a test match. I remember the names of Davidson, Benaud, Simpson, Grout, and 'Slasher' Mackay. Who could ever forget a name like that? I learned that Australia was a big, wide-open place where people went to start a new life. Arthur said my father talked occasionally about going to Australia, much to the annoyance of my grandmother.

The blue half of the 'pool

On a Saturday afternoon in football season, you could hear the crowd roar miles away when a goal was scored at either Goodison or Anfield. It sounded like a marauding army. The mid-1960s at Merseyside football matches were marked by the playing of Mersey sound hits before and after the games. The PA systems shook with the Beatles, the Searchers, Cilla Black and, of course, Gerry and the Pacemakers. These songs were tribal, anthemic, and uplifting. Music transformed the 1960s and the city of Liverpool. The Pacemakers' 'You'll Never Walk Alone' remains the spiritual anthem of Liverpool FC.

It was Uncle Frank who ensured that I became an Evertonian, a 'Blue'. Frank took me to games with Billy Meffin. They bought me programs and lollies and taught me about Merseyside football rivalry. We were Evertonian blue shirts. Goodison Park was our hallowed turf. The red shirts were Liverpool Football Club, whose supporters worshipped Anfield. A derby game between both teams was an intense and volatile day in a city's calendar. It gave a buzz to Saturday. The *Liverpool Echo* amplified the pre-match rivalry and made predictions about players and the outcome. The pubs close to the grounds remained full until 2:45 pm, when throngs of intoxicated men poured onto the footpaths to dash the ground. They formed long queues, mindful of the mounted police who controlled them with their push and shove moves. The atmosphere was electric with cheering, songs, taunts, rattling noisemakers and the calling of 'Program, program, get your program!'

The police horses worked in pairs to marshal the crowd in the streets around the football grounds. The police riders wore immaculate uniforms and leather boots. Their leather saddles were highly polished, and their stirrups gleamed.

I usually stood in the terraces at Goodison Park with my father and Uncle Frank. Everywhere, men with cigarettes between their lips or between nicotine-stained fingers surrounded me. They wore flat caps and Everton scarves and had foul, beery breath. I often struggled to see the game through or above the tightly pressed crowd. The game kicked off at 3:15 pm and most of the men close by had probably drunk several pints of beer. It was difficult to find a way to a urinal in such a tightly packed crowd. Some men would relieve themselves at the back of the stand or even where they stood. Rivulets of steaming urine raced down the wooden steps between my feet. On one occasion, being a kid wearing shorts, I felt a warmth trickling down my calves. A 'Liverpool hot leg' christened me without choice while I was watching the game on the field. My father was angry, but there was nothing he or I could do. My baptism. There were no CCTV cameras in those days nor police officers nearby, just the crowd baying for the blood of the opposition and shouting for their heroes. It wasn't unique to Liverpool. At Ibrox Park, the home of the Rangers, they called it the 'Glasgow hot leg'.

Cheshire

The day came in 1955 that we – my parents, Jenny and I – left Liverpool to be closer to my father's work. Uncle Arthur rented a car and helped us to transport some of our items. We moved to the village of Barnton, Cheshire, where we stayed with Aunt Margaret and her family.

My father commenced a new clerical job in the shipping department at ICI Winnington. I went to school in Barnton, but I can't remember much about it except for a girl who gave me a pomegranate to eat. She showed me how to use a needle to pick out the seeds. This was an exotic delight for the egg and chips junkie that I had become. The pomegranate was a new experience that symbolised life away from Liverpool – silver birch trees in the garden, cows in nearby fields, and woods and forests to walk in for fresh air. My Scouse accent melded into the gentler twang of Cheshire. Three months later we moved again, this time to Sandiway, not far from Northwich, a delightful market town in the heart of the county.

***

We rented a freshly painted council house: 1 Beech Close, Sandiway. Friendly neighbours gave us seedlings and vegetables from their greenhouses. They had pets, and bird boxes nailed to trees. The world seemed a brighter, more benign place after the claustrophobia of eight souls living in a small semi-detached house in Westcombe Road. Unfortunately, my mother disliked animals in the house. Both my parents were obsessed with hygiene. The world was a germ-ridden place. Crapping, slobbering dogs and piddling, sycophantic cats were to be avoided. However, my sister and I briefly shared a rabbit and a guinea pig. Both managed to escape.

I spent happy years attending the new local primary school. It was a five-minute walk from home and under the direction of the Cheshire Education Authority. The teachers were relaxed. Most arrived every morning on bicycles. The headmaster walked to school from a council house not far from ours. Back in Liverpool our neighbourhood was the street and not much further. Here the open space and the friendliness of the locals were a joy. The school had a playing field with football goalposts. It doubled as a cricket oval and athletics track in the summer months. We had free milk and a hot lunch every day at a small cost. I still have some of my primary school reports, awards, and badges. I can almost smell the school paint, the exercise books, the school canteen, and the smoke of strong cigarettes wafting out of the teachers' staffroom. I found it tough on the sports field, but I looked forward to school on most days. I judge my satisfaction from the fact that I can remember some teachers' names, including Miss Bettany, Mrs Armitage, Miss Kinvig, Mr Gallimore and the Headmaster, Mr Powell.

One unhappy memory of school life, however, was the teasing and bullying about being born of a German mother. Understandably, the suspicion towards the German people would take a long time to decline. Some kids called me a Nazi, but I did my best to ignore this. When my German grandparents came to stay with us in Cheshire, I looked forward to seeing them but didn't want to advertise their presence. Hermann and Bertha Oppermann couldn't say more than a few words of English.

There was a cultural shift in our house while they were with us. They shared the cooking, and we were treated to German dishes that featured mince, cabbage, onions, and herbs. Coffee grounds provided a new aroma in the kitchen. Bertha, whom I called Oma, prepared potato salads, rice dishes, stewed apples, and pears. She brought her plum jam from Germany. There was liver sausage, pumpernickel bread and *pfeffernusse* biscuits. Oma was very affectionate. Hermann, whom I called Opa, was a towering physical presence next to my father. He scared me. I didn't know much about his life, although my Aunt Christa, my mother's sister, told me that he was detained for a week during the war. The local command thought he might have been Jewish or anti-Nazi. There was suspicion about the surname Oppermann because it was originally a Jewish surname. He was released and went back to work for the railways.

While my father was at work, Hermann was mostly in the garden, weeding and planting. Opa was a fix-it man. He put his hand to everything that needed repairing and more. He lime-washed paths and repaired our swing. One Saturday morning he came in from the garden and asked my mother for nails. My father said we didn't have any; Hermann demanded we get some, and I was given the responsibility of taking him to the village hardware store. I would be his guide and translator. I asked my mother for a couple of phrases in German for 'Opa, this way please?', 'How many nails do we need?', 'Let me count the money' and 'We can go now.'

Off we strode in the morning sun to the shopping village. He was wearing his black beret and a collarless white shirt with rolled-up sleeves. Handmade leather braces held up his navy work trousers. He wore round-rimmed glasses close to the tip of his nose and nursed a half-smoked cigar between his full lips. No one in rural Cheshire looked remotely like my Opa. I dreaded being confronted by kids from my class. I wrote this poem years later:

Mein Opa, Hermann Oppermann, comes to Cheshire

'Er war so laut'
when he spoke his booming German at me and the
   shopkeeper.
'Ich will ein paar Nägel?'

Mein Opa, Hermann Oppermann.
All he wanted was nails for the fence.
Remonstrating, 'Nails,' with the intimidated
   shopkeeper.

Mein Opa, Hermann Oppermann.
After dinner, out-schnapps-ing my beer-drinking father
nonplussed by Hermann's table-thumping hands.

Mein Opa, Hermann Oppermann.
Clocking me 'auf dem Kopf' when I stole a puff from
   his cigar.
Everyone laughed at my embarrassment.

Mein Opa, Hermann Oppermann.
Leading me on a brisk hike
deep into the Harz Mountains.
How I marvelled at his difference from others.

Mein Opa, Hermann Oppermann.
'Echt Deutsch' my mother's father, a big man, like a Prussian guard,
now Bahnhof inspector retired.

Mein Opa, Hermann Oppermann.
He was so loud and intense; it frightened me.
Shiny black boots, tramping into the shop.

Mein Opa, Hermann Oppermann.
Round-rimmed spectacles, cigar-fuming fleshy lips,
forearms like tree trunks, he wore a dark blue beret.

Mein Opa, Hermann Oppermann.
In navy blue, silver buttons, immaculate braces and grey stubbled chin,
thumping the counter, asking for 'Nägel, bitte?'

Mein Opa, Hermann Oppermann
In just one day, he white-washed all the brick paths,
repaired a fence, tilled the veggie patch, drank a bottle of Schnapps,
and spoke for hours!

In 1962, we moved to 9 Manor Road, Cuddington, a suburb adjacent to Sandiway. The family was expanding quickly, with my brothers Anthony, Christopher, and Andrew born in the space of four years between 1958 and 1961. Time for a larger house. We gained an extra bedroom, a garage space, an outdoor coal house and a bigger garden with silver birch trees. We had hawthorn and privet hedges and grew vegetables including potatoes, marrows, carrots, green beans, lettuce, and shallots.

The four-bedroom house became a full house for a family of seven. My mother felt tired most days. My father was full of doom. They bickered regularly. I turned inward, deeply troubled, and often pessimistic. My schoolwork suffered.

My closest friends came mostly from one- or two-child families. They had watercress on their sandwiches and went on summer holidays. They got new bikes for birthdays. While their parents owned cars, I had to pester my father to pay for my school lunch. Visits from Arthur and Tilly were not only a solace and joy but a respite from the unhappy atmosphere at home. I was a sensitive kid and found it hard to handle criticism. I got a lot at home from my father. Rebellion never entered my head. I did what I was told, and that was that, although my face must have shown my displeasure at some of his demands. My father made a big thing about his deprivation and hardship as a child and adolescent. He wanted me to have a taste of the same because, to him, it was the way to build character. I felt he gave me more chores than other parents. There were stormy days between us, and the train ride to Liverpool became my escape route. I ran away to Liverpool twice. I developed severe tonsillitis on the last occasion, became delirious with fever and barely remember being driven back to Sandiway by Uncle Arthur. My father was still angry with me for leaving, and I overheard my uncle saying, 'Don't be so hard on him, John.'

Snow time
Winter was more fun for kids in mid-Cheshire than Liverpool. There were great places to play in the snow. Most kids built their own sled. My grandparents sent us a German *Holzschlitten*, a mahogany sled made for one adult or two kids. Local kids made fun of it – calling it the rocking horse. It was light and was very fast. We gathered at a place called 'Granny's Hump' to join in impromptu sled competitions. A solo rider had to lie face down on their sled and go down the big hill. They had to dangle their feet over the back of the sled to steer by dragging a gum-booted foot in the snow to turn or act as a brake. I made the detractors eat their words about my 'rocking horse', which always went faster and further. However, some of the

local sleds were more fun. They built them from planks of wood to support several kids. Tipping the sleds or ploughing them into snowdrifts was unsurpassed.

I spent hours in the snow building ramps to shoot over when going downhill. I could sit on the sled, stand on it and go down backwards. Sometimes we went down Granny's Hump on baking trays, spinning around on the way down. There were so many rosy cheeks, runny noses, and cold feet. You were often so cold that when you came home and jumped into the bath, the sudden change stung your skin and made you lobster red. I was often reluctant to come home until dark, extracting as much of the daylight as possible. I couldn't wait for the next day, especially if there was new snow overnight.

Fresh snow meant snowballs. You might be walking home when out of nowhere, came a volley of snowballs. Ambushed again, probably by kids who had a ready-made stockpile of 'ammo', you responded by gathering snow and launching as many snowballs back as you received. Some delinquent types put stones inside the snowball. These hurt, as did snowballs made from ice. When the cold set in after the snowfall, we stamped on the snow to make slides on the footpaths and skated on them in our shoes. We took a long run-up and then slid to see who could go the furthest. The slide improved as more people slid on it.

Heroes and villains

When I was ten, I discovered Robin Hood, as portrayed by English actor Richard Green. Robin was a hero, an outlaw, and a friend of the poor. He looked after his band in the forest. The TV program *William Tell* also captured my interest. I made longbows for my Robin Hood fantasies and crossbows for my William Tell re-enactments.

I made catapults, and someone showed me how to make a Zulu *assegai*, a short spear or dart launched with a single string, like an

Australian Aboriginal woomera. I used bamboo and carefully split one end into four and inserted four cardboard arrow flights. I could carve a point at the other end. Sometimes I included a metal weight to improve the performance of the assegai.

A crossbow was more difficult to make than a longbow, but it was more interesting because it had a trigger mechanism for releasing the string. I never perfected my trigger. The arrows or bolts were short and easy to make. They looked and sounded deadly whacking into a shed door. My parents warned me often about the risk of poking out someone's eye or breaking a window.

My next weapon carried the same risks: I pestered my parents for an air rifle. My father said no, but I coerced my mother to convince him. After all, he told me that he had won prizes for his shooting during military service. With my birthday approaching, my mother ordered an air rifle through a mail-order catalogue.

The rifle arrived in the mail while my father was at work. I unpacked it and went into the garden to shoot at jam tins. My father came home after work with a brown package under his arm. He saw the mail-order rifle and was very annoyed because he had not approved it and said that it wasn't a rifle, it had a smooth rather than a spiral bore. He then produced a superior air rifle from his package, a 'Diana' model, named after the goddess of hunting. It surprised my mother to find that he had relented. We boxed up the mail-order gun in its packaging to be returned to the mail-order company forthwith.

After dinner, my father and I practised shooting at a bullseye target hung up inside the laundry. Occasionally, we missed and hit the wall, much to my mother's dismay.

Air rifles required a licence obtainable from the local police station, allowing one to carry a gun, say from the house to a woodland. My shooting enthusiasm was also shared with Peter Horsfield, an older boy who lived across my road. His parents were very active sailors. They loved motorbikes and fixing cars. Peter followed all his parents' interests. He owned a Diana air rifle. He introduced me to shooting birds. One day we went too far. I put bread out on the lawn, and we waited to pick off starlings as they flew in. My mother severely chastised me, and rightly so. The bloodbath was appalling. I never shot at birds again.

Meanwhile, Peter graduated to a 12-gauge shotgun. He had an agreement with local farmers to shoot crows that menaced their crops. I was impressed but forbidden to go with him because of the risk of live ammunition. I stuck with the air rifle and sometimes took it fishing to fill in time when the bites were slow. I liked to watch and listen to airgun pellets hitting or skimming across the lake. Ceramic relays on telegraph poles were suitable targets, as were garbage tins and inflated balloons.

Summer walks and other recollections

Encouraged by my father, because we didn't own a car, walking became a frequent pastime on summer evenings and weekends. Our favourite walk was via Granny's Hump, where we played with our toboggan in winter. Granny's Hump led to paths through woodlands and villages. We used right of way paths between fenced-in fields. We crossed stiles, walked up and down hills, ambled through bluebell-covered woods and explored streams that led to a millpond. After Liverpool, the fresh air was blissful on summer evenings when we picked the bluebells and other wildflowers or paddled in the streams.

On warm, summer Sunday afternoons, my sister and I sometimes walked through the lanes of Cuddington to reach a tiny shop where we bought lemonade. On the way, we picked wild blackberries growing in the laneways. We took some home to serve with fresh cream or to make into jam.

I gathered horse chestnuts when in season, not to eat but for playing a game called conkers. We made a hole in a horse chestnut and passed a string through it and made a knot. It was ready for battle. One took turns swiping at an adversary's conker with one's own. To win, one had to smash an opponent's conker.

Some horse chestnut trees had abundant seedpods that were high in the foliage. I threw heavy sticks up into the branches to knock them down. Thinking that 'bigger was better', I chased after the largest chestnuts, because they would have more weight in them. One could become a local legend in conker season. But some science was needed. New conkers, no matter how big, were softer and greener inside than the older, seasoned ones. The secret to becoming a conker champion was to use an older, harder conker, which was seasoned by soaking it in vinegar for a week or more. I learned that some small, well-seasoned conkers could take out the big ones.

Glass marbles was another duelling sport at school and on the housing estates. We played for keeps. Some kids came to school with pockets full of marbles and went home with nothing. Ball bearings augmented one's cache of glass marbles. You could wager several glass marbles for a good ball bearing.

One joy of childhood was the summer twilight. In midsummer, it went dark at 10 pm. This meant all kinds of recreation after dinner, or 'tea' as we called it in Cheshire. I loved roller-skating, rounders, and football nearly all year round. We shared a lot of things. Television certainly changed that. We didn't get ours right away, so I watched it at a friend's house. We had a valve radio when I was a child. I peered into its open back, fascinated with the glowing light in the valves and the smell of the Bakelite case. It was a magic machine. I turned the dial to find different stations or switched wavebands from short, medium to long, listening to Morse code signals from ships. As an adolescent in the 1960s, I listened to the so-called 'pirate radio stations' that played the latest pop music broadcast from boats in the English Channel or off the West Coast. Transistor radios powered by batteries came on the market. It was liberating to carry the 'trannie' and hear favourite songs broadcast by the pirate stations because they focused on popular music. We called them pirate stations because the broadcasts came from boats and thus were not subject to licences and taxes.

On weekends and during holidays, mothers in the 1950s and 1960s were unlike the 'helicopter parents' of today. Your mum told you to 'go outside and play and be back by teatime'. If it was raining you wore a duffle coat, if it was snowing you donned a balaclava and woollen gloves. Whatever the case, you went outside and played! You might knock on a friend's door or find them in a local park. There was no slide too high, no swing you couldn't jump off. You got bumps, scrapes, cuts, and bruises. You 'scrumped' apples and plums, looking out for the local bobby riding his bike. You took your punishment at home and school because you deserved it. You played doctor-nurse, and you tried smoking cigarettes. You shared your pennies, chewing gum and chocolate bars. Play was an adventure, and a mystery.

We worked in groups to collect wood, old orange boxes and even bits of discarded furniture to build our bonfires for Guy Fawkes night. As the night drew near, we guarded our bonfire to stop others from lighting it. We made our 'Guy' from newspaper and straw stuffed into old pyjamas or jeans and shirts tied at the legs and cuffs. We came out before dark to hoist Guy into the bonfire. Soon, the neighbourhood was glowing with orange and yellow smoke and embers. Rockets crisscrossed the sky and loud firework explosions could be heard beyond midnight. Bonfires also provided hot ash to roast chestnuts and cook potatoes wrapped in foil.

The risk of being burned by bonfires or blinded by fireworks never stopped our parents from giving us free rein. There were no permits, no 'firies' at hand, no safety glasses, no ambulances standing by. We were careful but accidents happened. I suspect I sustained some permanent hearing loss in my ear due to my silly act of holding the ends of a penny 'banger' (cracker) between my fingernails. For a dare, I would light the fuse, stretch out my arm to point the firework away from my body, and wait for the explosion.

Train travel and train spotting

Travel between Sandiway or Cuddington to visit our relatives in Liverpool was always an exciting adventure. We walked to Chester Road to catch a Northwich bus. We alighted at the station in the village of Hartford to catch the train for Liverpool. I remember stops, including Acton Bridge and Runcorn, where you could look west towards the escarpments of the Wirral Peninsula. My father told me that most of the surrounding land was undersea some millions of years ago. After Runcorn, we crossed the Mersey from Cheshire into Lancashire. I noticed the build-up of heavy industry. All kinds of steam and yellow-grey smoke belched into the air. Everywhere was greyness, waste, rusting pipes, and crisscrossing railway lines. Depressing if you think about it but fascinating for a young boy. Here was the evidence of post-war productivity and its detritus. This was the landscape of the industrial revolution.

The train journey finished at Liverpool Lime Street Station after a series of long and dripping tunnels. You opened the carriage door and were engulfed by the puff and hiss of steam locomotives, the footsteps on the platform in counterpoint with whistling guards and porters pushing barrows. The loud chugging of the boilers releasing steam, and the sudden metallic clanking of tender and carriages being coupled were unsurpassed.

We left the station to catch a green double-decker bus and alighted in Townsend Lane, Anfield. From there it was a short walk along Priory Road to the corner of Manningham and Westcombe, where we turned right and reached the gate of Number 4. The outward journey to Liverpool was the most fun, especially if we were surprising my grandmother. We were always welcome, and uncles Arthur and Frank doted on us immediately.

Trainspotting was a pastime in the early 1960s not to be confused with the 1996 film of Irvine Welsh's novel. I particularly enjoyed the steam locomotives on the Liverpool line and became a regular train spotter. As a lad growing up in Northwich, I went out all-weather on my rickety self-made bike to wait near viaducts and bridges, to spot trains. It was a non-stop cavalcade of Jubilees, Black Fives, Eight Freights, Jintys, Dub-Dees, Standard Nines, Crabs and Four-Fs with the occasional Royal Scot or Patriot. Trains all had numbers, and their numbers were printed in an Ian Allan Publishing train spotter's book. You collected the numbers and underlined them. A new sighting was a 'cop'. Express locomotives had names of famous regiments, warships, naval heroes like Nelson, racehorses, far-flung parts of the British Empire like the Solomon Islands and Tonga. When a train passed, I checked my books for their number and class. I ruled a line under the entry. How I wish I had but one of those books now, with all the lines ruled under a plethora of numbers.

Football and cricket

My first cricket match was at primary school when I was in Fifth Class, playing against the Sixth Class boys. I was a good bowler and fielder but average with the bat, hence I batted down the order. I could deal with spin but wasn't much good with short ball pace. I didn't have any footwork. One relied on natural talent, as there was little, if any, coaching like today. Teachers organised the game, picked the players, suggested fielding positions, and umpired. I played cricket out of school with friends from the housing estate wherever we could find some space. We used a cardboard box for stumps and played with a tennis ball.

I captained the Cuddington County Primary cricket team in my final year. This was a great honour, given we played matches against the other local schools. I'll never forget winning my first toss and deciding to bowl against a visiting school. I bowled someone out first ball. Everyone cheered, and we were off to a flyer. It was a limited-over game, and we won easily by hitting fours to all our short boundaries. It was good to be on the winning side and to win away games. Playing against another school meant playing in different conditions. The pitches might be larger or smaller, the grass different according to the mowing. The line markings were lime white or creosote, and the size of the grounds varied. Once I recall picking up a ball that was smaller than what I was used to. It had a pronounced seam, and it was harder. I loved the grip I could get on it and enjoyed hearing it hit into the stumps.

Protection was minimal. 'Don't get hit' was the rule. There were no helmets or boxes, only pads and flimsy gloves with thin strips of spikey rubber sewn on the finger tubes. We wore white shorts, white shirts and plimsolls, with or without socks.

I became obsessed with football and cricket. Just two of the four seasons captured my interest: winter going into spring for football and summer into autumn for cricket. My paternal grandfather once visited. My father offered to show him around Northwich and took me along. I told them that I was selected for the football team and needed some football boots and socks. Our school jersey was a short-sleeved shirt with a V-neck. The colours were black and amber. The V-neck had black edging and the shorts were black and baggy. My grandfather bought me the socks, also amber, with the regulation double black stripes on the rollover. My father bought me second-hand football boots. These boots would be illegal and uncomfortable today. Imagine a thick sole and sides of leather that came up well and truly over the ankle, with white laces that always turned black in the mud. Each stud comprised three or four small discs of leather nailed with tacks and glued to the sole. If kicked on the thigh, you knew about it, not only because these discs of leather were very hard but also because nails would likely protrude through the leather. Contact created grazing and cuts.

My first game was against the older boys at school. I played full-back because I was good in defence stopping goals and had a very long kick. It felt good to be out there on the field even when playing against the big boys. I remember running all over the field and being incredibly red-faced by the end – it was exhilarating. The sports master picked me for captain of the team for the inter-school competition.

Sir John Deane's Grammar School

In 1961, my final year in primary school, I sat for the eleven-plus. This was the British education system's exam for deciding who went to a grammar school and who did not. They consigned the rest to a coeducational 'secondary modern'. It was a selective school system that favoured a university track via grammar schools. Only the top stream in a secondary modern school could prepare A levels for university. Although I was a beneficiary of the eleven-plus, I would later reject what I came to believe was an unfair and forced separation. One lost contact with friends who went to secondary modern schools. Some parents were smug about their child getting into grammar school. I remember pupils in my class being promised gifts such as the latest racing bike if they scored a place.

Sir John Deane's, a redbrick grammar school founded in 1557, was a rugby-playing school for boys, with lots of tradition. My parents scraped the money together to buy me the uniform, which included short trousers because I was starting in Third Form. I had a blue blazer and cap, V-necked long- and short-sleeved pullovers, scarf, light and dark blue tie for Wilbraham house, and white and grey shirts. Then there was gym gear, football gear, cricket gear, and so it went on. The school was free, but all this was a lot of money for my parents.

On the first day, it was like a cattle yard. We third-formers were the butt of jokes and taunts. We were the wrigglers, ankle-biters, runts or 'turd formers' with a lot to prove, being inducted into a highly competitive environment. It could be overwhelming if you didn't cut it intellectually, emotionally or in sport. I was assigned to 3H. My classroom was a working cricket pavilion! I would come in on a Monday morning and tread on a cricket box, or find a glove or a sock under my seat and used chewing gum under the desk lid. It was fine in autumn but arctic in winter when the radiators bubbled.

The sixth-formers, especially those who played rugby, seemed as tall as trees. They had shaving shadows and seemed to live in a bubble. Masters wore their university gowns, and the headmaster in his mortarboard suggested powerful authority. I recall lots of tweed jackets and pipe-smoking. I received a standard-issue hymnbook for assembly each morning. This was always carried in the side pocket of the school blazer.

A staple of the English education system in the 1960s was to ensure every pupil was adequately nourished. We paid five shillings a week for a hot lunch, including a dessert. Jugs of custard would be served with what we called 'stodge' – steamed pudding. The custard usually had thick skin. One of the senior students, presumably a rugby player or weightlifter, was often seen devouring a plate full of custard skins. I disliked watching him polish off these slimy-looking pancakes. I came to write:

> Predictably, it was boiled mutton again, drowning in salty gravy and bordered by soggy peas and mash, followed by a serving of warm stodgy pudding spooned from baking tins and splattered with tepid custard poured from jugs.
>
> A master ordered silence and called on the head prefect to say grace: 'God let us be thankful for the food we are about to receive', to which a voice audibly whispered, 'And God let us become eternally grateful for a friggin' new cook!'
>
> Sniggers broke the silence, followed by a crescendo of cutlery attacking cheap china plates. A prefect with canine hearing collared the insubordinate and ordered him out of the canteen to pick up litter around the school and to copy out Genesis, Chapter One, verse by verse, line by line, three times over, to be delivered before assembly tomorrow. Amen.

We said grace before we ate. We sat down at the same table every day of term, and each table had a leader from an older year. We always haggled over seconds, especially over a dessert called 'toothpaste pie'. It looked like a sort of pastry with white, somewhat scented icing. I ruined my teeth on these desserts and the lollies I collected from the bus stop shop on the way home.

We used to burn the lunch off as soon as we'd eaten it, running onto the playing fields to kick a ball around or play cricket. Older boys might roam around in gangs to taunt the newcomers.

Some of the teachers were proverbial tyrants. Others were young and revolutionary. There was Mr Jack Hetherington, always smiling, always ready to crack a joke. We called him Hethers. He once began a lesson standing in front of the class, with the long sleeves of his academic gown folded over his forearms. He held two sticks of chalk. The first he threw at the boy at the back of the class, who was chatting away to a lad behind him. Bull's eye. Pinged his neck. Laughter. Hethers gave the victim a mock severe look, then turned to the board. With the second piece of chalk, he wrote confidently, the word rhythm, all letters in lowercase but the 'h' taller than the others. 'Boys, this is how you spell rhythm.' Then he burst into a simple rhyme, singing r H y t H m, singing each letter – from middle C up to A (major 6) then down to F (Major), repeating the sequence. He shrugged his shoulders on the letter H, which he referred to as the goalposts. Hethers asked us to stand up, forty 12-year-old boys, and sing it over and again, until we became overly exuberant with added foot stamping and were told to sit down. The experience was never to be forgotten as a connection between language, music, and gesture. I've shared this story for years, striving to make the connection in my teaching.

Hethers warmed my heart with his jokes and innuendos, darting as he often did in between rows of desks, twirling the sleeves of his chalk-dusted Cambridge gown, exhaling pipe-smoke breath between stained teeth as he bent over my exercise books to check classwork. Whenever I see, hear, or must write this, I am likely to recall my teacher's smiling face and the day I learned to spell rhythm by linking language with music and gesture. Lest I forget this musical epiphany.

Then there was Mr Nicholson. We called him Nick. He was straight out of Oxford, had a girlfriend and sports car. He captured our attention; he rarely wore his gown.

In going to Sir John Deane's, I was masquerading as an Anglican (I had no desire to be marched into Northwich town centre with the other Catholics for religious instruction at a Catholic school). I had trouble with Religious Knowledge, or RK as we abbreviated it. My teacher was a former Welsh rugby star, Taffy Evans. He was as boring as a termite. He would ramble on inaudibly as we sat there 'listening'. No chalk, talk, discussion – just listening to a monotone. I was unmoved. Our homework was summarising passages from the Bible. Interestingly, minor infringements incurred the writing out of the same; we parodied Rolf Harris's new release, 'Sun Arise', by singing 'Summarise every Thursday evening.'

Scholastically, I had entered the school in the third stream out of four. My father, who hoped I would study medicine, wanted me to study Latin, deemed a hallmark of a grammar school education and useful for medical study. But I had to move up to the second stream to do that. I studied diligently with this goal in mind.

While I did poorly in music and RK, I topped other subjects and came to be known as a form 'swot', or nerd in modern vernacular. I was rewarded with a stunning report, which praised my efforts and promoted me to study advanced Latin. I studied French and German, as well as maths, English, physics, biology and history. My parents were very impressed. After being lost in the crowd, I had caught up with my mates from primary school and friends who were placed higher than myself in the eleven-plus.

I started in the Lower Fourth along with improved status and puberty and, at last, long trousers. The competition was stiff, and it took me time to be accepted by a group that had already been together for the year.

The school was high on academic success, rugby and athletics, and the Anglican faith. There were lots of prizes and incentives for good work. One prefect taught me chess. This was good on rainy days. But I loved to go outside. I made my mark with my peers by taking an impossible cricket catch. Respect was guaranteed from then on.

I have often reflected on life at school, sometimes turning to poetry. One thrill-seeking activity was to go to a shop that sold single cigarettes in a brown bag to the Sir John Deane's lads. I could duck off at lunchtime to buy a little stash and came to relish the exotic scent of tobacco wafting from a little bag of illicit treasure, folded carefully to hide the contents. One felt like a senior slipping back into school with two Woodbines secreted in a blazer pocket. One for me and one for my mate.

> I pondered the thrill of a 'smoko' in the bog.
> Heard the scrape of the match and saw the flash
>   of phosphorous
> and inhaled just like Dad while keeping watch
>   for prefects.

I vividly remember school sports, especially cross-country racing, in which I showed representative promise. But it was hell in winter when we ran out of school, shivering in singlets, shorts, and plimsolls (sandshoes). At the same time, the master on duty, usually late, sauntered up, cosy in his duffle coat, with his kid gloves and Oxford scarf, swinging a stopwatch nonchalantly in one hand and toting a thermos in the other. Much later, I wrote a prose poem:

The master swigs a mouthful of tea, and steam momentarily fogs his specs. He squints and barks, 'Ready boys?' Pauses. Stopwatch enabled. 'Run!'

I sprint like a Cheshire hound to the front of the pack. My heart is thumping as we jostle our way out of the gates and into The Crescent, running past its imposing houses, before taking a narrow laneway down to the river.

Feet thunder across a wooden footbridge that spans a short arm of the River Weaver, and we pound the gravel path towards Hunt's Lock. It's over the gates, one at a time, or become a headline in the *Northwich Guardian*: Sir John Deane's boy, 13, elbowed into a freezing lock, couldn't swim, drowned.

Father

I was thirteen when my youngest brother was just a year old. We had become a large family, and my father developed the tragic demeanour of a man who must have felt he was failing in a country riddled by class, with barriers to upward mobility. He worried about our future and felt burdened by a low wage to support us. Unlike most of my classmates' families, we did not own a house. We rented and were on the other side of the divide and struggling economically.

As a man supporting five children, my father was worried about becoming sedentary in an office job; he felt that this had led to the early demise of a couple of his office colleagues at ICI, with men in their early forties succumbing to heart attacks and thrombosis. My father saw an escape in becoming his own boss, more active and entrepreneurial. He resigned from ICI and gave up the weekly paycheque for his own painting and decorating business. He bought the gear: some ladders, paint, and overalls. He installed a phone for business and bought a second-hand, beige-coloured Hillman estate car, the type with mahogany wood reinforcements around the cabin. It was low to the ground and had a column shift and faded red leather seats. It carried the decorating gear to the jobs.

The business started well. There was plenty of demand, and I would help scrub walls and strip wallpaper on weekends for my pocket money. But the venture foundered in the winter of 1963, England's coldest for more than two hundred years. I remember blizzards, snow drifts, frozen rivers and blocks of ice for months. Frozen pipes led to burst water mains, treacherous roads, and the endless stoking of coal on the fire and then going out to purchase oil for our heaters. No one cared for having their houses painted, inside or out, when temperatures plummeted to minus 20 degrees Celsius.

The phone stopped ringing. Business slumped. We struggled to pay for groceries, but John F the entrepreneur, the fighter, had a plan. He approached some of the wealthy landowners of nearby Cheshire estates, and we went out with axes and saws to chop and cut firewood. We bagged the timber and door-knocked local housing estates. Unfortunately, the Hillman wasn't suited to hauling bags of firewood. We swapped it for a 1953 Thames van. It was dark blue and black, with a bull-nosed front and large mudguards, enormous headlamps, and prominent wing mirrors. It was the pre-loved workhorse of a milk vendor. It had two bucket seats up front and wooden floorboards. There was ample space to carry loads, and it doubled as a people-mover, carrying the seven of us on day trips to Wales. We sat in the back on the wheel arches or little stools and cushions – no worries about seatbelts in those days. The van, which I named Marmaduke, continued to support my father's business enterprises. He went from clerical work to decorating, to firewood, and then to chimney sweeping. Again, I was occasionally conscripted on school days, and I dreaded the day I would be spotted by a classmate or a teacher and called a truant or the son of a chimney sweep.

Sweeping chimneys was always messy work. First, we covered the fireplace with a metal cover, sealing its edges with tape to prevent soot from entering the rooms. We pushed a series of rods, attached to a brush, through a rubber seal in the metal cover that looked like a funnel. We screwed another length of pole to the brush head, and then another, pushing and pulling the brush through the insides of the chimney. It took several metres of rods before we cleared the chimneystack of some of the three-storey Cheshire mansions that we swept. As we pushed and pulled to dislodge the soot, an industrial vacuum cleaner, about the size of a washing machine, sucked it up from behind the screen. We emptied the cleaner regularly, filling bags with the soot, but accidents occasionally happened. They were not funny at the time, but in later years we roared. Once, we were more vigorous than usual with the sweeping because my father wanted to finish quickly, to get to a pub and place a bet. Suddenly, a massive amount of soot dropped down and knocked the hearth covers backwards. The parlour, with its white carpet and new furniture, looked like a black-and-white photo. We cleaned up the mess and were shown the door rather early that day. We scarpered quickly!

We might light a wad of newspaper to test the draw of the chimney. This helped to convince the customer that we had done the job well. There was an occasion when my father lit the paper just as a gust of wind blew down the chimney. It scattered a fairy-light shower of burning paper sparks all over the room. We had to dance around like boxers punching at the air, trying to catch the bits before they landed on the Persian carpets and furniture.

My father swept chimneys for a year before saying he'd had enough and selling the gear and van. He gave up his dream of being his own boss and went to work at Electrolux selling vacuum cleaners for a basic wage plus a bonus for each unit sold: if he made a sale, he was entitled to take a coloured tag out of the box and forward it to the Electrolux office. The number of tags submitted determined the size of the monthly bonus. My father was sometimes given to taking tags out of boxes before the units were sold, a practice he learned from other salesmen. The 'tagless wonder' was born. Week by week, these unsold vacuum cleaners began to pile up in our house. That was until Electrolux eventually spotted the scam and ended his career as a vacuum cleaner salesman. It was also the end of a sideline, for we had collected old vacuum cleaners to refurbish. I had learned to strip both Electrolux and Hoover machines, replacing parts in the motor, greasing the spindle, cleaning the filter chambers and polishing the outer shell. We were able to make a few bob flogging these cleaners, which we called 'time bombs', being unsure how long they would last.

My father recorded in his papers that his military service lasted 6 years, 285 days, 13 hours and 7 minutes. He had perfect eyesight, good health and physical development. He joined the 5th Kings Liverpool Regiment as part of the Royal Army Reserve from 12 April 1936 to 7 June 1937. He served on weekends to raise money for his parents before joining the Royal Air Force in 1937, only to leave on 14 November 1938 to join the 6/3rd Maritime Regiment. Called into action, he went to sea as a DEMS gunner on merchant vessels coasting the UK, going to the US and Canada. DEMS was an acronym for Defensively Equipped Merchant Ships. He was at sea from January 1941 to March 1943, protecting his ships from German planes and surfacing submarines. Two of the ships were the *Brisk*, a 2,000-ton Norwegian coal carrier, and the *Empire Tamar*. He saw active service as a soldier in Operation Overlord at Normandy, described in his papers:

> On 6 June 1944, I left Oban Harbour, Scotland, as a gunner on a merchant ship that was part of a convoy of warships. I was in a battery unit called 144 LA Regiment. After our regiment went ashore, they scuttled the ship I boarded off Normandy on D+4. They pounded it with anti-aircraft shells, to be used as a breakwater. On the nights of D+6 & 7, the Luftwaffe flew low over our beach to blow up their own ammunition dumps. We were preparing to capture Caen.

My father's experience as a gunner highlights the sense of duty and the futility of war. I cannot comprehend how he felt, standing exposed on the decks of small merchant ships behind an 'iron pole with a WWI Marlin gun mounted on top', waiting to fend off well-armed Junkers German JU88 bombers or surfacing U-boats. He watched and waited for planes and the periscopes of surfacing submarines. It was four hours on duty and four hours off. His gun came from an American aircraft. It was a synchronising gun with a belt feed from an ammunition box. It fired one armour-piercing bullet followed by a tracer then an ordinary bullet. Sometimes it went off by itself. Its effective range was only 300 yards skyward before the bullets curved into the sea. By the time he got an aircraft in the gunsight, it was already too far away. Risking insubordination, he told his superiors that it was a 'bloody peashooter'. They agreed it was imperfect, but they told him to 'fire it anyway and be sure to make lots of noise to put the Germans off their aim!'

By nine days after D-Day, surrounded by incessant bombing, my father was incapacitated with shell shock and shrapnel wounds. They evacuated him from Normandy on a hospital ship. The exact counting of his service days was, on the one hand, a way of saying he had served his king and country, but on the other, it alluded to the crippling shell shock and trauma of a long war. Those who experienced it – and there were many – thought they were going mad. In the 1940s there was little understanding of its effects on wellbeing, unlike today, with expertise in the rehabilitation of individuals suffering from post-traumatic stress disorder.

With a father struggling to find work and often unable to meet the repayments on our furniture or cover the rent and pay the power bills, I began to worry about our future. He increased his alcohol intake to dull his pain. Supporting a wife and five kids on one wage was never easy, and unemployment benefits were both lean and demoralising for him. We were sometimes restricted to living mostly on baked beans, sausages, mashed potatoes, macaroni cheese, corned beef or bread and jam. Bickering and reconciling became a continual pattern in my parents' relationship. The shouting matches, the slamming of doors and the smashing of crockery that followed were difficult to watch. My mother twice ran back to Germany to Hermann and Bertha's care. Sometimes I sought temporary refuge and a meal at friends' houses. I became unhappy at home watching my father's increasing dependence on alcohol and his going out every night.

He began to talk incessantly about a new start. Australia must have seemed to him like an escape route for a better life. Although my grandparents thought that leaving England with a wife and five children and migrating to the other side of the world was just idle talk, it became his fixation, and Australia dominated his thoughts.

My father collected stories and brochures about Australia and showed them to Arthur and Tilly. He tried to convince them to emigrate with us. But Arthur knew his history and read every newspaper. He told my father about the 1961 recession in Australia. Employment would not be guaranteed, and without a sponsor, we might find it difficult to adjust and settle.

We clashed repeatedly. I wanted to stay behind and live with my Uncle Arthur and Aunt Tilly. It would have meant my moving to Liverpool and starting a new school there. But he knew this would be impossible and ignored my rebellion. My mother tried to placate him, but he was obdurate. She was bruised from the hardship of the previous years, not just in her relationship with him or the burden of three children born close together, but also the consequences of my father's business decisions.

Going fishing became my escape route. My grandfather and father had shown me how to fish. It was a solitary recreation. I got up at dawn, tiptoed downstairs to the kitchen, guzzled cornflakes and wrapped up bread and cut some cheese. If there was no cheese,

I would make two 'jam butties' – sliced white bread sandwiches containing thick smears of margarine and strawberry jam. I might take lemon cordial if available.

I tied two rods to the crossbar of my bike and slung a wicker tackle basket over my shoulder and slipped away while everyone was still asleep. I rode to a favourite place accessible via the Winsford Road, several miles from home, past tree-lined fields and unique Cheshire fences with a recurring pattern of uprights, some painted in black, then some in white.

Nearing the lake, I rode along an invariably deserted road and turned off to a village called Foxwist Green to reach the last section, which went through a wood. A secret pathway led through an opening in the trees, just wide enough for my bike. I meandered downhill towards the lake. It was like travelling into a secret world where light danced on the water. Tall deciduous trees fringed the lake. Arriving just after sunrise was magical. I could smell the trees, bracken, and moss. The birds' chorus greeted my arrival at my favourite spot to fish – a small sandy bank between two dense patches of water lilies and reeds.

Fishing was about peace, the fresh air and sunshine, and the sound of moorhens and other birds – this made it an interesting hobby for me. Wind and rain never deterred me – only snow and ice prevented me from fishing.

I felt sorry for a fish when it died in my keepnet, but this was rare. However, remorse overtook me after I brought a large carp home in a bucket of water. It turned on its side. My father decided on swift action. 'It's dying. You couldn't have kept it, anyway. Scoop out a hole in one of the flower beds.' I did as he asked and laid the fish in it, and he chopped it in two pieces with a spade. Seeing the shiny, golden fish lying there made me sad as I covered it with soil. I didn't fish for some time after that and stopped altogether after I turned fifteen. Football, cricket, popular music, and eventually girls, became more important.

Music at school

My direct musical experiences up until 1965 were mostly confined to what I heard in the Catholic Church, such as plainchant and hymn singing. Playing recorder in primary school was not much fun, because of the strict infection control applied to the school-supplied instruments. After a lesson, we put all recorders into jars full of milky white concentrated Dettol. This resulted in frantic attempts to rinse and dry them before the start of the next lesson. I could always taste Dettol and became averse to recorder days, not to mention the wheezing and whining of overblown notes!

My parents and my relatives enjoyed music on the radio. They listened to Lonnie Donegan's skiffle music. They liked Frank Ifield's 'Wayward Wind' or Cliff Richards's 'Summer Holiday'. But there were still adults in my world who derided pop music and its musicians. For example, I was potato picking to earn some money. As we stood in a cart at the back of the tractor sorting the day's pick, a lively discussion about the Beatles ensued when the tractor-driving boss and his girlfriend dubbed the Beatles and their songs as moronic. I'd never heard that word before. I kept my thoughts to myself and looked in my dictionary at home to discover it was an adjective derived from a moron. I was annoyed by the denigration of my teenage world. I wished I could have told her so, but I was too polite then.

It was the hymns of Anglican devotion that awakened in me both the joy of singing and the recognition of melodic contour and harmony. In grammar school, we assembled in the hall every morning for hymns, prayers, and the business of the day. Assembly attendance and singing were compulsory, and we received a detention if we turned up without hymnbooks or were caught not singing.

Singing verse after verse surrounded by a few reasonable voices in a sea of groaning adolescent boys, I noticed variations in word structure and setting. I enjoyed soaring phrases, which led me to improvising harmonies amidst the massed voices. Assembly singing often lifted my spirits for the rest of the school day. My school 'family' was more ordered and predictable, removed from the claustrophobia of my chaotic home life with three younger brothers, always with colds, a sister with acute eczema and asthma, a depressed mother and a depressed, often shouting father.

I topped the form in both classwork and examinations in my first year, but my music score was below average. The teacher was also my form master, Mr Andrew 'Andy' Horrocks, a short and stout man with a ruddy complexion and closely cropped hair. He wore an ill-fitting grey-green suit with a waistcoat and fob watch, and shiny black shoes with rounded toecaps. Andy was also the organist at Witton church, a thirteenth-century Anglo-Norman edifice close to our school, where he played for Founder's Day and other special assemblies on the school calendar. He was approachable and mostly fair, but he used a school report to highlight my lack of interest or skill in his music class, most of which consisted of rhythm dictation produced from his tapping a pencil on his desk. Our task was to repeat the same over and write it down.

There I was in the cricket pavilion-cum-classroom, poised behind a hundred-year-old wooden desk replete with carved initials, notches and scrapes, a full inkwell, and a nibbed pen, ready to write the rhythms and blot the page in my exercise book. Morse code would have been more fun than *ta tefe* on an ancient desk. Elgar, Handel, and class hymns didn't touch me. In one lesson, someone dared to mention the music of the Beatles. There was a frisson of expectation, but Andy was immediately dismissive, referring to the group as the 'Be-artles' because they couldn't spell 'beetle'. Andy was either unable, or refused, to recognise 'beat' in the name, the essential element of their music. We groaned in disappointment. However, when he called for a show of hands to learn a brass instrument and join a junior concert band, I was one of a few to put my hand up, although not without trepidation as Andy counted me in. The visiting bandmaster, Mr Yarewood, was summoned to class. He handed out instruments and gave me a tenor horn – a brass wind instrument derived from the cornet and the valved bugle or flugelhorn. He told me the tenor horn was first played in Prussian cavalry bands in 1829. I was encouraged to take the tenor home to practise.

It was usually riotous on the upper deck on the afternoon school bus. My tenor horn was sometimes snatched from my hands by older boys. This resulted in a cacophony of farting noises for a few miles, much to the annoyance of other passengers on the upper deck. The same boys told me it wasn't cool to play in a brass band. In sixties parlance 'you couldn't pull a bird with that rubbish.'

I persevered for a few months and attended group lessons to learn scales, fingering and a few short concert items. Our first performance came up at the end of term. I struggled to sight-read the music, and I needed to pencil in the valve number fingerings for my part. By the concert, I could play a few notes, fluff a bit, play a note, and fluff a bit more. It wasn't fun, especially the collective need to clear spittle and condensation by ejecting the same from slides and taps onto the stage floor. So, I retired from tenor horn after just one term and hoped it wouldn't confirm in Mr Horrocks's mind that I was inept. When the call went out for band the following year, I sat on my hands and looked out of the window. I decided that learning music formally was not for me. It was popular music songs that stirred me, and they were to change my life.

I kept humming the earworms of the popular music that was sweeping the land. A curiosity for rock-and-roll guitar gripped me in March 1965 when the Rolling Stones released 'The Last Time', the first number one hit for songwriters Mick Jagger and Keith Richards. I went to a dance somewhere in Weaverham village and heard a band playing this song. I walked into the darkly lit venue and was immediately enveloped by a wall of sound. On stage, in bright lights, was the now-standard combination of lead, rhythm and bass guitarists plus a drummer. There was high energy, colour, and movement. This music was a million miles from the pencil-tapping rhythms of my classroom, farting into a tenor horn or the cacophony of classmates singing 'All People That on Earth Do Dwell'. How could this happen in Weaverham, with a fifteen-year-old from my school playing electric guitar and singing at a professional gig, just like my heroes – Keith Richards, George Harrison, and Hank Marvin of the Shadows? I was spellbound by the skill of the musicians and the volume produced by their amplifiers and drums, entranced by the stage lights shining on the red, black, silver, and green lacquered solid body guitars, the cymbals and chrome on the drum kit.

The guitar riff – 'dadada, da-da, dadada, da – was raw, loud, and alive. It was mesmerising and I wanted it to go on forever. There were no teachers or parents in the hall. Girls were dancing everywhere. Although I was too shy to dance, I felt the sound pulse throughout my body. I had found my portal, and the dress code was an awakening for me. The lads wore straight-cut or narrow jeans, shirts and pencil ties, and pointed shoes or gym boots. Some had copied the mop-top Beatle haircut, while the girls sported the bob or pigtails. They wore knee-length, pleated woollen skirts in dark colours or patterns such as navy or plaid, and blouses reflecting the conservative styles of the late 1950s with rounded Peter Pan–style collars.

My heart was on fire. How long would it take me to learn to play the guitar like that and sing? If only I could join a band. I was in a buzz and forgot about going fishing or playing football and became distracted from schoolwork. I listened to radio stations and recorded and played tapes made from television of British bands. From 1963, the explosion of the Mersey sound had changed everything. Gerry and the Pacemakers' 'How Do You Do It?', the Beatles' 'Please Please Me' and the Searchers' 'Sweets for My Sweet' changed the country and the world.

Nothing would stop me becoming an aficionado, listening to diverse songs from the foot-tapping 'Glad All Over' by the Dave Clark Five to the captivating performances of female vocalists such as Cilla

Black in 'Anyone Who Had a Heart' and Sandie Shaw in 'Always Something There to Remind Me'. All of these were hits in 1964.

I didn't go back to potato picking, instead finding a job in the supply store of a café on the M6 motorway at Knutsford. Here I might catch glimpses of bands on the road as they travelled to gigs in Liverpool or Manchester. I just missed out on seeing Bob Dylan and the Rolling Stones in person, but it's likely I peed in the same bowl as Bob or Mick! There was a well-stacked jukebox in the main café, and I would nip out of the storeroom in my white coat and load the jukebox with coins. I set up repeats of favourite hits, including the Supremes' 'Baby Love', the Animals' 'House of the Rising Sun' and the Rolling Stones' 'It's all over now'. I desperately wanted to play in a band. All I needed was a guitar.

My first guitar was a mail-order guitar from my café earnings plus some money from my parents. It arrived wrapped in old newspapers, inside a cardboard box. I unpacked it and relished the smell of the varnished timber and the shine of the untouched steel strings. It was a no-name Spanish guitar purchased sight unseen for £3, which in today's currency is about $80. Later, I dubbed it the time bomb. Its neck was warped, the strings were too high above the fretboard and the timber top looked like it came from a fruit box. Nonetheless, I was thrilled to own an instrument. It would soon feature strongly in my life and helped to shape my career. It was my friend, my talisman to help me adjust to and embrace a new country.

2

THE POMMIE TEENAGER

All you need is three-chord trick and a catchy riff.

In June 1965, my father stunned everyone when he confirmed a compulsory family medical appointment. We bundled into our dodgy green Vauxhall Victor and drove via Chester, our nearest city, to Crewe Memorial Hospital, where we met a migration officer from Australia House. My mother and my sister were anxious about having compulsory X-rays, medical examinations, blood tests and psychological interviews. It took until the early evening to complete these requirements, before the migration officer met us again. He thanked us for our patience and said we seemed an ideal family, the kind that Australia would welcome. He requested we visit our family doctor as soon as possible to have the mandatory vaccinations and said we should expect a letter in the mail confirming our selection and assisted passage. My father seemed relieved, and it would only cost £20 to emigrate: £10 for himself and £10 for my mother. We children would travel at no cost.

The officer continued talking about Australia and all the good things waiting for us. We wouldn't need heavy winter clothing. There was no snow or icy roads, only sunshine nearly every day. Jenny and I would have a pony and live near the sea and be healthy and bronzed just like the faces in the brochures. We would have to stay for a few weeks in a migrant hostel, but in the end, we should think of migrating to Australia as a long holiday.

I was intrigued by his spin but troubled by thoughts of losing my friends and schoolmates. My father ordered me not to start in the Upper Fifth because I was going to Australia and could go to school there. I challenged him: 'What about my going to university, becoming the first in the family ever to do so? You encouraged my interest in studying medicine. I will fall behind, then what?' He countered by saying I should now get a part-time job and save some money. 'Go and pick strawberries, and don't tell your friends or teachers about emigrating. No one should know except our immediate family.' We were going because it was 'best for the whole family, and that's that'. I replied sarcastically in grammar school Latin: '*Sic dixit tyrannum!* (So said the tyrant!)* My father turned to me, flushed, demanding to know what I said. Being a smart alec, I said nothing. We were to leave everything behind and travel by plane, with just three large suitcases. 'Why not go by sea?' I asked him, having heard about six-week voyages on the *Fairstar* or the *Orcades*, relaxing in the sunshine with other families. 'Why can't we tell our friends and say our goodbyes?' But he would hear none of this. He had seized the opportunity to be among the first cohort of assisted migrants to fly to Australia and he didn't mind which city we ended up in if we left England soon.

We waited for confirmation of an offer to migrate and the date of travel. Weeks went by and my father became anxious and grumpy. Eventually, my sister Jenny owned up: she had intercepted the letter and hidden it from my father by secreting it under loose floorboards beneath the carpet in her bedroom. She sheepishly handed over the letter, dated 1 July 1965. I remember him snatching it from her hands, then running his thumb over the embossed Commonwealth of Australia coat of arms, his hands shaking as he ripped the seal to pull out several neatly folded pages. There it was. At the bottom of page one it read: *On behalf of the Commonwealth of Australia, I am pleased to offer you and your family the opportunity to migrate. You will be accommodated in Sydney.* He was relieved to read out a departure date, the airline, a flight number and other details about vaccinations and travel documents. Our fate was determined. We were to leave Manor Road at 9 pm on 19 September 1965. I called it D-day!

My grandmother was devastated by the news, as I'm sure were my German grandparents, Hermann and Bertha. They would have been heartbroken, as my mother had neither the time nor the resources to travel to Germany to say goodbye. A letter and a photograph of the children would have to suffice. We were soon visiting family in Liverpool and sharing a customary late-afternoon Sunday roast dinner of beef, vegetables, and rice pudding. After the meal, the children played in the garden while the adults talked about Australia. This meal was the last time we saw my father's parents.

It was a quiet evening in Manor Road, Cuddington on 19 September when Arthur and Tilly arrived from Liverpool. They brought food for our last meal together. Words were few. My mother looked pale, and my sister was curled in a foetal position on the sofa. My young brothers, two, four and five respectively, played with their toys, while I put labels on the things I wanted Arthur to keep for me – my air rifle, books, fishing rods, stamps, and coins. My father stuffed our suitcases with clothes, references, testimonials, school reports and photographs. Arthur listed items he would store, dispose of, or sell on our behalf.

I saw my grandmother give my father a bundle of £1 notes. They were old notes from my grandmother's mattress. She distrusted banks and hid her savings from my grandfather who was addicted to betting on horses. My father's hands shook as he accepted the money. Tears rolled down his mother's cheeks. She was in deep pain feeling she would never see us again.

I helped my mother dress my brothers and tried to reassure both of us by saying, 'We're going on an adventure, and going to fly for the first time!' Just after dark, we closed the door at 9 Manor Road. The curtains were not drawn, to suggest that we were still there the next day. We exited quietly and loaded ourselves into Arthur's car plus a waiting taxi. I carried one personal item – my mail-order Spanish guitar, which I had wrapped in a plastic bag.

My sister sobbed as we drove away from our home of ten years. I held back tears and spoke only three words: 'Farewell Cheshire, forever.' My father, clearly rankled by my fatalism, glared at me, whereas Arthur reassured me quietly from his driver's seat, 'You'll come back.' I could see his eyes moisten as he swallowed. Arthur was always smiling, always upbeat. But this moment was raw. I felt the powerful bonds of family and understood the bittersweet shifting of emotions around the comings and goings in our lives. Arthur was not just an uncle; he was like an older brother and a close friend. I carried the painful knowledge of my parents' dysfunctional relationship and the image of my mother's loneliness while my father was out drinking. Just the same, it would always be a family, no matter how far-flung.

Arthur drove us slowly to Crewe Central. We were in two black cars. It could have been a funeral cortège for the passing of an entire family. Tilly stroked Jenny's head on her lap. And my brothers huddled against my mother in the taxi that followed. The moon appeared briefly from behind the clouds, and I tried to imagine what it would look like from a plane. I imagined leaving the ground and travelling contrary to the earth's rotation. Would this increase our speed? For now, such thoughts were fanciful. We had terrestrial business to attend to such as collecting the train tickets, portering bags along the platform, and saying goodbye to Arthur and Tilly. Crewe beckoned.

Once aboard the 10 pm night train to London, I watched Arthur and Tilly waving from the platform smiling stoically as we disappeared from each other's lives. The rattle of the bogies and the blasts of steam, things I loved to hear when we used to take trains to visit Arthur and Tilly in Liverpool, spoke forebodingly as we clunked through points, crossed converging tracks, and gathered speed.

Out of my window, I saw another train pass from the opposite direction, its carriages brightly lit. Passengers with newspapers underarm were donning hats, putting on scarfs, pulling luggage from the overhead racks, making ready for the journey's end. I wanted to tell them I was just setting out and where I was going, and what it felt like to be in a bubble floating away from my home, my friends, my possessions, and my school. Look! I'm a truant, a sneak, and a runaway! I breathed heavily on the window and my finger started to write in the condensation, 'I miss you, Arthur.' Our train jolted, and so did my thoughts. And I looked across the seat at my mother. Her head was drooping. She was asleep at last, a welcome respite from this sad chapter of her life's journey. No turning back now. A plane was waiting.

The trip to London was tiring. There were no sleepers available, and we sat upright all night in a stuffy carriage. My brothers, Christopher and Andrew, both had colds, and they coughed intermittently. My sister's eczema troubled her, and she scratched her wrists in her sleep. My father slept and snored open-mouthed, sometimes grinding his teeth. I looked out of my window at the moonlit fields of the midlands and allowed myself to conjure images of life in Australia. While I was attentive in geography classes, I knew little of what to expect and honestly believed that its cities were more like towns, with kangaroos as prevalent as domestic cats. Television had provided me with images of bushrangers and surf beaches. Radio offered humorous ditties sung by pint-sized Irish comedian, Charlie Drake ('My boomerang won't come back') and bespectacled Perth-born novelty entertainer Rolf Harris ('Tie me kangaroo down sport'). Judith Durham of the Seekers was the only example of an Australian woman's face I recognised.

We arrived in London at 5:30 am, a bedraggled flock shuffling through King's Cross Station and into a reverberant lounge room with garish pendant lights and smells of fried bacon and stewed coffee. My father scurried off to hail taxis to take us to Heathrow airport for BA 712, the 9 am flight to Sydney.

Unwelcome news awaited us at Heathrow. Our flight was delayed for a day due to insurgent activities in Saudi Arabia, under our flight path. It was 7 am and we didn't have enough money for a hotel room in London. We had to stay in the terminal and wait for better news. So, we slept on the chairs and the floor in the departure lounge, using the bathrooms to wash as best we could and eating the stale greasy food from the café.

My father was irritable and kept looking around nervously as if he was on the run. It was then that my mother confided in me that he was worried about being apprehended while leaving England without settling a hire purchase debt and the unpaid gas and electricity bills. He was also evading a pending court appearance to answer a charge of culpable driving in a minor car accident whilst under the influence of alcohol. Many years later my mother told me that Arthur sorted out 'the mess' we left behind and acquitted most of the debt.

Our flight was listed again, and we almost missed the call due to feeling displaced and disoriented. We had stopped listening to the incessant airline announcements. However, it was now a huge relief to be on the move again – somewhere, anywhere – escaping the frustration of camping in a terminal lounge for eighteen hours, seemingly the only people in this predicament. Airport staff must have known we were emigrating and left us alone. We were Australia's problem now. We were doing a runner, a midnight flit, a Houdini.

A new life in Australia

We touched down in Sydney on 22 September and descended the gangway bathed in sunshine. It was a humid day and 26 degrees Celsius. I squinted at the brilliant blue sky as I walked jelly-legged across the tarmac clutching my guitar, my future talisman, in its plastic bag. I didn't know then the significance of this object in the career I would follow.

Inside the terminal, a uniformed driver met us and helped us retrieve our suitcases. We showed him our papers and he asked us to wait for another family coming off the same flight. Together we left Mascot Airport in a grey Volkswagen Kombi with a Commonwealth of Australia number plate. We drove to Matraville to drop off the other family and then to Bunnerong, our destination, named after a clan of now dispersed Indigenous inhabitants of the Eora nation.

The drive from the airport was unmemorable. Things looked drab and uninviting in the industrial suburbs of Alexandria and Mascot, but some Cook Island palm trees seemed to welcome us. That was until the driver veered onto Bunnerong Road and to our destination. He turned off at a ten-block complex of huge, barren-looking rectangular blockhouses.

'Here we are,' he said politely as he drove into the front of Block 9.

'You're kidding?' said my distressed mother. 'Surely, not here!'

'Yes, Mrs Jones, my instructions were to collect your family and transport you to Bunnerong Migrant Hostel. It won't be for long.'

Tears welled. I was speechless. Where was this in the migration brochures? But I said nothing, I just wanted to wash, drink water, and fall asleep somewhere.

The deputy hostel manager came out of his office, thanked the driver, and greeted us cordially. He gave my father some keys and a large brown envelope containing a contract and a list of the hostel rules. He then showed us to our rooms and amenities.

We walked along a narrow roadway that ran through the centre of Block 9. There were several entries and exits. Inside were rows of partitions. Being a large family, we were allocated four rooms in a row: 3.5 metres by 3.5 metres, with double-decker beds for the children and a divan-style bed for my parents in the central room, which doubled as the family meeting room. The walls were not much thicker than cardboard. Privacy was minimal.

Each room had linoleum flooring, chipboard and Formica tables, spring coiled beds, frosted glass window slats and uncovered light bulbs. The walls were painted in a duck-egg blue colour. Big cockroaches and mice could run under the poorly fitted doors.

Looking towards Blocks 8 and 9, 1967, Bunnerong Migrant Hostel.
Photo: Brian Little

The manager showed us the communal showers, toilets, and laundry situated at the end of the block. In the canteen, he asked us to record what meals we had in a large book. The tally would be billed to my father at the end of each month and added to the accommodation tariff. He was given credit until he found a job to pay these fees.

Alone at last, with the guide out of earshot, my mother and sister turned on my father. How could he have done this to us, forcing us to leave our home in rural Cheshire for this prison camp? In his defence, we knew we were coming to a hostel, but even he had had no idea what Bunnerong was like, and conceded it was dilapidated and military-looking.

Recently, I found a government paper entitled *Report relating to the proposed erection of a Migrant Hostel at Randwick, New South Wales* (1965) for the Parliamentary Standing Committee on Public Works. It stated (pp. 6–7):

> Bunnerong hostel is located in the Municipality of Randwick and occupies part of Heffron Park ... the fact remains that the buildings were originally built as stores and subsequently converted to meet a post-war emergency. Bunnerong Migrant Hostel must create a poor impression on newly arrived migrants.

Travelling by plane halfway around the world on a one-way ticket had left us with little sense of what day or time it was. We had been on the go, travelling for 52 hours from Cheshire. Zombie-like, we took showers, made our beds, and succumbed to jet lag. I slept for eighteen hours until lunchtime the next day, feeling utterly disoriented, as if I was still at Heathrow terminal.

I recall getting up, locking our doors, and walking en masse to the canteen where we queued for a meal that comprised of burnt chops, mushy carrots, peas, and crunchy mashed potatoes – about as appetising as the food in a Cheshire piggery. I had just become a 'whingeing Pom'.

The next day we did what other hostellers did and went to Maroubra Junction to buy an electric frypan to enable us to cook meals in our rooms. We told our electrical goods salesman what we wanted. He could tell by our accents we were from England or 'the Old Dart' as he called it. He said he sold a lot of pans to hostel folk. We purchased thongs (flip-flops) to walk to and from the showers, as well as cotton shorts, T-shirts, and hats to deal with the hot weather of the coming summer, with its humidity and afternoon thunderstorms.

Hostel life for ten-pound Poms

Was my father seduced by the Australian advertising showing beautiful beaches and lovely detached homes, the promises of employment and housing, a more relaxed lifestyle, and a better climate? Probably, but he also had personal problems and other matters on his mind.

At only £10 fare for each parent and kids for free, with the promise of low-cost accommodation, Sydney looked like a way out. Of course, there was a cost. The assisted migrant scheme asked you to agree to stay at least two years or repay the full fare plus the return.

The 'ten-pound Pom' scheme remains the colloquial name for assisted British migration. It was part of the 'Populate or Perish' policy developed by the Curtin government before the end of World War II. It aimed to increase substantially Australia's population, in response to the vulnerability of a country with unrealised economic potential through under-population. 'Ten-pound Poms' had to be in sound health and under the age of forty-five. In 1947, more than 400,000 Brits were registered for the scheme at London's Australia House.

Some migrants had local sponsors to help them with employment and housing. However, the promises made to immigrants were not always fulfilled. Many faced lengthy stays in hostels, especially those who were unable to get suitable employment. Understandably, families missed their relatives and communities. I made great friends in Bunnerong, but I also saw the sadness in the faces of some of the adults. Migrant homesickness was severe, and some depressed souls were prepared to pay the Commonwealth to go back home again within a few months. Around one-quarter of the ten-pound Poms left Australia within a few years of their arrival.

The peak year was 1969, with more than 80,000 coming to Australia. By 1973, the cost of assisted passages had increased to £75 per family. This was still a cheap fare, but numbers of assisted migrants from the United Kingdom dropped off significantly, and assisted passage schemes were gradually phased out in the 1980s.

Bunnerong was not what we had expected, but we had no choice but to settle into hostel life.

A wire fence surrounded the hostel, giving it a prison-like ambience. Our units were essentially partitioned rooms in a massive shed with common amenities at either end. Most of the tenants were British and Irish. There was another hostel at Daunt Avenue reserved for other Europeans – for the 'wogs' as they were derisively called.

Some vivid memories for me are the sound of thongs or flip-flops made by people on their way to the communal amenities, the loos, the laundries, and the canteens. I remember domestic arguments that you could hear between the blocks word for word; peanut butter sandwiches and oranges in the canteen to be collected on the way to school; dust on the window slats; Mormons knocking on the doors; Geordie, Londoner, Scots, Midlander accents counterpointed in the canteen with the Yugoslav, Polish and English accents of the cooks.

The food at the canteen was barely edible but it was included in the tariff. The camp chief cook in our canteen was a friendly Yugoslav immigrant from another hostel, a big man with a moustachioed smile, who cooked like filling a cement mixer. I'm sure that running a kitchen for large numbers wasn't on his curriculum vitae. The smell of dampness after heavy rain would blend with the aromas of fried food at dinnertime from residents who avoided the canteen in favour of their own fry-ups and salads.

I recall block parties, too; teenagers hanging around the roadways and corridors being told to shut up during the day because shift workers were trying to sleep.

I wrote a poem about living in the hostel:

Hostel Kids, 1965

The western desert air rolls in,
making us breathless under dusty skies.
Heatwave at Bunnerong:
no relieving nor'easter or southerly buster today.

Night is falling.
Radio and TV are blaring news: Bob Dyer's Pick a Box;
Joe the Gadget Man; and the nostalgic Coronation
    Street.

Eerie neons flood each blockhouse with dim flickerings.
Mouse-sized cockroaches scamper on egg-laying
    missions
avoiding the flip-flop procession of towel
and toothbrush-toting residents
scurrying to communal bathrooms.

We, the hostel kids, the hope of our parents,
loll late on outside benches,
watching bogong moths zapping in the floodlights.
We chatter in adolescent tongues of Britain –
Scouse, Glaswegian, Mancunian, Eastender and
    Suffolk twang.

New connections: football and music

Two weeks after arriving at Bunnerong Migrant Hostel, in October 1965, I started at Matraville High School, a coeducational school nearby. I was hoping to play football, my favourite sport. I was surprised to be told by new classmates, 'You mean soccer, mate. Here, football means league!' Matraville was in Rabbitohs territory; the South Sydney Rugby League team were the dominant figures. League ruled.

I was told, 'Only wogs and dagos play soccer. You're a Pommie, you should be following league, not girly ball.' There was no real harm intended in Pommie. But wogs and dagos were racist terms. For me, it wasn't prejudicial to be called a Pommie, although some migrants differed on this. I treated it as a term of endearment and an acronym for 'Prisoner of Mother England'; the dictionary mentioned Pommie as a diminutive of Pomegranate, referring to its colour and likeness to the red hue of English people's faces when they arrived in Australia. At least I was slightly tanned from living in rural Cheshire and spending a lot of time outdoors.

I made friends quickly and shared my story about how I didn't want to come to Australia or go to Matraville High – a drab structure with a playing field of sand held together with tufts of coarse grass, at the centre of which was a 20-metre concrete slab used as a cricket pitch. The school was close to Long Bay Correctional Centre and not far from ICI and other industries, so different from the lush summer cricket pitches of Cheshire and the playing fields of my school. Worst of all, some of the teachers were indolent and wore drab clothes.

After navigating a different school environment, I sometimes dreaded the bell at 3 pm and the walk back to Block 9, Bunnerong Migrant Hostel, with its linoleum floors, Formica-topped tables, naked light bulbs, and cockroaches as big as mice.

Things looked up when I took a part-time job at Scott's Beefburgers, a meat-processing factory in Hillsdale. I made friends with my supervisor, Bill Austin, a cheery man in his late fifties, although he looked older due to years of labouring outdoors and the constant smoking of cigarettes rolled from strong tobacco. Bill showed me how to cut and grind large sides of beef, blend in breadcrumbs, add salt and pepper and pack the mixture into aluminium tubes to store in a freezer. I had to retrieve these a week later and take the frozen meat out of each tube ready for slicing into burger patties. Once thawed and cut they went to a posse of women who covered and heat-sealed the slices in plastic bags stamped *Scott's Nourishing*

Beefburgers. I never cooked one, knowing that the meat was cheap and fatty and that when thawing the frozen tubes and taking out the meat logs, flies would swarm.

One smoko, Bill told me about his three sons. I said I was the eldest of five children. He asked me what I enjoyed about England. I told him I liked fishing, football and listening to rock-and-roll. He said his son Paul was my age and liked football. Would I like to meet him and have a kick-around? My spirits lifted when he invited me to a Saturday lunch at his housing commission flat in Maroubra, where I met his wife and three sons. His wife was lovely but quite frail.

After lunch, Paul contacted some friends and arranged an impromptu 'friendly' kick-around in a small park at the confluence of Beauchamp Road and Anzac Parade in Maroubra. It was a hot day, and a game of attack and defence was played between rows of palm trees, with a pair at one end of the park used as a goal.

It felt great to kick a ball again, as if I was rediscovering my roots. I hadn't played for a few months but must have made an impression, because later that afternoon Bill invited me to join his son's team, South Sydney Juniors. After the first training session, I was given the captain's armband, a responsibility that gave me a sense of pride and purpose; I hadn't been a sports leader since my final year of primary school when I was captain of the cricket and football teams. No longer just another hostel Pom, I could boast Aussie friends and forget about the stigma of being a Bunnerong Hostel Pommie. Soccer, like the guitar, raised my self-esteem and provided me with feelings of belonging and acceptance in my new homeland.

Our South Sydney team uniform consisted of a green shirt edged with red, white shorts and red socks. The manager was Harry Gully, a jovial and rotund man, who openly disliked 'wogs' because most of the teams in our league were branded with ethnic names such as Pan-Hellenic (Greek), Hakoah (Jewish-Israeli), Apia (Italian), Prague (Czechoslovak), and Yugal (Yugoslav). We had a few English boys in our team – Jeff Coates, another hostel lad from Newcastle upon

Tyne, and Doug Gladden from Suffolk. The others were Australian born and included David Boyd ('Boydie') and of course Bill's son, Paul Austin.

Harry Gully always wore a green blazer with gold braiding, proudly sporting the Aussie coat of arms and a New South Wales (NSW) Soccer Federation insignia on his lapel. He was a local football administrator and became our manager and coach. But he couldn't run on a field, nor could he give instructions other than 'go out and win, lads!'

Most fixtures were played at Queens Park in the Eastern Suburbs. Unfortunately, we lost more games than we won, but our team spirit was strong. Opposing teams had more players to draw on. They had coaches and trainers in tracksuits who were on the field before the game and at half-time, leading the warm-ups. We had no reserves, and just getting eleven players was a struggle. We often played nine or ten against eleven. And when things went against us, Harry was always quick to shout at referees or argue with his opposite number.

Despite his apparent lack of experience as a player, Harry was an enterprising manager. He felt we needed a bonding excursion and an opportunity to 'toughen up'. He arranged an out-of-town fixture at the Emu Plains Correctional Centre. I knew this was a suburb on the outskirts of Sydney and at the foot of the Blue Mountains. I had driven this way before.

Bill generously wanted to show me some of greater Sydney. He drove a vintage green 1200 cc Austin A35 with leather seats. It was his pride and joy, and I went with Bill's wife and son, Paul, to a picnic at Warragamba Dam. It was a long, hot trip without air conditioning in the small Austin, and Parramatta Road was congested. However, I appreciated both Bill's kindness and the size of Sydney as we travelled west.

So, when the day came for the prison friendly, Bill drove Paul and me to Emu Plains on a sultry Saturday, where an enthusiastic warden welcomed us. As ever, Harry was already there, in his immaculate green and gold blazer, reciprocating handshakes and mopping his brow with a huge handkerchief.

He led us onto a small, parched field enclosed by a high wire fence. The Centre players came out and eyeballed us. They were in their late teens and early twenties. We were sixteen-year-olds. They were bigger, more muscular, tattooed, and missing teeth but we weren't intimidated. As I shook hands with the opposing captain, I felt his calloused hand grip mine like a vice. Was this deliberate or was it just his strength from working in farming like his inmates? It made me feel glad we were here to play football, not rugby or, indeed, boxing that was part of their exercise routine. They were very fit and played a bustling game. When they kicked, they kicked hard, and it hurt through the shin guards. It was not malice on their part, rather a lack of technique and a physical approach used to counter our skills. We were a fit and nimble team after playing for a full season. We easily out-dribbled the prisoners, and it felt as if we were giving them a masterclass. I expected the result to be much closer, but we won the game 5–0. The opposition were good losers and clapped us off the field. We finished by giving them a case of oranges, which they devoured like hungry lions. Unfortunately, other than handshakes, we weren't allowed to mix and talk with them. We were happy to have visited the Centre at Emu Plains and especially proud after its warden told us that a men's team that was asked to play declined over concerns with possible injuries.

While football offered me respite and hope in my world turned upside down, bringing a guitar on the plane to Sydney would eventually become a foundation stone of my future life. The guitar was the one thing I had brought with me, and I was determined to learn how to play it. I caught a bus into the city and went to Palings music and bought a pitch pipe, which comprised six notes for tuning strings of a guitar. Thus began my first bit of self-teaching in music. After a few broken strings from over-tightening towards the higher octave, my ear was good enough to approximate reasonable pitch and now the open chord sounded tolerable.

I had also bought Nick Manoloff's *Spanish Guitar Method* to help me with the tuning and to work out a basic musical scale, but I found the amount of theory daunting. There was no current popular music in the book, and it looked like a lot of work when all I wanted to play was something 'catchy', and quickly.

Once I'd mastered holding the plectrum, I started to work out how to play melodies and chord patterns from the music of my favourite groups. It was slow going at first, but I persisted. The breakthrough came one evening when I was sitting at the entrance to Block 9, plinking a couple of notes on the guitar for the pleasure of new-found friends. A long-haired blonde man in his early twenties walked past. He stopped, turned, and said,

'Hey, give me a look at your axe!'

'Sure,' I said, somewhat baffled by the word 'axe'.

'I'm Ron, Ron Edwards. I live here. My dad is the deputy manager.'

Ron was well-spoken and confident. He wore blue jeans, red suede boots and a loose-fitting shirt. I handed him my 'axe' and he played a twelve-bar blues riff. It was jaw-droppingly good and sounded authentic, like real Chuck Berry or Keith Richards of the Rolling Stones. I was speechless and Ron became the centre of my attention.

After he'd finished playing, I asked him to show me how to do what he just did. Without hesitation, he said, 'Sure, I'll show you. Wait here.' He went to his room in the block and came out with a sunburst Fender Stratocaster. I had never seen an electric guitar up close. The varnish was worn in places, but it was a thing of beauty. Ron sat down and propped the head of his guitar on the bench to amplify its resonance and played the same twelve-bar blues pattern over and over. Then he showed me how to fine-tune my guitar, told me which fingers to use and made me play the riff over and over until we could play in unison. This was manna to me.

I was hooked. What a hero. Within half an hour I was playing twelve-bar blues. Nirvana; I had finally welcomed music as my life's abiding passion. Ron and I met often on the bench, and he would talk about his time in a professional band called MI4. He had returned recently from a long residency in Cairns. I heard about his friend and colleague Dave Burke, a brilliant guitarist from London, who lived near the hostel.

I got to meet Dave and hear him play with Ron. They knew all the runs and licks, everything that was good and catchy on the charts. Dave, who couldn't read music – neither could Ron – had a gift for working out almost instantly the melodies and chords of hundreds of songs. Both were inspirational, and I spent many hours listening to their jamming on rhythm and lead guitar chord patterns. I watched every finger movement, pestering them to repeat whatever they played.

In Britain, I'd seen the style revolution of the Mersey sound, rhythm and blues, Motown, pirate radio stations, concept albums, discotheques, and much more. And in Australia, there was also surf music. Australia adopted American pop culture and the Stomp was born. It belonged to beach culture. Bands included the Atlantics, the Delltones, the Telstars and Little Pattie and the Statesmen. They played to packed town halls and surf clubs up and down the coast of Australia. But American musical influences were also countered by the music and hysteria of the Beatles and the Rolling Stones. Not only did migrants, especially from Britain, bring records and buy locally, but they also brought a performing culture. The Easybeats, for example, emerged from British and Dutch migrant teens that met at the Villawood Migrant Hostel, NSW.

I craved Ron and Dave's company, watching, listening, and emulating tricks. I was a sponge, an acolyte, and a fan-club all in one. I wanted to know about playing in a band and what it was like. This was the kick-start to my music education.

I practised constantly, and often heard my mother and sister shouting in unison through the thin walls of our hostel rooms: 'Michael, give it a break, no more guitar.'

Within a couple of months, I was playing rhythm guitar and starting to sing and play simultaneously. At last, I felt a connection to what I had left behind – a teenager in the sixties, growing up during a social and musical revolution.

This Jenerayshun

I met Brian Little at Matraville High School. Brian, his sister Jan and parents Alan and Irene lived in Block 3 at Bunnerong. Although not a musician, Brian was into tape recorders and electrical circuits and wanted to become an electrical engineer. He would come over to my block and record me on his BSR (Birmingham Sound Reproducers) Riviera reel-to-reel tape recorder. I played the few guitar licks I knew. He could speed up the recordings and slow them down and splice the tape to create loops. He could also amplify my guitar by attaching the recorder's microphone near to the bridge on the guitar body and then forcing the BSR into simultaneous 'record' and 'playback'. We had a lot of fun with feedback. We filled the void of Block 9's dingy corridors with my thrashing power chords, annoying the odd neighbour or two on the way. For me, it was a cathartic moment, recalling the first dance I attended and being overawed by the volume of sound. Brian offered to build me my first 'fuzz box' – a 1960s-designed distortion unit that made an electric guitar sound grungy. He was, in truth, an electronics whiz-kid.

One day, following a game, I invited Doug Gladden, a football mate, to come to the hostel for lunch. Doug worked at HG Palmer's electrical store in Maroubra. Doug was the eldest in a family of eight children. They were sponsored migrants and lived in a house in Little Bay. I introduced Doug to Brian, and they became instant buddies. Doug liked coming to the hostel to kick a ball around and enjoy the attention of some of the hostel girls, who liked his curly hair and Suffolk accent.

Brian, Doug, and I listened to a lot of music. We swapped singles and LPs. We liked The Who, a band that exemplified 'Mod' – the name of a London style movement in fashion. Their December 1965 hit 'My Generation' inspired my first band name, This Jenerayshun, which we pronounced in as best an Aussie accent as three Pommies could muster. How we relished singing the lines of that song. The name would look great on a kick drum skin. All we needed was a drummer with a kit.

I taught Doug some guitar fundamentals by playing the chords of his favourite songs plus the bass line for each one. I showed him where to finger the notes, with one note at a time, and one tune a day. It was an act of friendship because he had no prior musical experience and struggled initially with the patterns. But I was pleased to pass on what I had learned from Ron and Dave.

My sister, Jennifer, never attended any more school in Sydney. She took up full-time employment. Serendipitously, her first boyfriend, Alan 'Aldo' Guarino, knew how to sing in quasi-Elvis style and play rock-and-roll guitar, with a good vocabulary of licks and chord progressions. He became our lead vocalist and lead guitarist.

Alan knew a drummer, John Price. He had a drumkit and a car – a grey 1964 Holden. Both were priceless assets in the swinging sixties. Equipment-wise, we had John's complete Australian-made drum kit by the Drouyn company, and Alan played a black English Burns guitar and a 60-watt Fi-Sonic amplifier with four inputs. He, too, had a car, a green Falcon with chrome detailing. We practised in Doug's garage. All of us could sing a bit, but we needed to complete the instrumental line-up with a bass. The instrumental core of the British pop explosion was lead and rhythm guitars, bass, and drums.

I think I was the first to badger Doug to use his hard-earned HG Palmer's pay to buy an electric bass guitar and amplifier. He did it in style by choosing the iconic Hofner viola-bodied bass guitar popularised by Paul McCartney. Now Doug had both a bass guitar and a bass amp. We could use two microphones, one of which we plugged into a second channel on Alan's amplifier, as well as my first electric guitar, a bright red $39 Canora electric that I purchased with a down payment from money earned during my summer job at Scott's Beefburgers. The guitar was Japanese-made. It functioned well for playing rhythm. The other microphone was plugged into Doug's amplifier.

This Jenerayshun was born: two Pommie migrants (me and Doug) teaming up with Alan, the son of an Italian immigrant musician living in Maroubra, and John the drummer from Pagewood. We rehearsed for several weeks, learning each other's favourite songs. The passion was all there for sixties music, plus a reasonable skill set and enough equipment. We were well behind the mercurial Easybeats, the lads from Villawood hostel who were right 'up there!' And of course, there were the Bee Gees (brothers Barry, Robin, and Maurice Gibb), originally from the Isle of Man, who were making an impact around Australia. I found out recently that from 1963 to 1966 the Gibb family lived at 171 Bunnerong Road, a kilometre from Bunnerong Migrant Hostel. Sadly, I also learned that in 2016, a developer knocked down their 1929 Californian bungalow. I can but imagine the brothers writing great songs there and perfecting their vocal harmonies.

Our rehearsals were productive, and we made our debut in the hostel's recreation hall. It was loud, fast, and fun. The hostel girls loved to dance. My sister turned up in a sequined go-go girl dress. Brian was our sound engineer. He took photos and kept an eye on the girls. And, of course, a little bit of alcohol was smuggled in via the windows. It cost a 5-cent piece to get in, and most of the hostel kids came along. I recall we knew about fifteen songs, about sixty minutes' worth of music. When we ran out, Alan would announce 'by special request' to enable us to repeat songs. We were celebrities for a week after our first gig but needed another event.

In 1966 the confectioner, Hoadley's, maker of the much-desired Violet Crumble Bar, sponsored a national band competition called 'Hoadley's Battle of the Sounds'. We found out about it on the radio and in *Go-Set* magazine. There were local heats in country towns and capital cities, leading to semi-finals and a grand final in either Sydney or Melbourne. Like most young bands, we saw participation as a way of getting our name out there. The first prize was a full return ticket to England on a Sitmar cruise liner, with two booked concerts in London and $1,000 cash. We secured a spot in a preliminary heat in the Capitol Theatre, Sydney. There was a quick turnaround on stage – run on, plug in and play. Bands were at the mercy of the front-of-house sound engineers and, in our case, stage fright at playing to our first large and rowdy audience. Unfortunately, we were a bit too raw to make the cut, but I was thrilled that we gave it a shot.

Doug reminded me recently of another gig we did for the Catholic Youth Organisation (CYO), which organised and chaperoned dance and disco nights for teenagers. We played at a CYO event in Todman Avenue, Kensington. Our setlist included the 1961 Bobby Darin song 'Multiplication'. Alan, who always sang this with gusto, launched into the song. Halfway through the second chorus two priests approached the stage and told us to stop performing this inappropriate song or we would have to leave. It was too risqué for them, because multiplication was a euphemism for sexual intercourse.

We capitulated to the Holy Roman Empire and switched to another song, not out of my fear of Purgatory, but we wanted to get paid and enjoy the girls dancing in front of us!

The Silver Stars
Just a stone's throw from Randwick Racecourse and the confluence of Doncaster Avenue and Anzac Parade stands a Masonic temple. The shape of the building and the symbol above the door, a pair of

dividers, are distinctive. My entry into this building was for a different kind of fellowship: the first real gig. I carried my entry-level Canora guitar proudly through the front door and over the polished parquet floor to a high stage. I suddenly thought I was entering the dance hall at Weaverham to the sounds of the song 'The Last Time', unaware that it had an ominous ring to it. Today was my big day, a time shift to this resonant yet austere Masonic temple, hoping to be spotted by radio DJs and promoters. I was shaking with excitement as I helped set the stage, carefully positioning the amplifiers and setting the microphones.

But how we got to perform there is a convoluted story. I met a Londoner, Jim Geering, and his wife. Jim was a big man – tall, stocky, with slicked black hair and a mischievous smile. His accent was pure cockney and he meant business. He took a job at Long Bay jail as a 'screw' – the slang name for a prison officer.

He heard This Jenerayshun blasting out of the hostel's recreation hall on Saturday nights. He came over to me in the dining hall and asked me about the band. He told me that he had a bunch of lyrics.

Jim invited me to his rooms in Block 8 to meet his wife, who served us tea. He persuaded me to add music to his lyrics. I agreed, then he talked about managing and promoting the band. He talked big and I listened. I cobbled some melodies and chords together for his lyrics. His eyes lit up when he saw what I had done, as he could not read music. My theory was basic but enough to satisfy his sense of achievement.

Jim then had to keep his part of the bargain to help the band. But first, he wanted a name change. Our band name, This Jenerayshun, didn't work for him. He wasn't interested in the link to The Who, to the rebellious Mod music of London. No, Jim wanted something a bit more solid, obvious, and classy. He told us to find a new name. This wasn't an easy task because it was difficult to please everyone.

However, the problem was solved the next day, after I told Brian about the meeting. Brian said he saw a laundry van driving through Maroubra with Silver Star Laundry painted on the side. He suggested we use it. Da-da! The Silver Stars became the new name. It sounded showbiz. We changed the sign on the bass drum to Silver Stars for our first gig at the Masonic Hall in Kensington. Would this be the catalyst for the charts? Could two Pommie lads and two locals cut a path in the pop music revolution? Look at the competition: the Easybeats, the Bee Gees, Billy Thorpe and the Aztecs; the Atlantics; the Masters Apprentices; and the great Johnny O'Keefe himself.

After I'd set up my amplifier and guitar on a chair on stage, I realised I was the only one at the Masonic Hall besides the caretaker. Where was Jim? Where were my bandmates? The gig was due to start in an hour. Where were the hostel girls, friends and brothers and sisters and of course the protective mothers? I was so keen that I'd misread the time and arrived two hours early.

Eventually, the rest arrived together with our friends. Jim made his entrance with his wife on his arm. His hair was slicked down, his collar starched, shoes polished like a mirror. She wore a newly purchased pinafore dress. It looked like their debut, Jim walking in like an impresario. The fledgling manager launched immediately into a pep talk, as if addressing a football team before the big match. He puffed his chest out and spoke as if to impress the girls as well, 'You play, you do well, and I'll do the talking, right? I've invited a talent scout and a radio DJ to come to hear you play!'

We did our soundcheck. A couple more friends trickled in, then a few people unknown to us, to witness the birth of the Silver Stars. And what an auspicious moment it was. As Brian said to me recently: 'A couple of strangers walked in, listened and walked out again. I think the audience totalled about twelve people, excluding the band of course.' In the words of a friend quoting a showbiz personality, Bill Brady, 'There's nothing like walking off to the sound of your footsteps echoing around a silent hall.'

I can laugh now, but at the time, I was shattered. I had expected a good audience and a step up the rock-and-roll ladder, but this turned out to be nothing more than a minor rehearsal, with Jim scratching his head while reassuring us that he had big plans. A DJ did come. He said nothing, because he was too busy ogling our sisters and girlfriends, and slipped away before we finished. Alan and John left quickly after the gig. They were disappointed, and the situation confirmed their dislike for smooth-talking Jim.

Apart from musicianship, to sound good you needed a proper public address system. We couldn't make a big enough sound with only two amplifiers shared between three guitars and two microphones. We couldn't deliver any volume or any clarity in the sound. And that's what we were judged by. To play in a crowded hall required many decibels as well as good music to carry the day.

I needed a better guitar, a Fender or a Gibson, an instrument that sounded the same as those on the records we loved, not the cheap Canora that I bought for its looks. It had a bright red lacquered body, white buttons, and chrome pickups, but this was not enough. I pointed this out to Jim who, to make amends for the failed Masonic gig, took me to a local pawn shop near Central Station to look at a guitar he might buy for me. There was a white Fender Telecaster on a stand in the window; it would be mine if the next gig went well. It was an inducement I was prepared to accept, and I continued to add melodies to his rather insubstantial lyrics.

My doubts about Jim began after he told me he had fallen in a ditch at Long Bay where renovations were taking place. After the fall he took himself to a doctor and asked for a neck brace. Jim sought compensation and told me in confidence that he planned to sue for as much money as possible. However, his injury was minor. I was very uncomfortable with this knowledge. If he could cheat them, he could cheat us. I found out, a year later, that his case had been dismissed because private detectives had been following him and discovered that he would go to Maroubra beach, take off his neck brace, and go bodysurfing. They took photos. That was that.

However, we fell out long before that. When I turned his lyrics into songs, I made recordings of my voice and guitar on cassettes. I gave him the final songs and asked him to alter the manuscript to include my name as the composer. He looked up, gave me a wicked smile and said, 'No, my boy, they're mine, not yours, I wrote them.'

I spluttered and said, 'No Jim, you're the lyricist, not the composer. We composed the songs together.'

'Not in my world,' he said, pointing his finger accusingly at me. 'These are mine, that is what we agreed to.'

Meanwhile, his wife, a gentle and rather shy woman, said nothing, looking down at the sink and rinsing crockery. Never one for a fight, I acquiesced but told him it was not the done thing. I only wish I'd had the temerity to tell him his lyrics were mediocre. Anyway, I didn't see him again because he left the hostel for a home unit somewhere in Hillsdale. I was glad he was gone because I never wanted to cross him, as he seemed capable of violence.

The Silver Stars went on to play two more gigs – a wedding and a party, but without Jim. It was good to play the music we liked and to see our friends having fun. However, the experience of Jim undermined individual ambition in the Silver Stars. We split up by mutual agreement, with each member looking for different opportunities. I joined another band in 1967, the Charles Stanford Movement, named by its founder Stan Charles, nothing to do with the Irish composer Charles Villiers Standford (1852–1924). We jammed about four times and played at a wedding. The real significance of the band was meeting the drummer, John Mamo, who introduced me to his circle of friends, mostly lads of Greek and Italian background. One of them was Les Vella. He had wheels, and John used to give him petrol money to take him to Sylvania to see his girlfriend, Elizabeth, strictly chaperoned of course. One day, after a jam, John persuaded me to go with him to a party in Sylvania because there was a girl he thought I should meet.

Julie

I had had crushes on girls. The first one was when I was in Sixth Form. Lyn Carter was a class leader. She was confident, academic, athletic and the teacher's pet. I wanted to meet her at morning recess, but she was aloof and unattainable. She was out of my league, as she lived in a mansion in Oakmere, whereas I was a council house lad. Also, I had some competition. A couple of older football mates from Winsford Grammar School declared their interest in her. I shied away.

Similarly, when I was fourteen and working in my first job at an M6 café, I became interested in a girl who worked as a waitress. I plucked up the courage to meet her on a date after school. We sat on a bench in London Road. I tried to chat her up and must have bored her to snores by talking about school, Latin, cricket, chess and cross-country. She went home. So did I. At least I learned that she detested the school she attended – a secondary modern school in Hartford. I went to her school a couple of weeks later, hoping to meet her at the gate. I arrived and saw her hop into a British Racing Green MG sports car driven by a much older boy, and off they went. I was still a gangly fourteen-year-old curious about the opposite sex and goaded by peers who urged me to think about 'birds' – not the ornithological type, but girlfriends. I was simply shy, uncomfortable, and restricted to a rickety pushbike. My courting career would lie dormant until sometime around my seventeenth birthday.

I met Julie on a Saturday afternoon at her friend Elizabeth's place in a quiet street in Sylvania Heights. Elizabeth had invited a few school friends over. Like Julie, all were fifteen and attended Gymea High School. Elizabeth had a brother, but Julie was an only child. Elizabeth's mother served lemonade and potato chips in the living room. We played LP records of the Beatles, the Hollies, and Cliff Richard and the Shadows. I found out that Julie was learning Spanish guitar, something we had in common, as John had already told her about my passion for music. We talked about my first guitar and band, and how it all started in the hostel.

Meanwhile John and Elizabeth 'pashed' on the couch, in between her mother's frequent surveillance of the living room to dust the coffee table, pick up chip crumbs and top up the lemonade supply. A couple of hours rushed by, and it was time to say goodbye. John and I left reluctantly and piled into Les's 1963 Holden. They drove me home to Bunnerong – John went to Pagewood and Les to Maroubra. John winked at me and said, 'I told you Julie was someone you should meet.' He could see the mutual attraction. No doubt, Elizabeth would give him some feedback.

Would I go back to Sylvania again? I began to count the days and hours, hoping Les would repeat the drive. I phoned and asked him if we could go again. He wasn't sure because he was low on gas, and his Holden was a guzzler. But he did come. I dropped a bunch of silver coins into his palm, and we drove to the garage, fuelled up, and then headed to Sylvania. We arrived at Elizabeth's house and Julie was there at the door to greet us. Les said he would come back later and took off to a friend's place a few streets away. Julie asked me to say hello to her parents. We left John and Elizabeth in the clutches of her vigilant mother.

Julie's house was three doors along the street from Elizabeth's. I was all sweaty palms on meeting her mum and dad. This was new territory for me. They welcomed me warmly. Following a relaxed and brief chat, Julie said she wanted to show me her guitar. They left us alone in the living room. I listened to her play a flamenco guitar piece, her delicate fingers caressing her guitar in a version of 'Malaguena'. It was a real flamenco guitar with wooden pegs, a very well-made instrument acquired from her teacher. She invited me to play it. I knocked off a couple of my Beatles songs and improvised some twelve-bar blues. I noticed a striking painting on the wall and learned that Julie was skilled at visual art and calligraphy. We had much in common, the friendship was growing, and my heart was beating fast again. I went home in the evening to Bunnerong and told my mother I had a girlfriend; her name was Julie and I wanted to see her again.

I couldn't expect Les to keep taking me to Sylvania, so I began to use public transport. I would take a government bus to Central Station, then a red rattler to Hurstville, followed by a private bus close to Julie's house. The trip, including waiting times for the connections, took about ninety minutes back in 1967.

Meeting Julie was another nirvana moment in my adaptation to life in Australia and exorcising the demons that troubled me when I had been ripped away from my life in England. First, Bill Austin and football had made me feel welcome, and now Julie and her parents. I became a regular dinner guest, and I enjoyed public transport, using the time to unwind from work and to read on the train. It was always a joy to walk into Julie's house not only in anticipation of seeing her but marvelling at the tall trees, the scent of flowers and the clean air, and in the cooler months, the smoke from log fires.

Julie's parents, Grant and Helen, welcomed me like a son. They were caring and supportive. They saw that we were happy together. Helen had a part-time job in a local antique and old wares shop, and loved classical music. She played me records of Schubert songs and the piano music of Ravel and Debussy. Her dream was to travel to Bavaria and see places such as Neuschwanstein Castle. She was intrigued by my German mother and my ability to speak some of the language. She caught on that I was interested in poetry in school and wrote poems and song lyrics. She liked *The Prophet* by Kahlil Gibran and asked me to read some to her and Julie.

Grant wasn't a 'romantic' as such. After serving amidships in the Royal Australian Navy, he enjoyed a job in marketing and sales for a leading hosiery company. Grant was a superb handyman. He made furniture and cupboards. He also repaired lawn mowers, fixed cars, anything. He was quietly spoken, methodical and never uttered a bad word about anybody or anything. He and Helen had achieved the 'Australian dream' by saving up a deposit to build their own home, a lovely cottage surrounded by tall trees, regularly visited by possums, hungry magpies, and copperhead lizards – wildlife all new to me, the hostel boy, used to metal wire fences, Nissen huts and no trees on site.

Due to the travel distance from Maroubra, where my parents had finally rented a house so we could leave the hostel, Julie's parents offered me the spare room on weekends. I helped Grant in the garden, chopped wood for the fire, or assisted him in his workshop under the house. If the weather was good, he took me fishing with his mate, Len Sharpe, a successful solicitor from Sylvania Waters, a suburb built on reclaimed land east of the south side of Tom Uglys Bridge. The suburb was once nicknamed 'mortgage flats' due to the number of mansions built by couples that over-committed themselves.

Sharpie, as he was called by Grant, owned a flash motorboat. We loaded it with tackle, and refreshments, to fish near the heads of Botany Bay, close to the Kurnell side. We trolled to catch kingfish and tailor. On calm days we went out of the heads to fish over a reef. We caught fish in all conditions, enough to feed two to three families and Julie's tortoiseshell cat. I loved the freedom of the boat and the avuncular company of Grant and Len. As a boy, I had only known sitting on a riverbank or a lakeshore to catch freshwater fish. Len's boat led me to marvel at the orange-turquoise glow of the sea at sunset in the middle of Botany Bay, heading south-west back to Sylvania Waters. After tying up the boat and gutting and scaling the fish, we would always go to the Sylvania Hotel for a couple of beers. This was my new adult world; I was one of the blokes. After socialising at the pub, Grant drove us back to Edwards Street where Helen would either cook some of our fish or have a baked dinner ready to serve. Life was good and I felt safe after dinner to share some of the stories of my family's migration to Australia and my former life in rural Cheshire.

Julie and I wrote each other letters and poems. Those I wrote to her, she complemented with lovely illustrations. During the week between visits and outings, I relished coming home from my job in the Boral office to find a letter in the postbox. We enjoyed trips into the city to eat at one of the Cahill restaurants. I recall favourites such as Chicken Maryland or Beef Stroganoff, which we washed down with non-alcoholic cider. We went to movies, walked around the Rocks, and took ferry trips to Manly. We signed up for a four-day Christian retreat near Gerringong on the South Coast. It was our first time away together, in separate dorms of course. We went especially for the long walks on Seven Mile Beach, rather than the bible study sessions.

By this stage in our relationship, I had introduced Julie to my parents and siblings. Although we had moved to Maroubra, I wanted Julie to see the hostel, to show her where her Pommie boyfriend once lived in Block 9. She praised me for my resilience. My mother responded to Julie's outgoing nature immediately. They became instant chatterboxes. I was tickled that Julie would comfortably address her – at my mum's request – using the diminutive, Gizzie, rather than Mrs Jones. When I introduced Julie to my dad, he was his usual taciturn self, showing little emotion. Our relationship swung like a pendulum. He seemed surprised that I was growing up and never once volunteered any knowledge or insight into relationships. I was expected to learn all by osmosis. However, he realised that I had to travel some distance to visit Julie. He listened to my request for driving lessons. I told him about my plan to save for a car. He gave me some lessons and took a day off work to support me through the test.

He had a rather posh second-hand English car, a Humber Vogue. It had a wood panel dashboard, gorgeous leather seats and stylish chrome appointments. The engine purred and the floor shift was a dream to operate. I soon mastered driving it and began to think of a day when I might pass my driving test. Alas, it wasn't to be at the first attempt. The examiner urged me to do more gear shift practice to slow the car more downhill. My father obliged and gave me more time in the Humber. I took the test two weeks later, passed and even earned a compliment from the examiner about my driving and the stylish Humber Vogue. The next day, licence in hand, I popped the question: 'Dad, may I borrow the car tomorrow and visit Julie after lunch?' Although he didn't appear ready for my claim on his wheels, I managed with my mother's help to convince him that I was capable and that he could trust me to bring the car home by sunset without a scratch. Guitar on the back seat with flowers for Julie, I drove to Sylvania feeling like the cat who'd got the cream. Independence Day at last. Wheels! Lucky me. But I knew I had to get my own car as soon as possible.

Triumphant though I was with my new licence and freedom, there was something in my life that still held me back. It made me feel sad that I'd never learned to swim – swimming wasn't much of a thing in Liverpool. It was a curse on my self-esteem from the moment I arrived in Australia. Everyone I met could swim. I was embarrassed when I had to admit to Julie that I couldn't swim and that I dreaded being asked to go to the beach with her and her friends.

Whenever I glimpsed the ocean while on a bus or train or driving past Brighton Beach on my way to Sylvania, I looked longingly at the blue water. I envied the lads of my age who could surf and knew I could be called a sissy, a sheila or a poofter. I had a fear of water and would only wade gingerly up to my knees at the beach. How desperate was I to become a part of the sun-struck surf culture of coastal Sydney? I could play surf songs, but I couldn't swim. Not only was I a Pom but I was an impostor who played 'Wipeout' and couldn't swim.

As I turned eighteen, in February 1968, my three younger brothers could all swim like fish. My dad, seeing my angst, came to the rescue. He spoke to the swimming instructor at the Coogee-Randwick RSL where my brothers had learned. The instructor agreed to meet me at the pool after it closed for the day. This was good because I would have been out of place in the kids' class. He gave me a free lesson and several tasks to complete. The conditions were perfect. A large indoor heated pool all to myself for half an hour a day for a week, and nobody to stare at my Pommie-white body flailing around in the water. He encouraged me to use goggles and to put my head underwater. I learned to float with a device, then stretch out and glide forward while looking underwater and blowing bubbles. I did this over and again, reassuring myself about the freedom and joy of moving through water. I was getting it right! I had self-belief at last, and the experience of my first comfortable swim, face-down while looking at the black lane markings at bottom of the pool, was pure magic. It took me three sessions to go from getting my feet off the bottom to a basic breaststroke. Then came treading water, which I soon mastered.

Next, I pushed myself to swim across the pool. Again, I did this by myself. There were no teachers, no parents, no cameras, just my doggedness to succeed. Eventually, I managed a 50-metre length. It was a gift, another nirvana. Time to buy the speedos and board shorts to hit the beach. The next task was to tan the white skin. I even tried to advance the tanning process by using coconut oil and other products. Ouch. I burned easily with my fair skin. This led to extreme sunburn with yellow blisters. Pommie-white became Pommie-red, and the pain was agonising. But I was a true-blue sun-burned Aussie ready to catch a wave, perhaps a little one! I was eventually monstered by a large 'curler' at Maroubra.

3

WHITE-COLLARED, SELF-SCHOOLED

A life in music is a gift of life itself.

After arriving in Australia, I recall great apprehension starting school almost at the end of the academic year – in this case, Year 10 – not knowing anyone or which subjects I would study. How would I cope, having not been in school since the end of July at Sir John Deane's in Cheshire? It was intimidating to join a classroom after school had started, find a seat at a desk after a brief introduction, and follow a lesson. The collective stare was for another Pommie arrival. I was used to being in a large class of boys in uniforms, strictly monitored by prefects and teachers and studying Latin, French, and German electives. But I entered a history class. The subject was Australia in World War II. I knew nothing and felt lost, hoping for the relief of the electric alarm sounding the end of the lesson – nothing like the brass bell rung in corridors, as was the procedure in my last school.

The students were relaxed and ambled to their classes, with only some in uniform. Matraville High was a smaller school than Sir John Deane's Grammar. The architecture, while functional, was close to brutalism in style, relying on rectangles and squares. There were no trees or shade, only concrete fringed by sandy, grassed areas around the buildings. It was drab and soulless. However, the students were friendly and forgiving. Never did they call me a Pom or bully me. They just chatted casually during break times and allowed me in the conversation if I chose to join in.

I had returned to school in the first year of the newly developed School Certificate, and I was bewildered because the syllabus was different from the system I was used to in Cheshire. Matraville High School listed me for examinations in English, Mathematics, French, German, Latin, History, Geography, and Science. It was stressful, but I passed all my subjects very well except for one: I missed sitting the Science examination due to a school administrative error, and I received an automatic F grade, the only one in my career. It was my first taste of education bureaucrats.

Importantly, getting back to school after the disruption of immigrating to Sydney was stabilising for me. The mix of boys and girls at Matraville High reflected the hostel population, and I liked hearing them talk about surfing and music in the idioms of their Australian dialect.

The summer break arrived, and I looked forward to playing my guitar and exploring Sydney. I took on casual work to earn pocket money and went back to school in 1966 for Year 11. There was a buzz at school because on 14 February 1966, Australia switched to decimal currency. It was fun spending shiny coins at the school canteen.

However, I still found it difficult to settle. None of my language electives were available, and I regretted the disruption of the shift from England. My father was also pressuring me to take a job to help the family get out of the hostel. So I took the big step of discontinuing school in April, with a plan to start again in 1967, and found a book-keeping job in the Mascot office of the (now-defunct) Airlines of New South Wales. Each day, listening to the nearby planes flying in and out of Kingsford Smith Airport, I would think about my friends in England. It seemed so near, yet so far.

The job provided an income, but I didn't get to know my colleagues, except for saying hello to the friendly receptionist who handled the pilots' papers and messages. Sadly, one Monday I came into the office and heard that she had died from gunshot wounds in Darlinghurst. It shocked me to recall her at her desk on Friday, and dead by Monday, likely the innocent victim of a gangland payback in Kings Cross. A few weeks later, our elderly tea-lady dropped dead on the footpath at Matraville shops. My adolescent world was turbulent, especially when an Irishman in the office dragged his chair over to mine while we were examining logbooks and surreptitiously pushed his leg against mine and put his hand on my knee. Confused, I pulled away and shared my surprise with another clerk that I trusted. He told me 'Harry's a fairy, a homo, he's making a play for you.' I simply didn't know what this meant. I had never heard such words before. Such was my naiveté at sixteen.

Working in this office might enable me to save for an airline ticket and return to England, something I often considered. My dream that I might study medicine was slipping away. My father wasn't forthcoming about his promise to support my education. The Airlines of New South Wales job was enough until the end of September, when I pleaded with my father to let me return to school. He agreed reluctantly, on condition that I work a part-time job to pay my keep.

I enrolled in Randwick Boys High School for the last eight weeks of Year 11. The school felt more robust and focused than the coeducational environment at Matraville High. It would be difficult catching up on the missed work, especially for Maths and Science. There was much to read in English, and my French and German were rusty. I had to pick up an elective subject. I chose Ancient History. The teacher was very understanding and loaned me her personal texts and notes. I felt deep enthusiasm for this new subject. It tapped into my grammar school background in Latin.

Here I was again, playing catch-up, attending school out of sync with the year, as I had done in Year 10. Despite pushing myself to the limit, it was like climbing a mountain. I hadn't fully prepared for the exams. There were too many gaps in my learning, and I was at a disadvantage working in the first Year 11 syllabus under the new system. My results were ordinary, with low marks in maths and science. My English mark was good, and I did very well in Ancient History, scoring one of the highest marks: since it was a new subject at the school, I caught up quickly and was able to show what I might achieve in a fair competition. But the school principal's comment on my report annoyed me: 'Matriculation prospects doubtful.' Failure was never part of my script, and I aimed to prove him wrong.

My classmates at Randwick Boys appreciated my situation and gave me moral support. Many of these boys were from Jewish families that lived in Bondi, Clovelly, and Bronte. They were confident, focused, and excellent conversationalists. If I wasn't their scholastic equal, a few had music in common with me, as four of them played in bands, three in a band called the Pink Fits. I lost contact with them after I left Randwick High, but I heard one became a nuclear physicist in the US, one became a holistic GP, and another, a highly successful advertising mogul.

Disruption ruled again in my home. My parents were arguing all the time. I felt alone and left to muddle through things. I'm not sure why – possibly depression – but I didn't return to Randwick High School for Year 12, which would see me sitting for the Higher School Certificate. Instead, I applied successfully for an office job at Boral Oil Refineries in Matraville. I took the job with thoughts of a cadetship to study accounting in the evening.

My job consisted mostly of collecting and delivering mail around the various offices and workstations at the oil refinery. It was large enough for me to use a pushbike. I made two runs a day, rain or shine, and did book-keeping in between the runs. A regular salary meant I could buy a decent guitar and amplifier, go out with friends, and buy good clothes. I suppressed all thoughts of study. I rode my bike between the refinery installations including the catalytic crackers and a maelstrom of tanks, pipes, and operating rooms, all for refining oil to make kerosene, solvents, bitumen and more. Here was science and technology at work, but they meant nothing to me as a seventeen-year-old. I lost science, or it lost me, somewhere between the ages of thirteen and seventeen.

I enjoyed the office environment at Boral and made new friends. I embraced the South Sydney Rabbitohs as my rugby league team, and found myself locking horns with colleagues during in tea breaks. They comprised St George 'Dragons', North Sydney 'Bears' and Newtown 'Bluebags' supporters.

Travelling around the refinery, I could hang out briefly with the engineers, the electricians, refinery operators, and the men on the bitumen loading and dispatching trucks. I listened to yarns and enjoyed the jokes. There was a small lawn in front of the office, and the lads had set up a putting circuit. Weather permitting, we competed on most days of the week. I listened to office banter, including the occasional bragging about football, horse racing, cars, and sexual prowess. I was a seventeen-year-old among men aged twenty-five to fifty years. They treated me well and I found them to be easy-going most of the time. However, a recently married Kiwi, a bookkeeper, once boasted about his stamina in the bedroom. He was mercilessly hounded ever after.

By June 1968, I was becoming restless again. My dream of going to university was fading. I made enquiries about attending TAFE rather than going back to a high school. Fortunately, I discovered the Department of Correspondence Studies, which offered the full syllabus for students unable to attend a high school due to distance. I talked a lot to Julie and her parents about my dilemma. They understood what I was feeling and encouraged me to make a choice.

It was impossible to leave work. My father wouldn't have me back as a dependent, so I enrolled in five subjects for the HSC examinations: English, French, German, Ancient History and Mathematics. This combination would allow me to matriculate. A few days later, a postal van delivered several parcels of printed materials. They contained lesson notes, reading lists, essay topics and worksheets. I went to Angus & Robertson's bookstore and purchased the required texts for my subjects, plus study guides. It would be a race against the clock to catch up on as much work as possible and prepare for the exams. I had a small bedroom off the kitchen in our rented house in Pagewood, where I could lock myself away.

Other than going to work, eating, and sleeping, I read and studied every day from late August to November without a break. I would get up at 5 am, wash, grab breakfast, and work until 8:30 am before walking to Bunnerong Road to catch the Boral work bus. My goal was to matriculate. It was a long shot. It was more likely that I was catching up before attending TAFE full-time in 1969, using my savings to pay my board. This cramming would be preparatory work to get into a study rhythm again. I had to complete the Year 11 work that I'd missed at Randwick in 1967 in addition to the entire syllabus of Year 12.

Contrary to my vivid memories of teachers at my previous schools, my Correspondence School teachers were only ever names to me in blue ink. They marked my work carefully, always including helpful suggestions and returning it within a week. They felt like friends.

I took two weeks of annual leave from Boral before the examinations to study more intensively. I was pleased to be following my goal despite the mountain of material that I had to cover – all the novels, plays and short stories plus grammar for English, French and German. I had opted to sit the basic mathematics exam because I missed a lot of work that required drill and repetition. In hindsight, I wasn't confident about passing, and failure in any one subject would not allow me to matriculate.

I had to stay well and highly focused all the time. Fortunately, my father and I kept out of each other's way. My mother just smiled and made my meals, and I locked my guitar in the cupboard to remind me that study came before everything. I hardly saw Julie for the last weeks leading up to the examinations, such was my focus and determination. She wrote me letters of encouragement and listened to bulletins on the phone about which assignments I was working on.

On the first day of the exam period, I walked to Maroubra Girls High School to sit the first English paper. This school was a designated centre for 'irregular examination students'. I walked into the auditorium in civvies – jeans, a snappy shirt, denim jacket and gym shoes. I took my seat amongst 120 girls. I had expected to be nervous about the exam because I hadn't read everything, and hoped to get questions that suited me. Indeed, I stayed calm by reassuring myself that it was an achievement to be back on track as a student. I felt lucky and gave it everything, going home happy. One down, five examinations to go.

The weather during the examination period was warm. The green of the garden shrubs tempered the light in my bedroom and I became accustomed to different bird calls in the day and the sound of frogs and crickets at night. These were my companions. I saw the sun come up and studied before going to Boral. I came home and worked until the early hours. I became a stranger to my parents and siblings. I hardly said a word or made eye contact, always lost in my thoughts, always with a book in my hand and pencil and notebook close by. I went back to work the day after my final exam, German. It was in the first week of December. It went well. I had run a marathon. And so, I counted down the days until 18 December waiting for my results to arrive in the post. Would I pass or do it all again next year at Sydney Technical College?

At last, I could see Julie again. I retrieved my guitar from the locked wardrobe. I cleaned my bedroom and listened to LP records. As I rode around the refinery delivering mail, I ruminated on the letter

I wanted to arrive at Pagewood. It arrived on the 19th. There it was, sticking out of the mailbox. I retrieved an ominously stamped Board of Studies envelope with my name on it. With adrenaline coursing through my veins, I shuffled into the house, clutching the envelope tightly. I threw my bag on my bed and went into the garden. I held my breath as I ripped open one side of the envelope and extracted a trifold letter. I scanned the subject list and saw a list of five subjects. It had the letter P for a pass next to each one. I read it over and again to be certain I understood what was in print. I was both shocked and elated because I hadn't expected to pass Mathematics. But there it was. I had achieved a matriculation pass. Nirvana! Was this how it felt to win a gold medal at the Olympics, because this was my moment? I phoned Julie. I told my parents. Even my father broke his silence to congratulate me. I don't remember eating or even sleeping that night. Instead, I played some of my favourite Who tracks from *A Quick One* and started to dream about not only university life but the possibility of feeling completely settled in Australia and having made up lost ground.

I went to work the next morning on cloud nine. I waited until morning tea to see my boss and give notice of my intention to leave Boral on Christmas Eve. He offered to take me off the bike, give me a full desk job and cover the costs of a part-time accountancy degree, but I declined his generous offer. I wanted to become a full-time university student, study arts, make new friends and enjoy the camaraderie of campus life. It was the upturn in my career path that I needed, one that boosted my self-esteem. The support from the entire refinery staff was overwhelming. They gave me a wonderful 'send-off' and a 50×50-centimetre farewell card with a hundred names on it. Not bad for an office boy from the migrant hostel. For the first time, I was no longer playing catch-up. I bought a leather briefcase, some new clothes, and a mountain of books. I could start university at the commencement of the academic year with other students.

University

The University of New South Wales (UNSW) was established on 1 July 1949, and Foundation Day was first celebrated on 4 July 1961 to raise the public profile of the university and collect money for charities. During my time, I witnessed pram races that ran from Liverpool Street to Circular Quay, and I tried to dodge the flour and water fights on campus. While at UNSW I sometimes encountered the jibe 'So you go to Kenso Tech?' This came from the snobby University of Sydney students across town that said UNSW was too young to be a real university. UNSW in 1969 was a vibrant place. It had a visionary and popular vice-chancellor, Rupert Myers. I was fortunate to be a student in an institution that reflected the new freedom and energy of the 1960s.

To do medicine, I would have had to pick up Chemistry and Biology and study full-time for a year and re-sit the HSC. This was financially, if not emotionally, impossible for me. So, I was happy to enrol in a Bachelor of Arts degree and study English, French, History and Philosophy of Science (HPS), and Psychology. I began to think about a career in teaching or using my linguistic skills to work for the Department of Foreign Affairs, perhaps even doing postgraduate research.

My undergraduate life at UNSW featured a different curriculum from those of literature courses today. The influence of Oxford and Cambridge shaped the content. The study of Old English and Middle English language and literature was compulsory. Exams were many. Studying Old English and learning the grammar of Anglo-Saxon, the foundation of the polyglot language we speak today, was important to me. I relished learning to read, translate and appreciate the surviving poems of the mostly anonymous poets of the eighth and ninth centuries. I still find Beowulf a remarkable piece of writing by any standard; an epic poem of 3,182 alliterative lines in pre-Norman English. It switched me to thinking about the connections between music and poetry and how this great epic involved recitation and singing with the accompaniment of a small lyre.

The study of the novel began with fiction and essayists of the sixteenth century. As an honours student, which I became, it was compulsory to study seventeenth-century religious prose tracts alongside the metaphysical poets. Shakespeare was the mainstay of Elizabethan and Jacobean theatre, which also included Thomas Kyd, Christopher Marlowe, Ben Johnson, John Fletcher, Thomas Middleton, John Webster, and John Ford. Each unit of study involved reading widely. The only shortcoming was that little scope existed for comparative literature from Europe and America or writings from the rest of the English-speaking world, including Australia and South Africa and other Commonwealth countries. Our curiosity propelled us to read Russian and French novels. I look back on the depth of the subjects and the research experience, grateful for the exposure to a wealth of enriching material.

I wanted to leave home but couldn't afford it. My father said it was okay to stay with the family as long as I could substantially contribute to the household economy. I took several part-time jobs and helped him with his latest venture as a floor cleaning specialist. One of his contracts was polishing the floors of wards and corridors at Prince Henry Hospital, Little Bay. This led to an offer of extra work for me as a hospital porter, wheeling patients to and from operating theatres. I didn't stay at this for long because it made me uncomfortable seeing how critically ill some patients were. My father was angered by my decision. He thought I gave in too easily. He was also spending longer hours at the Matraville RSL, and there was now daily friction between him and my mother. I worried about his addiction to alcohol. All this, just as I was coming up to my first-year exams. I had to cut back on casual work. He resented this. There was no leeway. But I did what I could to contribute to my keep and made it to the end of the exam period before I had to find work again.

Fortunately, I did well in all my first-year subjects and was awarded a Commonwealth Scholarship, which, in my case, provided an independent student allowance plus help to purchase books. So I moved out of my home by accepting the generous offer of a spare room with Julie's widowed grandmother, in her Federation house at Connell's Point Road, South Hurstville. It would mean a train trip to Central and a bus to Kensington, but it was closer to Julie's house in Sylvania.

New friends

Regarding friendships, I didn't know what to expect at university. Indeed, it was daunting in the first few weeks. I was all at sea following the crowds into lecture theatres, getting lost trying to find tutorial rooms, and filling in endless forms. I made friends quickly, and this helped me navigate the big world of UNSW.

I met Ted Hall outside the Faculty of Arts, which was housed in the Morven Brown Building next to the library lawn. I picked his Geordie accent immediately, and he acknowledged my occasional north-west midlands vowels. Ted was a tall lad like me but with long Mod-styled brown hair. He, too, was a migrant and we swapped hostel stories. Ted spoke animatedly about the Nissen huts of the Cabramatta migrant hostel, his first domicile in Australia. He went to Burwood Primary then Greystanes High School and played football for the Commonwealth Hostels team. He also managed to take part in one or two playground 'dustups'.

Ted's father was Polish and his mother, English. They immigrated to Australia in 1961. Ted was studying English, History, Philosophy, and HPS. We caught up after English and HPS lectures, where we met, if memory serves me, Sue-Ann Seaton, Jeanine Baddock, Peter Lanevaali, Ros Hinde, and Sharman Mellick, who is now a children's author. Ted and I would often meet at lunch and talk about migration, university, politics, history, and weekend social life. We kept in touch for a couple of years after graduation. He came to see me play in the Renaissance Players before he left Sydney to teach in Ballina. From there, he went to London to study law as a postgraduate, then to Scotland, and became an expert walking leader and a writer of Celtic mythology and legends. Today, he lives with several animals in a quiet village in Donegal, Ireland. We tracked each other down via Facebook and continue to chat via WhatsApp.

I became good friends with Robert Elliott, originally from Queensland. He was well read and highly articulate, and always asked lecturers complex questions. We met in English lectures. He majored in philosophy, specialising in ethics. We hung out together in the second year when he joined the Philosophy Honours stream, and I moved into the same in English. We lost contact in fourth year but caught up again in 1973 at the commencement of our postgraduate studies. He suggested we take a trip to Tasmania, that we sleep rough in parks and church grounds, but use a backpacker's hostel if the weather turned cold. Robert went on to a PhD and pursued an academic career as an ethicist, with a string of publications. He finished, like me, as an academic leader in his institution.

Undergraduate life

Several things embodied the energy of UNSW: The Roundhouse, *Tharunka*, and the Wizard. The Roundhouse became an iconic 'groovy' building of modern and forward-looking design. It was a hub of social and cultural life at UNSW from its opening in 1961. I discovered Café Society – a place to meet other students and staff. It held the *Tharunka* student newspaper office, and you could hire a breakout room for a club meeting or could go to a Roman ball or a Zoom Sunday event. The latter – implying a zoom camera shot – was an early type of 'rave' party with live bands or a disco. A lighting spectacle was a feature provided by 'Ellis D Fogg', the pseudonym for Roger Foley, an innovative lighting designer and lumino-kinetic sculptor. His shows were unforgettable, as was the list of bands who made the campus rock on Sunday evenings. Consequently, lecture attendance on Monday mornings was often low.

Then along came the Wizard, the hilariously manic, comical character Ian Channel (b.1932). He migrated from the UK in 1967, with double honours in psychology and sociology from the University of Leeds. He joined the teaching staff of the newly opened School of Sociology and began a PhD in the sociology of art. Channel proposed alternative modes of thought and social interaction underpinned by the persona of a wizard, suggesting magic, esoteric philosophy, sociology, and performance art as a means of dissent.

Channel, who was tall, bearded and with long flowing hair, wore a way-out variety of outlandish costumes. His antics in 1969 led to his PhD candidature being terminated by the head of the recently established School of Sociology, on the grounds he had made 'insufficient progress'. He lost his teaching fellowship and the associated income. But in an extraordinary reversal of fortune, the Vice-Chancellor, Rupert Myers, appointed Channel as the Official Wizard of UNSW, which he declared was an endorsement to pursue 'experimental teaching and social reform techniques' that marked 'the beginning of a new social role complex.' He had insight and power.

Channel formed a group called the Blackguards, which became the ALF, a movement for the Action of Love and Freedom. However, his irreverent behaviour and performances were a target of radical left students who saw him as a diversion from significant issues. I recall him speaking from a ladder and being willingly tarred and feathered by some radicals who dragged him into the pond below the vice-chancellor's balcony. Channel, who was always quick to seize the day, arrived in a loincloth and with his long, flowing black hair and wiry figure. It resonated with the persecution of Jesus.

The student newspaper, *Tharunka*, was irreverent, ardently socialist, and full of great concert reviews and poetry. The drive of the paper was to be controversial, iconoclastic, and strong in parody. It aimed to challenge the quietly complacent, backwater ethos of an Australia waking up from its post-war slumber. It was in *Tharunka* that its editors, Richard Neville and investigative journalist Wendy Bacon, honed some of their skills. Everyone read *Tharunka*, and we couldn't wait to get our hands on each new edition. How different today, when student-led newspapers are left in large piles, unread!

Women were prominent at UNSW and deservedly gaining a powerful voice. Bacon led a group called the Kensington Libertarians and encouraged the publication of an Australian edition of *The Little Red Schoolbook*, a book that was banned in many places around the world, including Queensland. The book encouraged young people to question social norms. It contained pages on sex, drugs, alcohol, and tobacco.

However, the book that shook everyone from their slumber was Germaine Greer's *The Female Eunuch*. It was the incendiary book we all bought in 1970. Sexual politics became a highlight of café discussion. Meanwhile, campus activist Sal Salby created a magazine called the *Bull Sheet*, which he distributed outside the Menzies Library. Sal was the first pro-Palestinian Israeli on an Australian campus.

We were swept into another dimension in the sixties. We had the writings of Noam Chomsky and transformational grammar, plus the scientific writings of Karl Popper. Conflicted, we became agnostic or atheist. We were liberated and liberating each other as baby boomers with adrenaline, free love, and popular music. It was a renaissance on campus for sure.

∽

In 1970, my second year of university, I turned twenty and my name went into 'the lottery of death': the ballot for conscription to serve in

Vietnam under the National Service Act. The mechanical delivery of this was via a Tattersall's bingo barrel. My birthdate wasn't pulled out, which meant all males, including myself, born on 17 February 1950 weren't called up. It's the best lottery I never won. I never became a 'nasho' but still feel sorrow for the 200 young men killed and the 1,279 who were wounded, as well as the shameful disparagement and neglect of our Vietnam veterans.

Student opposition to conscription was intense for the 1970 moratoriums, the first of which took place on 8 May 1970. We saw the ANZUS treaty as the motivation behind the Australian participation in the Vietnam War – to improve trade with the US and fortify against communism. Along came Jim Cairns, Labor's Shadow Minister for Trade and Industry, who became a student hero, advocating and taking part in our peaceful marches. Thousands of middle-class Australians joined hands with students to protest. About 200,000 took part on 8 May. There were marches in every capital city and some rural towns. Many UNSW staff postponed lectures to accompany students to demonstrations in the city.

I was no longer fearful of my father's physical presence, nor the memory of his clenched-fist threats during my childhood. While I never saw him lay a hand on my mother, he abused her mentally by calling her 'fat', 'a lazy cow' and 'just like her mother'. It reached a sad climax late one afternoon in April 1970 when I dropped into the Pagewood house to say hello. I walked into the middle of a terrible row. Insults were flying. My father was ironing his shirt, and my mother was berating him for 'living at Matraville RSL', seeing floozies, and begrudging her money for a pair of shoes. I watched his anger increase as he held up the iron threateningly. My mother was in tears and my three young brothers were close by. I couldn't bear it any longer. The same scene for years, with the potential for physical harm. My mother looked exhausted and pale. I puffed out my chest and told them both to cool it. My adrenaline surged, and I shouted at my father, 'Both of you have to stop this, now.' I turned to my mother and said, 'I'm taking you away, Mum! We're leaving the house immediately. I will help you pack.'

I was shaking as I helped her pack a few things before I let my young brothers into the garden to kick the ball around. My mother came outside. She hugged each one of them and said she would go away to her friend Doreen's for a few days. For once, my father didn't intervene and tried to comfort my brothers in their confusion. It was a terrible situation. She was close to a nervous breakdown, and he was an alcoholic with an abusive temperament. My mother never returned to him, and for custody of the boys, he spent a lot of money on a barrister to ensure that he would take them from her. She capitulated in the courtroom and agreed. I felt deeply sorry for my brothers not having their mother in the same house, although I knew he would care for them. He and I no longer spoke, and it remained that way for several years.

My mother rented a flat in Maroubra. She recovered her strength and continued to work as a ward assistant for Prince Henry Hospital, Little Bay. My father and brothers moved into the Kingsford house of an older couple, Percy and Ida. When Percy passed away, Ida became my father's *de facto*.

For a long time, I carried mixed feelings of anger, pity and sadness about my family situation. However, both my parents moved on and found new partners. I relinquished all resentment towards my father. My father never climbed Everest, penned a novel, or played for his beloved Everton. He never forgot the shells and machine guns that threatened his body and mind in World War II. He never found a job or career that satisfied him, but he achieved something greater in human terms. He wanted a better future and more opportunities for the five children he and my mother brought into the world. Bringing us to Australia was an act of love more than a means of escape.

Summer jobs

There are deep, winding, unused tunnels beneath Sydney's central station. They are cool, musty, resonant spaces. One leads to the now disused mortuary station. Every year the PMG (Postmaster General's Department, now Australia Post) hired a posse of university students to shift mountains of parcel bags in the glut of Christmas mail. I got lucky to get this job in December 1970 and worked in the mouth of one of these tunnels. I had to hump mailbags on and off large wheelbarrows painted beetroot red, with heavy metal wheels and long handles at either end.

It was hard yakka but a lot of fun, too. We student casuals lined up like a chain gang. None of the full-time workers moved a muscle. Many were overweight, chain-smoking, hard-drinking men in blue singlets, shorts, long socks, and steel-capped boots. They would lie around on mountains of mailbags, teasing us. Or they ogled Page 3 girls in the *Mirror*, rolled smokes and decanted thermoses of strong tea, some of which smelled of whisky.

It was our job to read and call out the bag type and destination to the tally clerk before hoisting the bag over the shoulder and heaving it into another barrow. For example, 'Mel – P!' was shorthand for a parcel for despatch on the Melbourne train. 'Coffs – L' indicated a bag of letters for Coffs Harbour on the North Coast Mail. I'm sure Christmas teddy bears survived the rough handling. One couldn't say the same for other goods such as baked cakes, salami, porcelain eggcups, bonbons, even fireworks!

We humped bags until our hands were raw, but we dared not say a word to the blokes, who called us long-haired sheilas. We worked while the regulars bludged, to use that great Aussie word. Despite the banter, we got on. It was all good fun, especially when they teased each other and played practical jokes. For example, one of the older blokes, Jim, often fell asleep after lunch. His workmate, George, planned a wicked wake-up call. Jim was cocooned in a pile of mailbags, snoring. George sidled up with his fly open. He whipped out his 'Jolly Roger' tattooed with a butterfly and positioned it a couple of centimetres away from Jim's closed eyes. 'Wakey, wakey!' snickered George. Jim woke up with a start, and gales of laughter greeted him. Jim had to endure a few days of being called a victim of the 'pork sword!'

Aside from practical jokes, we would entertain ourselves at lunch by playing cricket with a tennis ball in one tunnel, using a mailbag for stumps and a lump of wood for a bat. And we often shared a few beers with the blokes at the Agincourt Hotel, corner of Harris and George Street, on Christmas Eve, our last day.

I needed more weekend work, and Julie's father teed me up a job through his friend, Pat Meldrum, an expat from London who worked for Gilbey's Gin. Pat had contacts with posh hotels. He found me a job as a drinks waiter at the Chateau Commodore in Potts Point. I had no experience and had to rely on Pat and Grant to instruct me on the basics. I was going in at the deep end. The supervisor gave me a sailor's uniform to wear. It was small and a real squeeze to put on. It was acrylic and uncomfortable.

There I was in my first job at a swanky hotel, pretending to be a real drinks waiter. I was nervous, especially having to move through a crowded courtyard with a swimming pool in the centre. It took me less than ten minutes to break a champagne flute, spill two drinks on guests and come within centimetres of ending up in the pool. I felt the glare of those I offended and the heat of the sun. Balancing tall cocktail glasses and champagne flutes on a small silver tray was not for me. Embarrassed and disappointed, I went to the change room, tossed the uniform on the floor, got into my jeans, and quit the job there and then, vowing it was the end of my waiter's career.

Variety became my norm for holiday work. A year later, I was picking up glasses in the White Horse Hotel at Hurstville, where I felt more at home with a crowd of swearing labourers pouring schooners down their necks and spitting on the floor. And no sailor's uniform required.

Another job was at the Bendix Brakes automotive parts warehouse at Rockdale. I worked in the store helping to fill orders for small parts, including brake linings, carburettor parts and air filters. I enjoyed making friends there and seeing how the business worked.

I also tried dishwashing – becoming a *plongeur*, as they say in France. I found this job via the UNSW Students' Union. There was a small restaurant in posh Woollahra. La Goulue was French named but specialised in Indian food. It was owned and staffed by a Pakistani chef, Gulu, and his wife. The premises were tiny, especially the kitchen with its tiny sink that made dishwashing and pot scrubbing difficult. The cuisine was superbly aromatic, and the place was always full. It was like no other job. I had to arrive by 5 pm. My first task was to go to the Moncur Hotel with money from the boss and buy six long-necked beer bottles. The boss's wife then served me an early meal of curried beef and rice while Gulu pulled the top off a long neck, poured me a beer, and took the bottle to swig at his stove.

Wealthy Woollahra patrons arrived and ordered. Soon I was filling the sink with hot water and doing my job. Gulu looked at me regularly and filled my glass. By eight o'clock I was sloshing water all over the place and Gulu would sing in Urdu. What made all this fun is that he preferred to communicate with me in French rather than use his broken English. So, we conversed as best we could. He had picked up French while working in a Paris kitchen, whereas mine was language laboratory-honed university French. What a student job! Well-fed, half-tanked, and paid in cash.

Teaching guitar

I described earlier how I had taken up the guitar, which became both a solace and a tool of creativity and wellbeing. This instrument liberated me in another way. I was keen to play all styles, including classical guitar, because that meant reading music and learning how to compose. In 1971 I was in my third year at UNSW. My sister, Jenny, gave me some used LP records that were given to her. On top of the pile was Julian Bream's *Popular Classics for Spanish Guitar*. From the moment I dropped the needle onto the LP, the music and the quality of the recording utterly transfixed me. I pored over the sleeve notes to confirm it was just one player and one guitar, because his playing was superb for its colours, phrasing, and dynamics. This LP was a document of a recording made in the library at Kenwood House, London. It became my touchstone. I played it hundreds of times to let the music enter my soul, discovering the sonorities of Villa-Lobos, Turina, Llobet, Torroba, de Falla, and Albeniz.

Meanwhile, I discovered the Sydney Spanish Guitar Centre in Lower George Street at the Rocks near Circular Quay. It was above the Ox on the Rocks, a restaurant-cum-nightclub almost under the Cahill Expressway. I remember ascending flights of stairs to the garret-like rooms where I could hear guitarists practising or taking lessons. The atmosphere was superb. Paintings on the clean walls, simple lighting, wooden chairs, and seagrass matting. I met the director, Peter Calvo PhD, a suave, well-spoken academic from London. Peter had migrated to Australia to teach economics at UNSW, but he had a greater passion for guitars. I told him I had taught myself to play popular music, but now I wanted to learn to read and play classical guitar such as I heard on the Julian Bream recording. 'You've come to the right place,' he said, smiling enthusiastically.

Peter opened a guitar case and lifted out a superbly handcrafted guitar by Fleta, a gorgeous-sounding instrument. He gave me a two-hour free lesson on the spot. I watched and listened to him show left-hand and right-hand positions and play through a study by Fernando Sor. It mesmerised me, being so close to such beautiful sounds coming from his guitar. He then invited me to accompany him to the top floor of the building to a garret with views over Circular Quay. A shelf covered each wall, made from planks of chipboard supported at each end by Besser blocks. The blocks were 'borrowed' from building sites. I had one at home. It was a badge of student thrift and ingenuity to build (steal) such a bookshelf.

Peter's shelves contained neat piles of photocopied guitar music. The repertoire started with simple technical pieces through to demanding compositions, all arranged by Len Williams, the father of virtuoso John Williams. Peter was also one of Len's students and he was on a mission, with Len's blessing, to introduce his teaching approach to Sydney. The Len Williams technique became the gold standard at the Sydney Spanish Guitar Centre. Clarity and strength were to be achieved through correct nail shape, hand position and angle of attack on the strings.

I left the Guitar Centre carrying a sheet of scales and a study by Ferdinando Carulli, my homework for the week. It was the first step to becoming an acolyte of the classical guitar fraternity. By this time I could already read and write simple music charts – words, melody and chords; now my theory skills improved as I began to study classical guitar. I took a weekly lesson and enjoyed the camaraderie cultivated by the Centre. Peter encouraged students to drop in between lessons, to play and chat with other guitarists. And if one was at the Centre between one and two in the afternoon, Peter would press money into someone's hand and send them out to buy bread rolls, salami, cheese, ham, mustard, and pickles to share.

My experience of studying classical guitar and self-taught rock-and-roll led me to become a teacher. In 1971 I dropped into the Don Rankin Music Centre, a shop and teaching centre at 208 Anzac Parade, Kensington, where I had purchased my first electric guitar in 1968. I had a good collection of popular music LPs by now, but my purpose was to find some classical guitar music. I bought a copy of Andres Segovia performing 'Fantasia para un gentilhombre', for guitar and orchestra, by Joachim Rodriquez. Don asked me what I was doing, and I told him I was a student at UNSW down the road and now playing classical guitar. He must have been impressed because he offered me a job on the spot, teaching on Saturdays. I jumped at the opportunity because I needed money to help supplement my Commonwealth Scholarship Independent Student's

Living Allowance. The guitar students paid $3 per half-hour lesson. I kept $2 and taught eight to ten students between 9 am and 4 pm. Earning $16 from this job was a boon because my rented room was $12.50 per week, paid out of my living allowance of $19.95 per week. Food, books and travel soon accounted for the rest of the allowance.

While working there I met Don's son, Noel, a drummer. He organised a gig for me in a Thredbo pub from Boxing Day into the New Year. Noel introduced me to the bass player, Larry, and we formed a covers band. I had a decent guitar then, a Stratocaster, which I had picked up for peanuts. It was an early 1960s model. The original sunburst colours were worn, so I re-lacquered it in jet black. I regret selling it. We did the Thredbo residency in an always overcrowded barn where people drank as if there was no tomorrow. We played from 7:30 pm to 1 am. On New Year's Eve, we played until 2 am but the crowd wouldn't let us stop. They blocked the stage exits. We were exhausted by 5 am and heard glass breaking. It took bouncers to free us from a posse of aggressive drunks. Welcome 1972! I kept my job teaching at the Don Rankin Music Centre, but told Noel to find another guitar player.

Final undergraduate years, 1971–1972

Julie and I had continued our relationship, and in my third year of university we talked to her parents about our living together. Grant and Helen consented without reservation. I rented a one-bedroom compact unit for us in a Federation house in Perouse Road, Randwick. Julie would study art at Alexander Mackie Teachers' College, and I would continue my degree at UNSW. My scholarship and Saturday morning guitar teaching covered the rent, and Julie received a small allowance from her parents. We were young, happy, and part of the sixties revolution and the generation of 'the pill'. There was never any talk about marriage or a family.

After I embarked on my double honours major trajectory, the

amount of reading in English and French was massive by modern standards, because both subjects involved sixteen contact hours per week. It was possible at UNSW to take both embedded and end-on honours study from second year on. The workload for both simultaneously became impossible, and I pulled back to just the honours stream in English plus a major in French.

Professor Harold Oliver, a Shakespeare scholar, led the School of English. My meetings with this extremely conservative man reminded me of the more severe masters at Sir John Deane's. He was dictatorial to the extent that the honours cohort in fourth year had no choice of thesis topic. He chose the topic and would supervise and mark each 10,000-word thesis. Besides the thesis, there were eighteen examinations throughout the year. They covered Renaissance and Jacobean prose, fiction, and drama, plus Old English and Chaucer. Luckily, there were several approachable and inspirational lecturers in the School of English. Professor Harry Heseltine specialised in modern poetry and delivered captivating lectures, similarly Professor Ron Geering, an expert on nineteenth-century fiction, while Dr Doreen Gillam and Dr Janet Walker illuminated our lives with Anglo-Saxon poetry and Middle English prose fiction.

The School of French was the more dynamic environment, probably because of its leader, Professor Judith Robinson-Valéry, the first woman to be appointed as a fully tenured professor at an Australian university. The courses of language study in the syllabus included history, philosophy, politics, society, and cultural enquiry. Our honours tutorials were stimulating because of the small number of students. Our enjoyment would raise eyebrows today because a tutor might encourage us to bring a flagon of wine to post-lunch tutorials plus savoury biscuits and cheese. Some staff and students would smoke, too. University in the 1960s had a touch of the bohemian.

Students in their fourth-year honours program had more contact with the academic staff. Two lecturers helped to broaden both my literary and my musical interests – Bruce Johnson and Michael

'Mick' Crennan. Bruce hailed from Adelaide. He was an inspirational teacher. He was also a professional trumpet player in the Eclipse Alley Five led by reed player Paul Furniss. I followed the band to different gigs. My favourite was the Saturday afternoon session at the Vanity Fair Hotel in Goulburn Street, Sydney. The band played behind an L-shaped bar. The atmosphere was unsurpassed as they pumped out their traditional jazz. We lost track of how many schooners we tipped down our necks for over three hours. The audience bought beers for the band, and I watched the lines of full glasses of Toohey's increasing in front of each musician. The boys had so much beer they gave glasses away before it went flat. Bruce had incredible stamina. He could drink throughout the gig, pack up at 5 pm, and head off to another gig in Balmain and play on from 6 pm. Indeed, he was sometimes so busy with weekend music that he read novels during set breaks, preparing for his classes on Mondays. Bruce pointed me towards recordings of traditional jazz and Afro-American blues. So did Mick Crennan.

Mick invited me to his parties. He had an impressive collection of LPs to share around. I became a devotee of blues music by listening to Robert Johnson, Bessie Smith, Big Bill Broonzy, Lead Belly and Blind Lemon Jefferson. I listened to the jazz violin magic of Stephane Grappelli and Joe Venuti. Mick and I both shared an interest in classical guitar and swapped the latest LPs by Spanish guitarists, including Alirio Diaz and Narciso Yepes. Mick's classical guitar was an ordinary instrument, but I helped remedy this in 1974. One afternoon, walking past a pawn shop in Newtown, I stopped to look at a guitar that was propped up in a window full of cameras, tape recorders and military stuff. I went inside, tuned it up, and looked at the maker's name on the label inside the soundbox: John, aka Ben, Hall, a leading Australian luthier. I bought the guitar at a bargain price, intending that it to go to Mick. We met the same day and inverted the strings because he played left-handed. He still cherishes this guitar!

White-Collared, Self-Schooled

Sadly, the hours I spent at university with colleagues and buried in the library began to affect my relationship with Julie. I saw less of her. The university opened me up to complex ideas, causes, parties and eventually infidelity. It was in 1972, at the end of my honours year, when I became involved with a teaching fellow at the university. It happened after the submission of my thesis. Naomi made a play for me, and I didn't object. She was doing a PhD and gave tutorials to first- and second-year students. She had pageboy styled hair, dressed in loose-fitting gothic black clothes, and smoked expensive Russian cigarettes in a long holder. Boozing together in jazz pubs and at parties followed. She drove a peppy 1955 Citroen and flattered me with gifts as if I were her toy boy. I soon discovered that I wasn't the only one in her life. She was also on the rebound from a long relationship with a departmental head and had flings with other musicians while we saw each other. I was in a vortex. She was on the staff. I was technically a student until I got my results. It became an 'approach and avoid' situation.

Julie and I were building a life together, supported by her parents, but I was having an affair with an older woman. This wasn't part of the narrative. I returned to the flat in Randwick late one Friday evening to discover that Julie had left. Her mother had collected her and her things. She had pulled me aside a few months before to dress me down about ignoring Julie and my dominance in the relationship. The vehemence of her criticism didn't surprise me. I had messed everything up. I had lost my innocence. I was ashamed of my selfish behaviour and how I had hurt Julie. I pulled away from Naomi immediately and never saw her again. There would be no reconciliation with Julie. I went to tell my mother. She was so upset and cried about losing a 'daughter'.

4

MUSIC, POETRY AND MARRIAGE

Improvising at the edge of what happens next.

The turbulence of my final undergraduate year led to much self-evaluation. I had messed things up in my relationship and pulled back in the depth of my studies by spending more time on recreational music and less on the wide reading necessary for the final examinations. I felt jaded and thought about a rest, but as a high-achiever type, I completed my honours degree and qualified for a Commonwealth Postgraduate Scholarship to support two years of full-time research at UNSW, commencing in 1973. I intended to combine my competing interests and investigate the contiguity between music and poetry in sixteenth-century England. I commenced my Master of Arts (Honours) research degree program with the possibility of expanding the topic to a PhD-length study.

It was around this time that I changed my name. I chose Atherton after a school friend, David Atherton. He was one of several friends to whom I had been forbidden to divulge my family's imminent emigration to Australia. We'd done a runner, and I would spend several years afterwards atoning for it. The Atherton surname had rhythmic emphasis; it was Old English-sounding and similar to Aethelstan, the name of a famous king of the Anglo-Saxons. Taking a new surname was a signal of self-esteem and establishing individuality and purpose in my life. It would help me find an identity in academia and in music.

The Renaissance Players

I wanted to become creative and perform again, to pick up from where I had stopped playing in rock bands. I practised classical guitar regularly and discovered a repertoire that included transcriptions of attractive lute music. Going to more concerts, I found early music and the Renaissance Players and became an instant fan. I thought about buying a lute because this prince of instruments connected closely with lyric poetry in the Renaissance. The European lute, developed from the Middle Eastern *oud*, became the prime accompaniment to songs and lyrics and, therefore, was relevant to my poetry research.

I discovered myriad sources of lute music that I could adapt for the guitar. The lute is an instrument that came to Europe through the Crusades and with the Moorish occupation of Spain. It developed into a perfectly designed Renaissance artefact, with more music written for it than any other instrument. The lute enjoyed a revival in the 1960s, but it was difficult to get an instrument in Australia. I had a chance meeting with Martin Hendy, a Welsh rugby player who owned a lute made for him by Sydney architect and guitar maker John 'Ben' Hall (the same maker of the guitar I later found for Mick Crennan). Martin gave me Ben's contact details, and I tracked him down. Ben had not long returned from a trip to England, where he had made a lute for himself, with the help of the luthier Thomas

Gough, who made guitarist Julian Bream's first lute. Ben was a lovely man, softly spoken, deep thinking and generous. He divided his time between teaching architectural design at Sydney University, making guitars and lutes, and painting abstracts.

I asked him to make me an instrument. He agreed and said it would take six to eight weeks and suggested I call him occasionally for an update. I called him often, such was my new obsession. I was so desperate to get my hands on one of these multi-stringed, pear-shaped instruments.

The day arrived. The lute was ready. I drove to Wentworth Falls in the Blue Mountains, west of Sydney. It was on a cold July morning that I entered his house and walked into a family room full of abstract paintings, sculptures and lovely handmade furniture. Ben led me to his workshop and there it was, a new lute sitting in its custom-made case. He took it out and told me he had strung it up a week before and played it every day to help it settle and make any minor adjustments necessary. The lute had fifteen strings. Ben had made it from sycamore, spruce, rosewood, and ebony. It was my first handmade instrument, and it was love at first sight. I had a new talisman. It marked the start of my career-long habit of commissioning Australian-made early music and folk instruments.

I put the lute back in its case and drove home enraptured with my purchase – another milestone in my musical journey, one that soon presented a significant challenge navigating the lute's fifteen strings and different tuning from the six-stringed classical guitar. It would open a portal to early music.

I plucked away for a few weeks and moved around the fretboard with more ease by using tablature, a schematic notation that shows the player where the notes are on the fingerboard. The first piece I learned to play was an anonymous arrangement of 'Packington's Pound', a popular ballad tune from the mid-sixteenth century. Within months, I could explore the music of John Dowland and other Elizabethan lutenist composers. I loved the smell of my newly made instrument with its combination of seasoned timber, varnish, and wood glue, and, of course, I admired its proportions and the hand-carved rose covering the sound hole.

I continued to practise the guitar while teaching myself the lute. Leaving the Sydney Spanish Guitar Centre after my usual weekly lesson, I glanced casually at a noticeboard next to the stairwell. I saw an advertisement that read, 'Lutenist, Jonathan Rubin, is soon going overseas to study in Basel, Switzerland, and the Renaissance Players group is looking for a guitarist interested in playing the lute.' This was serendipity. I ran downstairs like a greyhound and out into lower George Street to find a working phone box to call the director, Winsome Evans, to request an audition. She answered the call. My heart racing, I mentioned the notice at the Centre and told her about my musical background and that I owned a lute. She invited me to her office in the Music Department at Sydney University. I cancelled all social activities and practised throughout the weekend before going to see her at 9 am on Monday morning.

I believe Winsome warmed to my firm sense of rhythm and my capacity to improvise freely, something that came from my rock-and-roll background. However, I wasn't much of a sight-reader, not surprising for a self-taught rock-and-roller, although I was learning to read through studying classical guitar. I mentioned my Masters at UNSW, how I was researching Elizabethan and Jacobean poetry, including the lutenist-poets of the Elizabethan period, and how this connected to the performance practices of medieval and Renaissance music. I told her how my work included reading medieval troubadour poetry and the music-poetic traditions of courtly love. Winsome subsequently invited me to join in rehearsals for an upcoming concert.

I played in the first Runnymede Pop Festival in September 1973, held in the gothic ambience of the Great Hall at Sydney University. This festival became a major event in the Sydney music calendar for the next thirty-five years. It included music, poetry, and mime.

Runnymede, of course, was significant as the place for the signing of the Magna Carta. The concert featured popular songs and dances in medieval Europe at that period of history. We wore red and yellow minstrel tunics and processed down the aisles singing plainchant, accompanied by a set of bells made at the Whitechapel Foundry in London. It was an exhilarating experience for me to play a role in such a well-prepared and professional ensemble.

The charismatic Frederick May, a professor of Italian at Sydney University, selected and read the poetry. He chose texts from the early Middle Ages to modern humourists including Spike Milligan and Roger McGough. Fred, as we called him, looked like a slim version of Dumbledore in the Harry Potter movies. With his horn-rimmed spectacles, broken tooth, beard, lank hair, string bag and apple, Fred was one of the university's eccentric characters. He was an insatiable polymath and vehemently opposed to censorship. Fred delighted in reciting suggestive and ribald poetry in our concerts. He was so popular that enrolments in Italian studies grew exponentially. Students from other disciplines flocked to see him perched at the top of a ladder, speaking on many subjects. Sadly, he succumbed to viral pneumonia in 1976. He was only fifty-five. It was devastating for his family and the group.

Another element of our Runnymede concerts was the inclusion of Erasmus the Clown. For several years Jeremy Wright, a junior business executive, delighted audiences with mime interludes like those of Marcel Marceau, the world-famous French mime artist, and the antics of the Italian commedia dell'arte.

After Jonathan left for Basel, I became the group's lute and guitar player. Winsome gave us a lot of music to learn. In October 1973, we performed at two Musica Viva Coffee Concerts in the Sydney Opera House. I was apprehensive about my lowly sight-reading skills compared with the surrounding musicians, who were mostly students in the Bachelor of Music degree or had already studied their instruments at high examination levels. Like most guitar players with my background, I struggled somewhat with sight-reading. I had to establish myself by being able to sight-read the complex figurations Winsome composed in her highly embellished reconstructions of the music. But her confidence in me grew, as I maintained a vital continuo role as a plucked strings specialist.

The Renaissance Players at Sydney University just before the tour of Asia, 1974. *l-r*: Michael Atherton; Lyndon Terracini; Wayne Richmond; Barbara Stackpool; John McLoughlin; Stephen Stewart; Graham Pushee; and Winsome Evans at front. Due to overseas study commitments, Joanna Parkes and Jonathan Rubin were missing from this photo. Photo: Alex Ozolins, Australian Information Service (National Library of Australia, nla.obj 10844695)

The Kathy Kanga Fun Show

I was still teaching guitar at the Don Rankin Music Centre on Saturdays, and I usually took time off at midday for a cuppa with Don and his wife, Corinne. Don was a multi-instrumentalist who played in RSL clubs and musicals. He specialised in clarinet, sax, flute, piccolo and trombone. I got on well with him, but he could be gruff behind the counter and didn't suffer fools gladly. Corinne was much better in the shop.

I met Don's sister-in-law, Joy, and her husband, Richard Bamforth, both experienced pantomime actors. They described a show they presented in London – the *Kathy Kanga Fun Show*. Intrigued, I told them I composed songs and instrumentals. I played them some examples. They liked my popular and eclectic style. Richard and Joy were planning a new production of their show as a children's entertainment for the inaugural season of the new Sydney Opera House, due to open in October 1973. There was lingering doubt about the opening and the attendance of Queen Elizabeth. Given the construction delays, the media said that the building would have 'more openings than Dame Nellie Melba's never-ending farewells'. However, it opened to the public on 20 October, and I would perform there with the Renaissance Players and in the *Kathy Kanga Fun Show*.

Richard gave me a script, and I went back to my bed-sitter in Pagewood and read it a few times before composing songs and dances. Don offered to be the musical director. He told me not to bother with notation, just to give him a cassette of my songs and instrumentals. He would notate and arrange the music for the small ensemble.

The text of the *Kathy Kanga Fun Show* 'book' was a concoction of social and cultural satire. I composed signature tunes for the principal characters: Don Ramsino, Kathy Kanga, Mr Executive Turtle and Chop, the taxman. I included a dance called 'My gear is my caravan', a quasi-Indian piece for a small ballet ensemble dressed in lamb costumes. Keeping it 'family', Don played reeds and conducted. Corinne played the piano and their daughter, Kaye, sang the major role. They did everything on the proverbial smell of an oily rag. Richard built a set. Joy made the costumes. Richard paid the actors. The Rankins, being family, performed gratis. I performed for the experience.

Unfortunately, the production had just three hours to 'bump' into the Music Room, before the opening. The stage was just 4 metres deep and 20 metres wide, without any backstage area. It was a

400-seat cinema. History tells us that it was one of the many botched inclusions by the team of architects who attempted to develop the interior beneath Utzon's beautiful exterior design. There was no music pit. We had to huddle together in front of the stage on the right side and make do with an upright piano.

Then there was a more serious problem. The costumes and ballet dancing were wonderful, but the musical parts that were arranged for reeds, flute, guitar, piano, bass, and drums were full of errors. I didn't recognise some of my music in Don's notation. This, along with my rudimentary reading skills, was unnerving.

Don swore at the band when the music cues went haywire. He tried to correct missed cues himself by playing his clarinet and flute, shouting out letters and bar numbers. I lost my place several times. Actors forgot their lines. It was utterly shambolic. I wanted to hide. Inevitably, three days into the programmed one-week season, Richard and Joy canned the show.

I have vivid memories of some great one-liners in the script, gorgeous costumes, and the pirouettes of ballet dancers in sheep costumes, but I could not obtain any photos or recordings. All that survives from the project is a cassette of some of my song-sketches and a flyer. I never saw Richard and Joy again. Their return to pantomime must have been hugely disappointing, as they had once performed for the Queen at the London Palladium.

I learned from the shambles the value of thorough preparation, rehearsals, respect, and teamwork. I needed to improve my sight-reading and learn how to arrange for diverse musical ensembles.

Touring with the Renaissance Players

My lute and the Renaissance Players' multi-instrumental, theatrical approach to early music introduced me to a musical odyssey that would lead me to experience the sights and sounds of the world.

The impulses of the child in Liverpool identifying sounds, running sticks along fenceposts, using found objects to make sounds with running water, bouncing balls and jamming on pots and pans in the kitchen always remained. I used any spare cash to buy, collect and commission new instruments. The drive to find new sounds was central to my odyssey. It coincided with the push from Gough Whitlam's government to move Australia on from an Anglo-centric view of the world and assert itself as a thriving democracy in the Asia-Pacific region. The arts featured in Labor policy as part of Whitlam's Overseas Cultural Exchange initiative. So, in 1974, the Renaissance Players were invited to undertake a six-week international tour of Asia to present concerts in India, Thailand, Malaysia, Singapore, Indonesia, the Philippines, and Papua New Guinea. The Department of Foreign Affairs supported it as an opportunity to show how our instruments and diverse music reflected modern Australia as a multicultural, inclusive society. Many of our instruments, such as the shawm, lute, rebec, hourglass drum and bells, were related to Asian instruments. Furthermore, we presented Thai, Malaysian and Indonesian music arrangements to show goodwill and connection with Asia.

Swapping roles with a becak driver (cycle rickshaw) in Yogyakarta, Indonesia, 1974. Photo: Wayne Richmond

This was the first time I had been overseas since arriving in Australia. The itinerary was exhausting, but the camaraderie was great because the group included outstanding musicians, including the vocalists Lyndon Terracini and Graham Pushee. Both became internationally acclaimed opera singers – Graham, a Handel specialist, and Lyndon, a leading performer in twentieth-century modernist opera. Jonathan Rubin came home from Basel to join the tour. Jonathan enjoyed a successful career as a lute teacher in Switzerland and a continuo player with Les Arts Florissants. I've kept the plane tickets from the tour, as originally stapled together for the seventeen-flight, six-week itinerary. There were fourteen concerts, six television appearances and ten receptions. The tickets stretch across my lounge room!

I did some sightseeing between concerts, except for the visits to India and Thailand because I caught amoebic dysentery midway through the tour. I stayed in my hotel bed in the Ashoka in New Delhi for two days and should have seen a doctor. Unfortunately, the room boys kept giving me ice water to drink to address my dehydration. Ice water made the condition worse. I lost weight rapidly.

I missed out on a day trip to see the Taj Mahal and was so sick that I barely recall the flight to Bangkok where, on arrival, an Australian consular staff member took me to a private hospital, where I received excellent care and recovered with intravenous fluids. Soon, I could eat again, and regular doses of beef consommé, mashed potatoes and Coca-Cola tasted like ambrosia. I missed the two concerts in Bangkok, and also the group's scheduled departure for Manila. My strength returned, and I caught a flight the next day and was fine for the rest of the tour. However, I noticed that my colleagues, including Winsome herself, were sometimes dashing off the stage to find the loo.

Nevertheless, some highlights of the tour included concerts given by local musicians, as well as visits to see instrument makers, markets, and temples. In Medan, Sumatra, it was difficult to sleep because of the high humidity. I heard cockerels calling in the night and before dawn, the sound of a muezzin close by. My curiosity bade me get up and leave the hotel to find the source of the chanting. I followed the sound to a small mosque. The passionate intensity of the chanting and the musical intonation made a powerful impression on me, and I wondered at that moment how the Crusader knights felt when they heard Islamic calls to prayer in the Middle East.

Such experiences have enriched my life and work. I was a young man of twenty-four and saw Asia through the eyes and ears of a touring musician. I knew of the connections between Middle Eastern music and early European performance practices, enhanced through contact in the Crusades. Experiencing Islamic religion and culture in North Sumatra and in Malaysia, meeting Indian musicians in Delhi, and seeing Wayang Kulit shadow puppets in Indonesia all sparked my abiding interest in ethnomusicology.

I was one of the few group members who took a camera on the Asian tour, as well as a cassette recorder. These tools marked my emerging interest in the anthropology of music, especially in the evolution and making of musical instruments and sound-making objects in diverse cultures.

Playing football as a recent immigrant opened my eyes to multicultural Australia, but the tour of Asia aroused my curiosity about the music of ethnic minorities in our country.

The concerts on tour were very successful, except for the last one at the University of Papua New Guinea in Port Moresby. We thought this concert might have been ill-fated, because we had touched down in Moresby at 5 am after an awful night flight from Manila. We had a white-knuckle flight with severe air turbulence; even the experienced aircrew looked anxious as they strapped themselves tightly to their seats. I was frightened and fully expected that we would fall out of the sky in response to the sudden drops these events incur. We had experienced nothing like this during the tour. But our trusty Qantas Boeing 707 held together after what seemed like a severe beating. Clean air prevailed. Passengers chattered nervously, relieved that it was over, hopefully for the rest of the flight. Time for a night Scotch. Fortunately, there were no injuries, but on inspection, Jo Parkes's viola da gamba had sustained some damage.

Upon arrival in the terminal, it was dark and hot, and we were desperate for sleep. Clearing Customs was painfully slow. In 1974, Papua New Guinea (PNG) was newly self-governed and working towards full independence from Australia. They made a painstaking forensic examination of our instruments, luggage, and carry-on bags. Despite the polite ministrations of our Australian High Commission contact, the officers showed no concern for the wellbeing of a sleep-deprived mob of bedraggled white Australians. They took their time ransacking every suitcase.

Although exhausted, some of us could still smile. Stephen Stewart, our viola player, who was a finicky eater, liked to pack edibles, including leftover sausages, in his bag. He would not introduce his intestines to spicy tucker. It was a funny scene to see the food fall out of its loose wrapping onto the table. There was also an embarrassing moment, especially for a female member of the group, when her underwear was held aloft under the bright terminal lights before she was questioned about her contraceptives. I think the customs officers were delivering a bit of comeuppance.

Once cleared, embassy staff took us to our hotel rooms to rest for a short time before being whisked away for an early television spot. This usually happened before most concerts on the tour. There were no 'roadies' and we always lugged our boxes of instruments around with us, never leaving them unattended in a van, in rooms or backstage, because most of the objects were irreplaceable.

We began our last concert of the tour around 4 pm that day. Everybody seemed exhausted, severely jaded by the gruelling pace and conditions of the tour or they had 'gastro'. We were close to refusing to play, but with the end of the tour in sight – just two days away from returning home – we soldiered on.

The venue was a recreation hall on the PNG University campus. The audience comprised staff and students, as well as Australian High Commission staff and expats living and working in Port Moresby. About halfway through the first half of our program, a group of heckling students forced the doors open, just as Jonathan and I began playing 'Le Rossignol', an Elizabethan lute duet. They turned off the lights to disrupt the concert and stop us from reading our music. Jonathan and I continued playing undaunted because we had memorised the piece on the tour. Security arrived to herd the interlopers out of the auditorium. They went peacefully. We learned later that these students were angry because they hadn't received their living allowance that day. An administrative bungle was responsible. They used our concert to embarrass the university. The Australian High Commission staff asked us to finish our concert at the interval. Relieved, we packed up and had a light supper before much-needed sleep. The next day, we flew back to Sydney.

Life & relationships

By this time, early music and the frequent Renaissance Players concerts were my strong abiding passion. My musical commitments left little time for serious relationships. When I arrived home from the tour my girlfriend, Jan King, was there to meet me. I felt relieved to see her smiling face waiting for me at the airport and promised to share the full account of the tour with her and her friends.

We had met a few months before, when I was jamming on flamenco guitar riffs with a buddy, Brian O'Sullivan. Brian was a retired army helicopter pilot who ran a ceramic gallery called Crackpots. He and his wife, Ros, loved to cook Spanish food and would invite all and sundry to their terrace in Glenmore Road, Paddington, to share paella and sangria. Jan had not long come back from living in Italy, and I discovered she was (and still is) a practising artist, well known for her metal sculpture and teaching art. I was utterly drained after the tour, and Jan took me home and nursed me back to health. She was always so calm, positive, and delightfully untroubled. We were close for a few months more but gradually saw less of each other due to work and other commitments.

I met Judy Feher through music. She was an art teacher who liked my guitar and lute improvisations and interest in literature. We talked poetry and philosophy for hours. Judy was about to make a significant life choice; she was thinking of moving to Israel to live in a kibbutz, perhaps stay there permanently. I met her parents, Yehuda and Mariana. Yehuda was originally from Hungary. He had an impressive library, and I enjoyed discussing middle eastern politics with him over dinner. I'm not Jewish, and Judy's parents sensed that my relationship with their daughter was one of close friendship and not likely to upset their religious and cultural leanings. However, they were delightfully welcoming to me, as was their son, Michael. After Judy left permanently for a life in Israel, where she teaches art, Michael and I became close friends. He had just completed medical school and played the guitar recreationally. He would eventually become my best man when I married. He now lives in London and is an eminent medical specialist.

My friendships with Judy and Jan were welcome in my life, but I wasn't contemplating anything long term. I was a carefree bachelor living above Gallery 16, an art gallery in Elizabeth Street, Paddington. I was still drawing a scholarship stipend and working on my master's thesis, although the lute, guitar, and related instruments such as the Arabic oud and Turkish *saz* were my dominant interests.

I was living in the gallery thanks to the generosity of its owner, Joanna Anderson, also an Irish ceramicist. I met Joanna at another party in Paddington, where I was playing the lute. I discovered she lived in Olive Street with her two teenage children, having recently separated from her husband. I mentioned to Joanna that I needed to leave a share house and was looking for a flat. She told me about Gallery 16, over the road from the Grand National Hotel in Elizabeth Street. Joanna invited me to live above the gallery. This would help me out and help her make the premises less vulnerable outside gallery hours. She was understandably nervous about the prospect of intoxicated patrons of the pub trying to break in or lob bricks through the window. So, I became the resident musician to monitor the premises.

Gallery 16 was a repurposed two-storey terrace. Downstairs featured display cases for handmade jewellery, ceramics, and textiles. There were pots by some famous names: Peter Rushforth, Maria Gazzard, Derek Smith, and Shiga Shigeo. Joanna had built a studio with a mezzanine bedroom at the bottom of the garden; my room was upstairs above the main gallery. It fronted the street. I covered the floor in seagrass matting, and the ceiling featured a tie-dyed yellow parachute. Both features were typically seventies Paddington. Joanna and I became good friends. She was like an older sister. She encouraged me to learn transcendental meditation and to grow and use herbs in my cooking. This was an era when everyone's sitting room looked like an art gallery, with neutral and white dominant tones to set off fabrics, photos, relics and so on – even fabulous books with rich colours on their dust jackets.

On Saturday mornings, I might sit on a bench or cushion just inside the gallery door, with a pottery mug full of Turkish coffee. I played the guitar often, sometimes classical pieces, sometimes improvisation interludes while monitoring the objects as I greeted the customers. They enjoyed the ambience – the smell of brewed coffee and the strains of my guitar music. One day, a customer would change my life. A strikingly confident woman with henna hair stepped into the gallery. I was reading a book. My guitar was upstairs. She asked me questions about some ceramics on display and if I was a guitar player. Surprised, I said yes, and I asked why she asked. She said she noticed the manicured fingernails on my right hand, so I must be a guitarist. This was the conversation starter that brought us together.

I found out that Rosalind McGrath was an oboe and *cor anglais* player studying Arts-Law at Sydney university. She came to the gallery to buy a gift for Cathy Rawson, a school friend who lived around the corner from me. I helped Rosalind look at jewellery and trotted out a few facts about different makers that I had gleaned from Joanna. I think she bought a small ceramic bowl. I wrapped it up, collected her money, and she left the gallery. I told Joanna about the meeting, and like an Irish matchmaker, she said, 'O yes, I've seen her in here before and thought she is someone who'd be right for you.' Intrigued, I went off to the kitchen to make some coffee, pondering her comment, and went back to my reading.

Paddington was a good place to live. I made many friends, enjoyed the cafés and the proximity to the city, Centennial Park, and Red Leaf Pool (now Murray Rose Pool) in Woollahra, which was a favourite place to swim. While I enjoyed living by myself in Gallery 16, I felt it was time to meet new friends, and I moved into a share house in Comber Street. It was a small weatherboard cottage owned by Annette 'Nettie' Pirritt, a visual artist and dancer. It worked out well. We collected our friends for musical soirées sitting around on the seagrass matting floors, with incense candles and cask wine, and playing music. I played the lute and a medieval psaltery, and tinkered with a sitar I purchased in New Delhi during the Renaissance Players tour.

I met Peter Draper at Comber Street. He was an accomplished classical guitar player. He founded the Bennelong Players, which performed in the Bennelong Restaurant at the Sydney Opera House. When he and Nettie became an item, I moved out. Once again, my troubadour pretensions led to another invitation to take a room in a Paddington house. I went to live with Peter and Valli Moffitt in

Windsor Street. Peter, who is now a retired architect and intrepid ocean yachtie, won an award for his refurbished terrace. His wife, Valli, a designer of Italian background and born in the Venuto region, handled the stylish furniture, carpets and wall-hangings. Valli and Peter wouldn't accept any rent, only a modest contribution to food and playing a bit of lute and guitar in the lounge room after dinner, but only if I felt like it.

Valli was a superb cook. She introduced me to fresh ingredients, how to find the best olive oil and herbs, and boldness of presentation. Peter, as was likely common in Paddington, grew a few interesting 'herbs' in his overgrown rear garden (but never higher than the fence!). I remember helping him harvest some. He shared it around at a dinner party, to which I had invited Jan. When I ingested some of Pete's Windsor Street special, I expected to experience bliss. But the opposite occurred. My heart raced. I became nauseous. I felt as if I was spinning in circles. I needed air. Jan and another woman responded to my distress. I asked to walk off the loss of control that overwhelmed me. Both supported me out of the door.

It took me an hour to regain my composure and return to a normal heart rate. I fell asleep on a sofa and was much relieved when I woke up hours later feeling more settled. After this adverse and possibly allergic reaction, I vowed never to touch 'herbs' again. There would, of course, be endless opportunities, but when it was offered, I passed it on.

I stayed at Peter and Valli's house for six months. About two weeks after moving out, I was in a Renaissance Players rehearsal at Sydney University when Rosalind walked into the Music Department. She borrowed a shawm to take home to practise for the forthcoming Renaissance Players Christmas concert. I went over to say hello while she was chatting with Winsome Evans. She introduced me to her friend, the singer Henry Pritchard. Winsome asked the group to continue rehearsing. Rosalind and Henry stayed and listened for twenty minutes before leaving. I looked up from my music as she waved and smiled at me on the way out.

Meanwhile, I moved into another shared house, this time in Evans Street, Balmain. I was grateful to Peter and Valli for their friendship and support, but I felt it was time to move when I sensed some growing friction between them. The couple, who were also great business partners, eventually divorced. I lost contact with Valli, but Peter and another mate, Don Godden, have stayed in touch. We've sailed together and attended cricket and rugby tests.

Within two weeks of my seeing her at the rehearsal, Rosalind joined the Renaissance Players. Rosalind and I got to know each other while chatting during rehearsal breaks. She asked me to call her Ros and invited me to a party hosted by one of her orchestral friends at her house in Lindfield. I discovered she was a member of the ABC's National Training Orchestra; she played principal oboe and cor anglais and sat next to another oboist, Ivor Davies, who went on to fame as the leader of the band Icehouse. We talked endlessly about music, about the Renaissance Players, and about books, writing and my postgraduate research in English literature. We were soon inseparable, and a couple of months later, while we were enjoying a cuppa in the sun on the wrap-around balcony of the terrace in Evans Street, we talked mutually about getting married and decided to tie the knot. Ros was wearing a long summer dress and a headscarf she had made. I was, as usual, wearing my trademark black denim jeans and a blue shirt. It was a sunny afternoon, and I proposed. It was a gigantic leap for me, and I couldn't wait to tell Joanna that Ros and I were going to get married.

Since we were engaged, Ros's parents invited us to move into the family home in Martin Road, Centennial Park, a few doors down from novelist Patrick White. Ros was born in 1954, and so our first celebration was her twenty-first birthday. I hired some posh tails to match her handmade dress with its elegant colonial Australian styling. The occasion was an opportunity for me to meet many of her friends and extended family. We held the party in the ballroom of Neidpath, a Point Piper mansion owned by Charles Lloyd-Jones. John Cropper, one of Ros's friends, was our host. He was looking after the house for Charles. John, who loved champagne, could extemporise voice and piano arrangements on any Broadway classic. We sang and danced around the piano in a ballroom with tall windows looking into Sydney Harbour. The working-class boy from Liverpool, then Bunnerong, was now seeing the world through a different lens.

Performing, recording, touring

The Renaissance Players became the musical mainstay in my life for a few years. I was the group's treasurer and made myself available to support Winsome as much as possible, especially for our music theatre works, including Orazio Vecchi's *l'Amfiparnasso*, a commedia dell'arte–influenced madrigal drama. We produced the *Play of Daniel* and performed live to air on the ABC. Winsome encouraged me to write lyrics and songs for our Christmas Pudding concerts, for example, 'I'll sing you one-o, with a radum scadum rubidio' – a parody/pastiche of 'Green Grow the Rushes O' – in which each group member identified with an Australian animal.

> I'll sing you twelve-o,
> with a radum, scadum, rubidio.
> What is your twelve-o?
> Twelve young dingoes howling!
> Eleven white cockies squawking!
> Ten platypuses paddling!
> Nine echidnas rolled in a ball!
> Eight goannas on the run!
> Seven koalas on the gum!

> Six for the wombats waddling!
> Five old emus trying to fly!
> And four fat possums hissing!
> Three, three, the kookaburra!
> Two, two the kangaroo,
> The big red roo and joey too!
> One ol' swaggie and his swag and a jumbuck
>   in his tucker-bag.

During my time in the group, I took part in four LP recordings. The first album was *Memories of English Minstrelsy*. We recorded both the music and the poetry at EMI Studios, Castlereagh Street, between 7 pm and 2 am one night in 1975. It is a delightful collection of English folksongs, medieval songs, and dance tunes. My favourite recording was *The Cat's Fiddlestick*. Its whimsical title doesn't give a clue to what it contains. This LP draws on the embellishing accomplishments of the group's core of players, including Winsome, viol player Jenny Tebbutt, and myself on lute and mandoline. The music included the famous *Tratado de glosas* (1553) – divisions on ground basses by Diego Ortiz, who provided written-out embellishments. Following Renaissance performance practice, we added our own. The completeness and variety of music on this LP was ahead of anything similar in Europe, the epicentre of the early music revival.

While I played in the Renaissance Players, I was also a member of the Bennelong Players between 1975 and 1977. This was a trio, mentioned earlier, founded by Peter Draper. It comprised Philip Hartl on violin, Brian Strong on cello, and me on classical guitar and lute. We played chamber music arrangements of baroque, classical and popular music, performing in the Bennelong Restaurant at the Sydney Opera House, Thursdays to Saturdays. We also did regional tours and school concerts in and around Sydney. I shared the gig with another guitar player, Raffaele Agostino. In addition to sharing the guitar role in the Bennelong players, I played solo in the restaurant on Tuesdays and Wednesdays, playing both classical guitar and lute.

So keen was I to make a living from early music that I started a group with Ros and called it The Kynge's Mynstrels. It was a quartet with Jenny Tebbutt, the viola da gamba player mentioned above, and Paul Brown, a geology postgraduate student and folk musician who played guitar and percussion instruments. We were excited one day to get a call to play live on the ABC and eagerly prepared a program of songs and instrumentals. The venue was the Recording Hall (later the Broadwalk Studio), one of the best small venues at the Sydney Opera House. I had played there with the Renaissance Players in what was originally designed to be a giant lift well to serve the main concert hall and opera theatres. The internal completion of the Sydney Opera House was a nightmare. Even the so-called Music Room, where I had performed with the *Kathy Kanga Fun Show* in the opening season, was a small cinema with a stage just 4 metres deep. Unfortunately, performances of The Kynge's Mynstrels were but few. However, it became a vehicle for my development as a music director.

In 1976 I made another foray into musical theatre, in the production of *Sir Walter Raleigh*. The librettist was Ros's mother, Amy McGrath (aka Amy Cumpston; 1921–2019). Amy was a poet, writer and historian with wide-ranging interests from the Children's Crusade to Elizabethan politics, Genghis Khan, and the Opium Wars. *Sir Walter Raleigh* explored political intrigues in the court of Elizabeth I. I composed and arranged songs, dances, and instrumentals for period instruments. Amy and her husband, Frank, leased and ran the Australia Theatre in Australia Street, Newtown. It was their philanthropic contribution to the support of rising actors and playwrights.

I directed a group that comprised Ros playing shawm and recorders, Jenny Tebbutt playing a bass viol, Malcolm Tapscott on the spinet, and myself on the lute, recorder, and percussion. Ros, Jenny, and I were used to playing together in the Renaissance Players and the Kynge's Mynstrels, so we made a good ensemble sound instrumentally and vocally.

Sir Walter Raleigh was a thoroughly enjoyable and satisfying experience artistically. The stage director was David Freeman, who became a friend of the family. He was inspirational, and is now an internationally renowned opera stage director. The lighting was professional; the plot was sophisticated, and the set was attractive. *Sir Walter Raleigh* gave me an enduring interest in music theatre, although I didn't work in this genre again until 1986.

∽

Ros and I married in 1976 in the Great Hall of Sydney University. The Renaissance Players serenaded us from the rear balcony. The minister was Jock Barry, a friend of Ros's parents. He looked resplendent in his Presbyterian robes. Rosalind, named after the character in Shakespeare's *As you Like it*, would shortly write a history honours thesis on an Elizabethan diplomat, Sir Nicholas Throckmorton.

Michael and Rosalind Atherton outside the Great Hall at Sydney University on our wedding day, 1977. *l-r*: her parents, Frank and Amy McGrath, and my parents, Gisela Oppermann and John Jones.
Photo: Michael Feher

Music, Poetry and Marriage

She was in her element. I was the smitten troubadour. We held the reception at Martin Road. My parents (now divorced), siblings and friends, including ex-girlfriends, joined in the celebration. Frank, Ros's dad, was a delightful host. He spoke eloquently, befitting his station as a Chief Judge of the NSW Compensation Court. Frank's illustrious legal career took off when he was secretary of the Balmain Ironworkers' Union. He was a young legal eagle and discovered the forged ballot papers created by a communist group trying to rig the election of delegates.

Ros and I continued to perform with the Renaissance Players and featured on recordings. I found a press cutting recently and rewrote it for fun to share with family and friends:

> Medieval musician playing Galician bagpipe in Martin Place. What brought this 'ten-pound', fair-skinned baby boomer born in the 'Old Dart', to ply a vagabond trade in post-colonial Sydney? I bamboozled the photographer with the wailing bagpipe – a red bag and only one stick pointing in the air. Where were the three sticks and the obligatory plaid of the highland version? People chuckled at seeing a grown man swathed in a nylon tent of a costume, half red, half yellow, ending above the knees of 50 denier be-stockinged legs. A minstrel in tights run amok, escaped from an ancient musical zoo! Warning to all – Do not feed, do not approach, just pretend to listen! Beware his accomplice, a female jongleur with granny glasses, also oddly dressed, cheeks puffed, blowing with abandon a raucous reed pipe.

My master's thesis worried me. It was overdue, and my interest in completing it was waning. But Ros encouraged me to push on to submission. I took her advice. The problem began when I worked with a meek supervisor. He was a lovely, gentle man whose expertise was in the nineteenth-century English novel. But I was looking at the relationship between music and poetry in the Elizabethan and Jacobean periods. My topic grew out of exploring the song lyrics of English, French and Italian lute songs. I wasn't sure what to expect from the supervisor, but he was no match for me, and I drifted for a year and made excuses not to work.

I selected four major but different poets – Thomas Wyatt, Philip Sidney, Fulke Greville and John Donne. I investigated their poetic language to detect the bifurcation between music and poetry in the English Renaissance.

My supervisor was happy with my thesis argument, but he was only one voice. Unfortunately, it came back from the examiners with a request from one of them to do some rewriting and resubmit. I was crestfallen, having expected it to fly. I was numb and despondent. This examiner had pointed out that I hadn't mentioned his book on Thomas Wyatt. He was an English expert. But his book had been published just six weeks before I submitted, and it wasn't in the local libraries. There were no internet flyers from publishers and authors back in 1976, nor reviews of the book. I felt unlucky and had no recourse but to read his book and address a couple of issues that certainly would benefit from a rewrite.

I ripped up the marked copies as a symbolic gesture. Once more into the breach, with Ros lifting my spirits. I went to see my supervisor, only to find out that he was going back to England. Luckily, I met a new supervisor, Dr Mary Chan. She liked music; she went to concerts and understood lyric poetry. So, I refocused my work and made solid progress. I re-submitted the thesis four months later. It sailed, coming back with great reports. Mary showed it would have earned first-class honours had it been the first attempt. Indeed, with development, it would have been a PhD. However, I received a distinction (Honours Class Two, Division One) and was pleased to graduate. It would become crucial to my appointment to a professorial chair fifteen years later.

Heart, Head and Hand

My first film music job came in 1979, when Peter Weir contacted me via Film Australia to compose music for his documentary about ceramic artists Peter Rushforth and his Japanese friend, Shiga Shigeo. This was two years before the release of the feature film, *Gallipoli*, that led Peter down the pathway to an Academy Award for direction. It was a twenty-minute film that portrayed the life and work of Rushforth, examining his craft as a way of life of sharing his discoveries. It showed the respect and admiration he enjoyed personally and professionally from students, colleagues, and friends.

Peter was interested in the sound of medieval instruments and how I might incorporate some of their sonorities in the film score. I composed about ten minutes of music for him, which I multi-tracked on a TASCAM Portastudio, which was a four-track cassette tape recorder with a built-in mixing unit. I devised an opening theme, music for the credits and short transitions plus solos. I featured a *gemshorn*, a recorder made from a conical animal horn. It has a gentle sound, blending the tone colours of a recorder and an ocarina. There was a scene in the film in which Peter Rushforth and Shiga Shigeo load and light up a kiln. They watch it through the night, waiting expectantly for the pots inside to fire and cool. Peter asked me to play a solo flute theme as if we were watching slow motion. It created a mysterious and expectant feeling in the scene. I tried to emulate the sound of a *shakuhachi* (Japanese bamboo flute).

During one of the mixing sessions, Peter talked about his direction of *Gallipoli*, then also a work in progress. He felt that the young men were going on a crusade, hence his interest in medieval music. I kept my fingers crossed that I might become involved in the soundtrack, but he and his producers used mostly existing classical music for the score, including the famous Tomaso Albinoni's 'Adagio in G minor for organ and strings'. However, I learned a lot from Peter's careful listening to and placement of music and sounds in *Heart, Head and Hand,* especially when and where not to include music. He gave me tips on underscoring dialogue.

Beginning a teaching career

In 1977 I had changed from teaching individuals to play the guitar, to working as a music tutor with the Workers' Educational Association in NSW (WEA). The WEA grew out of an organisation founded in England in 1903. The Sydney branch began in 1913 as a joint undertaking by the trade union movement and the University of Sydney, to build a progressive organisation committed to enabling adult working people to gain a liberal education. It is one of Australia's oldest and most prominent providers of continuing education for adults.

Joss Davies introduced me to the WEA. He was Assistant Director of Adult Education at Sydney University and responsible for managing residential schools for adults. They held these at Mitchell College of Advanced Education in Bathurst, now part of Charles Sturt University. Included were courses in painting, literature, photography, architecture, poetry, geology and film criticism. Joss put me down for a week-long course in Mediaeval and Renaissance music and agreed to include Ros as my co-tutor.

These schools became my first sustained period in tertiary music teaching. There were twenty-five students in my group. They included recorder players, vocalists, violin players, guitarists, and brass and keyboard players. It was a workshop based on theoretical and practical classes for large and small groups. I had devised a program to suit different levels of ability but always to perform at a school concert shared with students from the other courses. Wherever possible, I ran one or two classes involving visual arts students. This encouraged the music to influence the visual artists and vice versa.

Ros and I repeated the course in 1978, but I taught courses by myself from 1981 to 1983. They became very popular because they included history, music, and dancing. This led to an invitation in 1981 to prepare and present live television tutorials for Channel 10 with the University of Sydney. I presented a variety of tutorials on early music, including music in William Shakespeare's plays. The content was my choice, and I included visual elements from books displayed on a second camera. I showed instruments by pulling some of them apart and then playing them. For this to work, I had to arrive well-prepared, focused, and ready to look into the camera. There were no retakes. The programs went live to air on Saturday mornings. Those were the days when commercial television willingly included programs relevant to adult education as a form of community support.

In 1979, Roger Covell, Head of Music at UNSW, invited me to become a tutor for summer vacation courses in Renaissance and Baroque music. This started my working with UNSW Opera as an assistant director to teach and direct a presentation of *The Play of Robin and Marion*, a thirteenth-century music theatre work by the trouvère Adam de la Halle. Roger's entrepreneurial spirit was legendary. Most will remember him as an exceptional music critic, but his vision for music included setting up a permanent residency at UNSW for the now-iconic Australia Ensemble. He built up an excellent music department in a set of demountables and wrote a watershed book on Australian music, *Australia's Music: Themes of a New Society*. It was the first comprehensive study of the history, development and performance of art music in Australia. Not only was Roger an inspiration, who praised the achievements of the Renaissance Players and Sirocco, but he once gave me a role as a banjo player in Benjamin Benjamin's opera *Paul Bunyan*. So, when the banjo is subject to disparaging musical jokes, I puff out my chest and stand up for the banjo, an instrument developed in the USA by African Americans and based on similar African instruments, including the *banjar*, a West African forerunner of the modern banjo.

5

HEALING MUSIC

The promise of music as therapy.

I first met Dr Marie Bashir in 1973, when she invited the Renaissance Players to perform in the Sydney Town Hall at the ball celebrating the appointment of her husband, Sir Nicholas Shehadie, as the Mayor of Sydney. It was a wonderful occasion, and Marie, who would go on to become a child psychiatrist, a professor and Governor of NSW, chatted with us as if we were family. However, I had no contact with her again until March 1978, when she phoned to ask me if I would teach guitar to one of her patients. Marie told me about a shy young man who wanted to learn classical guitar. I obliged and noticed he was both brilliant and very anxious. After a few weeks of lessons, I had to tell him I was putting my hat in the ring for a university teaching job in Canberra, but I would find another teacher should I leave Sydney. That same night, I answered a call from Marie. She told me about Rivendell and that a position was available for a music therapist. She invited me to her office, a large, wood-panelled room within the magnificent Thomas Walker House at Concord on the banks of the Parramatta River. After an informal interview, Marie gave me a tour of Rivendell, an educational and healthcare facility. It took its name from Elrond's house in the writings of JRR Tolkien – a sanctuary for those on complex journeys, a place to rest and recuperate.

Thomas Walker House is a fine Queen Anne building designed by the founder's son-in-law, the famed Sir John Sulman. The entrance is via a three-storey tower construction that includes a clock. At the rear of the building, there is a delightful hall that can seat approximately 200 people. It features a platform stage and a rear gallery that is accessible from the first floor. There are nine stained glass windows, six of which depict Faith, Hope, Charity, Temperance, Justice, and Prudence. Around the room, at ceiling height and in gold lettering, there is a legend: *This Hospital For Convalescents was Founded by the Late Thomas Walker of Yaralla In The Hope That Many Sufferers Would be Restored to Health Within It.* The hospital building was officially opened on 21 September 1893 exclusively for patients in need of rest and recuperation, to stay up to four weeks at no cost.

Marie and I paused in the hall. I noticed the fine eggshell textured plaster on the walls. I looked up and saw magnificent ceilings, Victorian rococo, gold edging and motifs. There were original candelabras fitted now with modern light bulbs. Out in the foyer were several marble plinths, but without busts. These had been removed for the protection of the patients. In contrast to the general opulence, well-worn, old-brown linoleum was fused to some of the floors and tacked with shiny brass studs.

One of the office staff beckoned Marie. She left to take an urgent call. As well as being the founder and director of the Rivendell Adolescent Unit, Marie was a practising child psychiatrist. With Rivendell under the authority of the NSW Health Commission and linked with the Department of Psychiatry at Sydney University, she was an exceptionally busy woman and mother. It's not surprising that the career trajectory of this remarkable woman – mother, doctor, violinist, leader, professor, an Australian born in Narrandera of Lebanese parents – would lead her to become an outstanding Governor of NSW.

I climbed the stairs and walked into the west wing to look at the view from the balcony. A tall, forked tree graced the grassy incline leading down to the river. The bifurcation of the trunk led me to ponder which path I might take: Join Marie's team, as a music therapist, or take up a university English lecturing post that was going in Canberra? My attention was suddenly drawn towards the river's edge where I saw a boathouse building reminiscent of a Dutch water tower. The boathouse is a well-known landmark to ferry hoppers on the Parramatta River. The convalescents who arrived by ferry from Sydney first entered this building. It also included a waiting room, storeroom, lounge, and smoking room for male visitors. I imagined the long-forgotten and hushed voices of the sick and frail disembarking here at Concord, escorted by nurses in starched white cotton uniforms. The poet Henry Lawson was once a convalescent at Thomas Walker House, and described his experience in 'The Unknown Patient':

> The moonlight breathes on Walker House and softens scrub and hill;
> The native trees are strangely stirred, the pines are very still;
> The nurse's lantern flits and flits, and pain and sorrow cease,
> For all the patients are asleep, and all is Rest and Peace.
> Not class nor creed nor race debars, and even Wealth is free –
> The suffering miser shares alike the Home with Poverty;

> The felon's past is never known when kindness 'sends him through'
> The stone says, 'many sufferers', but it means 'sinners', too.

The aroma of lunch caught my attention as a group of casually attired adolescents made their way to the dining hall, their footsteps echoed below in the eastern courtyard. Marie returned and repeated her offer for me to join her team. She would give me set-up time to research the discipline of music therapy, to purchase whatever equipment I required and to observe groups and meet staff members on an individual basis.

We continued to walk and chat while she described the Rivendell program. What would I be able to contribute? How could I, without training in special education or clinical psychology, fit in? How would a musician have a place here among the tears and fears of emotionally challenged young people, many of whom were under the yoke of potent psychotropic drugs? How does a performing musician transform the persona of public performance into one of deeper caring and sharing, where musical communication is process above product? These were the overlapping questions that busied my mind and fuelled my interest.

I walked back to my car an hour later, past the receptionist's open window, and heard the insistent chatter of her electric golf-ball typewriter. I glimpsed Marie, with her perennially welcoming smile, greeting an anxious parent. Later, I drove to my home in the Eastern Suburbs deep in thought. Time to reflect. If I accepted the position at Rivendell, it would invite significant challenges. I would be joining a unique cross-disciplinary team working with a small cohort of students. I discussed it with Ros, and called Marie two days later to accept the position of Music Therapist – an obscure yet intriguing title. There was no official pay award for a music therapist, and Marie had to persuade the accountants at the NSW

Health Department to provide me with a benchmark salary. This would be the same as an occupational therapist. I was probably the first full-time salaried music therapist in the state.

Music as therapy

On my first day at Rivendell, the caretaker led me to a room that opened onto a courtyard in the east wing. He unlocked a large cedar door covered in many years of paint. The room had a high ceiling, a wooden floor, and large windows. They had already found me a reasonable upright piano. I sat down and drew up a list of musical instruments, books, and sheet music, plus a portable sound system. Following lunch in the dining hall with staff and students, I went to the staff room to read about the policies, browse through clinical notes, and devise a timetable.

Rivendell's mission focused on emotionally stressed young people of high school age and ability, of either sex (ages twelve to nineteen approximately). It aimed to provide a therapeutic and educational program for those youngsters who would otherwise have to defer or leave their schooling through psychological illness. The unit offered residential and day care for only thirty-six students and, occasionally, short-term accommodation for country families in therapy.

Referrals included a wide spectrum of psychiatric disabilities, including schizophrenia and other psychoses, psychoneuroses in severe form, psychosomatic and organic disorders, and behavioural and personality disorders. Youngsters who were too physically disabled to be educated, or those with a long and repetitive history of aggression or deviant and delinquent behaviour, were ineligible for admission.

The Rivendell clinical team comprised three psychiatrists,

(including the director), one registrar in training, three social workers, one clinical psychologist, fourteen nursing staff, an occupational therapist, four teachers, a music therapist, and the part-time services of an instructor of design and technology. The model was that of a functional healthy family having problems that are not insurmountable and that can be constructively resolved by observation, analysis and understanding.

Once again, I felt as if I was playing the catch-up game, shifting from the more obvious pathway of an academic career in an English department to exploring my musical self in a unique environment. I was curious about music-making as an adjunct to psychotherapy and special education. Equally important to me was Marie's endorsement of my capacity to make this work. Her encouragement was inspiring.

After four months in the role, I had established a creative improvisation group, a music and movement group, and one-on-one sessions with students. The idea of improvisation has long been central to my music aesthetic. A performer becomes utterly, intensely absorbed, especially in free improvisation, where in theory one is in the moment and not bound by rules or referents. However, free improvisation is also coloured by the minutiae of the performer's life experience and projection of subjectivities. But to improvise is to be at the edge of what comes next. This has a significant role in music therapy.

It took me a year to feel part of the clinical team. At first, I aligned myself more readily with the occupational therapist and the special education teachers. My interventions were designed to use music to increase self-esteem and positive body concept. One program involved guided song writing to enhance communication, self-concept, and a sense of achievement. Another used one-on-one improvisation on an instrument as a learning task for self-expression. The improvisations became scaffolds for nurturing students in the acquisition of basic skills on guitar, piano, percussion, or the voice. This was a particularly effective approach with 'school-refusing' adolescents. Singing to peers and therapists about personal problems enhanced self-awareness. Creative activities were life-changing for some at Rivendell.

My practice at Rivendell

Wayne pushed at my open door and saw me sitting at my piano where I was arranging music for a spontaneity group session. His red hair and ruddy face contrasted with a blue flannel shirt and stovepipe jeans ending in oversized, beige desert boots. I'd noticed him before, occasionally stamping his way around the Unit, cursing angrily.

'What yer doin' Michael?'

'Preparing sheet music,' I said.

'Oh,' he said softly.

'This is an unexpected visit,' I added.

'I was thinking about the songs played by the band and stuff. Here are some words I wrote.'

A good sign, I thought. He's motivated. He trusts me.

'Have you written poems or song lyrics?' I asked.

He looked down at the floor, hesitated, then pulled a folded piece of paper from his pocket, thrusting it towards me clumsily, as if he was embarrassed or wanting to get rid of it. I unfolded it carefully and found the paper heavily marked with spidery handwriting in red biro ink:

> I'd like to fly
> fly away high,
> free as a bird in the sky,
> carried by the wind,
> fly away high,
> on a jet plane, baby,
> high in the sky.

Wayne struggled with dyslexia and poor peer interactions. He could be impulsive and often angry with his peers at Rivendell. I praised his words, encouraging him to write some more. I now showed him the basics of a blues song, and he came back the next morning with these words:

> I've got the stepmother blues,
> yeah, yeah, yeah!
> I've got the stepmother blues.
> I got the stepmother blues.
> My stepmother's crazy
> She treats me like dirt.
> I got the stepmother blues
> yeah, yeah, yeah!
> I got the stepmother blues,
> But I'll get back at her
> And treat her like dirt.
> I got the stepmother blues,
> yeah, yeah, yeah!

The words revealed his pain, as well as his anger and low self-esteem. They confirmed his difficult relationship with his stepmother and consequently with his father. Wayne felt unloved and became an underachiever and a 'school-refuser'.

I set up a regular session for him to explore his feelings through song writing and using the 'blues' genre. This helped him disclose things he found too difficult with either his therapist or the nurses who cared for him.

Song writing at Rivendell would ideally lead to performances. I encouraged students with evolving skills to form a rock band. The motivation was usually strong. The repertoire included sixties and seventies music – Beatles, Rolling Stones, Supertramp, Eurhythmics, Eagles, Queen, and Olivia Newton-John, plus ballads and Irish jigs. These were workshopped with varying degrees of participation, some members swapping instruments. I used improvisation to liberate self-expression in some usually shy students.

As a music therapist, I was alert to individual needs and difficulties. One student might be averse to amplified music, another might become over-stimulated by the excitement of drumming. Band members were expected to set up their own and others' equipment, tune up, and care for the instruments loaned to them. Playing together from memory and learning the theatrical gestures of performance were more important than learning to read music. I aimed to have a band memorise a three-song program to play at the end-of-term concerts.

There was an opportunity to branch out from music alone, to start a spontaneity group using theatre improvisation, drawing on the psychodrama techniques of Jacob L. Moreno and the improvisation games of Viola Spolin. I collaborated with the occupational therapist and included some of the nurses in sessions to provide support for the more anxious students.

Full support and performative involvement came from the staff at Rivendell, including the doctors. Following a discussion with Marie, I offered to produce and direct a yearly musical or a play in Term 3. My first project was a production of *Oliver!* in 1978. I chose this work for its uplifting and memorable score. The libretto was especially suited to a larger-than-usual cohort of younger boys and girls at Rivendell. I cast one of the psychiatrists as Fagin; our clinical psychologist as Bill Sykes, the murderer; and two popular nurses as the undertakers, Mr and Mrs Sowerberry. The cast and audience loved the irony of these choices, especially the deeply empathic psychologist as the murderer. The boy chosen to sing Oliver had never made it onto a school stage before and rose to the occasion, learning his part despite the burden of medication. His parents cried during the performance, seeing him succeed in the role.

In 1979, I produced *Bye Bye Birdie* for its themes of hero-worship, boy-girl relationships and rebellion. The rock-and-roll band that emerged in Term 2 named itself Eclipse, and I featured it in *Bye Bye Birdie*.

As in *Oliver!* it was all hands to the pump. I was the producer, director and set designer. Students and staff collaborated on all aspects of the production – costumes, set design and construction, lighting and sound. In twelve weeks, the relatively 'green' cast made astounding progress towards a professional-looking, lively, and mostly pitch-perfect production. The music was performed entirely by students – including the four 'Birdies' playing several rock numbers, with a gifted student playing the piano score. This was written by band members:

> We all came to Rivendell
> Then we started a band,
> We put our songs together,
> Everyone lending a hand.
>
> We found the name Eclipse,
> As we floated by the sun.
> When the moon cast its shadow
> Down on everyone.

I am grateful to Marie and Rivendell for all that I learned, as well as the opportunities that came my way while I worked there. It led me to the Australian Music Therapy Association (AMTA), then emerging as a voice for the professional status and employment conditions of music therapists. I gave talks to staff in hospitals. I participated in seminars and ran workshops, including for special education students in teacher training colleges. The New Zealand Music Therapy Association invited me to Auckland to run a short course, I published journal articles and linked up with art and dance therapists around Australia, and I supported the AMTA mission to have music therapy accepted as a professional discipline.

Redirection

While there was much joy in my role as a music therapist, some things were raw. I was beginning to take too much on board. I'd been having regular psychotherapy sessions with a psychiatrist, two days a week, using the free association technique. Marie had recommended a skilled Freudian analyst. The experience was to help me advance my skills as a therapist, which it did. But it also opened the past trauma of migration, my poor relationship with my father and a panic attack I experienced during my second year at university. The emotional barometer of Rivendell had become too difficult for me to handle. Leaving became a necessity.

One Friday afternoon late in 1980, I took a stroll around the grounds of Rivendell. It was after a difficult day managing the impulsive behaviour of a student and hearing that one of the nurses had criticised my position at Rivendell as 'charmed'. She doubted the efficacy of music therapy. I was disappointed, given the amount of work I put into my job. She had no understanding of the hundreds of extra hours that went into the musicals. I walked outside for fresh air, down to the mangroves at the river's edge, and I saw one of our students fishing alone.

Nick was a tall, shy, acne-scarred boy wearing a flannel shirt. I couldn't recall him having any friends. I watched him catch a bream and methodically take the hook out of its mouth then drop it into a bucket full of fish. Nick said he would take them home to eat and was waiting for his mother to collect him. Most of the students went home on weekends. He was only fifteen and had the manner of an old fisherman, with a skill and purpose unrecognised by any school system. Childhood and adolescence seemed absent from his life. He was one of several students during my three years at Rivendell that made me feel sad about their prognosis. Their clinical case notes described in detail some of the desperate circumstances many of them experienced in their family system.

While talking with Nick, I looked back towards the building and the clock tower, realising it was already 6:30 pm on a Friday. Most of the staff and students had gone home except for a few nurses and a cook who would look after those who couldn't go home. I was moved to reflect on a boy who had severe OCD:

Bobby

Bobby jumped me from behind the door.
His hands closed softly around my neck.
They were wet and cold, like raw meat.
A chunk of script from Dr Who came out of his
    ruby-lipped mouth.
'Hello Bobby.' I feigned a struggle with a crinoid monster.
Bobby's actions were his way of saying,
'I like you, but I must wash bad feelings away.'
After gently breaking his grip, I smiled at him.
He cackled with delight and left the room.
I sat down to write up my music therapy notes,
and I could hear the bathroom taps running
and Bobby washing his hands for the sixteenth time today.

Bobby was loud
Bobby was boisterous
Bobby was whimpering
Bobby washing his hands
Bobby was washing again and again
Bobby was washing and calling out
Bobby was medicated and pop-eyed
Bobby was murmuring the ancient tongues
Bobby's dad took him to hard-core porn when he was young
Bobby rocked 'to and fro' at the sink
Bobby's mum said, 'He's mad, keep him here!'
Bobby washed himself raw
Bobby's mouth hung open
Bobby's eyes looked red
Bobby was alone
Bobby washes
Bobby … is no more.

6

GOING FREELANCE

Celebrating unity in diversity.

I loved my work at Rivendell, its challenges, and watching students grow and get well. But Rivendell was beginning to absorb too much of me after three years. I was thirty and wanted to spread my wings. I decided to leave my full-time music position in music therapy and become a freelance musician, composer, and educator, knowing that I needed to take on whatever projects were available. Ros supported my decision.

Sirocco

I wanted to play music professionally but in a less score-based ensemble than the Renaissance Players and Bennelong Trio. I connected with Bill O'Toole, who played Irish folk, Balkan, and Middle Eastern music. He invited The Kynge's Mynstrels to participate in 'Chanters Tune', a concert sponsored by the Folk Pipers Society. The artists included Declan Affley (Voice and Uilleann pipes), Jim McBride (fiddle), Bill Hart (Highland pipes), Norm Potts (Northumbrian pipes), plus Bill's group, Sirocco. We performed on 9 November in St John's Church, Paddington. At this feast of reed playing, Bill told me about his time in Europe. He went to the London College of Furniture to study instrument making, where he founded the folk group Blowzabella. In Sydney, he founded Sirocco based on his London experience, teaming up with friends Andrew de Teliga and Guy Madigan. The trio played for weddings, parties, and house concerts. Bill, Andrew, and Guy heard me playing a swag of instruments in the Kynge's Mynstrels: *Gaita Gallega* (a bagpipe from northern Spain), crumhorn (sixteenth-century wind-capped double-reed instrument), recorders and cittern (a small wire-strung medieval guitar) and singing in different languages.

They saw that I was interested in exploring the Middle Eastern roots of medieval European music and had experience in arranging British folk songs for guitar and early music instruments. I felt a strong affinity with Sirocco, and to my delight, Bill asked me to play with the group at their next dance. I jumped at the opportunity. Soon, I visited Bill's wood-turning workshop in Chippendale, learning Sirocco's repertoire, which included Irish, French, Macedonian, Bulgarian, and Turkish tunes.

My first concert with Sirocco was on 23 January 1981 in Paddington Village Church. The poster described the gig as 'Wild Folk Music from the Middle East to Ireland'. The entry price was $4 at the door. This event immediately loosened my bonds with Winsome and the Renaissance Players. I felt rejuvenated by Sirocco's music and an immediate sense of brotherhood playing and sharing a stage with Bill, Andrew, and Guy. I picked my moment to tell Winsome I was leaving the Renaissance Players. She was disappointed and looked at me as a traitor, but I knew she could find other string players to replace me. Indeed, one strength of the Players was its capacity to 'blood' new players from the pool of talented Bachelor of Music students. The group always found excellent musicians ready to adapt their classical techniques to medieval and Renaissance instruments and performance practices.

I thanked Winsome for her faith in my music-making and assured her that it was an apprenticeship I would never forget; that I'd learned precious improvisation and ensemble skills within the group. By the time I left, I could play parts on the tenor viol, play the crumhorn, oud and Turkish saz, as well as small drums and metal percussion objects, and sing part songs. I carried this background into Sirocco.

A unique hallmark of Sirocco was that Bill made and played most of his instruments, including English and French bagpipes and the *kaval* (Balkan end-blown flute), and used mostly Australian timbers. He also specialised on the melodeon and the tin whistle. Bill generously gave me a 6-hole transverse flute made from brushbox wood, a *rauschpfeife* (wind-capped shawm) that he had made while studying at the London College of Furniture, and a *bombarde* – a double-reed wind instrument from Brittany. Years later, these are prized possessions in my instrument collection, and I've played them around the world.

Andrew, who had a background in punk rock with Jimmy and the Boys, played violin and *bouzouki* and penned great tunes for the band. Guy played a *dhol* (Indian side drum), a *bodhran* (Irish frame drum), and a variety of percussion including bells, tambourine, and seedpods. He specialised in the *darbuka*, a Turkish, hourglass-shaped drum, and played African-style between his knees as if it were a *djembe*. Like Charlie Watts (Rolling Stones), he was Mr Reliable, especially with music in 7/8 or 5/8 time. Guy was solid. Dress wise, he liked loose-fitting linen shirts and snappy waistcoats.

I focused on string instruments, including the cittern and the oud, and on the rauschpfeife, wide bore recorders and occasional percussion. I, too, brought a waistcoat into the mix – a superbly embroidered garment made by Kalash women in Chitral, in the Hindu Kush. I wore it over red or white billowing shirts.

My first gig was exhilarating. It connected me to a new audience hungry for multicultural music and dancing. Most Australian folk dancing was in the bush music tradition. It included ballads and dance tunes such as polkas and quadrilles. Sirocco's music was different. It went beyond this tradition and introduced audiences to Hungarian, Balkan, and Middle Eastern dances. Bill invited the dynamic Gary Dawson, a much-travelled, generous and energetic teacher, to teach us steps and how to call dances. Gary could bring people of diverse backgrounds onto the dance floor and create an exciting sense of community.

Sirocco played its music from memory, enjoying a beer between sets. It was also a true collective for deciding what to play. We were relaxed on stage and revelled in banter. Playing helped me to keep fit because Bill and I would also show dance steps to our audiences. The dances were usually line or circle dances from the Balkans, England, or France. They were easy to teach and learn, and the gigs went wild. I discovered an excellent musical resource, *Begged, Borrowed, and Stolen*, that added considerably to my Anglo-Celtic repertoire. Like the jazz musicians' 'fake book', this orange-covered, spiral-bound A4 booklet included all the popular dance tunes from the bush music scene and more. I picked it up for a few dollars and it gave me enough repertoire to sit in on most jam sessions at the big folk festivals. One gig became two, and then three, and I became a full-time member of Sirocco. We attracted attention as a folk group with a distinctive sound. Work opportunities came in fast.

I continued to perform solo. One memorable solo performance was playing a program of lute, recorders, and bagpipe music in 'Glensloy', a woolshed venue at the 1982 Lambing Flat Festival of Early Music. Lambing Flat was the former name for Young, NSW. It became a notorious scene of vicious race riots in 1860 following the discovery of gold. Within months of the discovery, Americans, British, Irish and Australians arrived, and the population grew to

20,000 new inhabitants. This included 2,000 Chinese, who were the focus of bitter resentment.

It might appear incongruous to hear such a delicate instrument as the lute, from pre-colonial Northern Europe, following the chaos of Young's history. However, music, conviviality and landscape were just as intimately connected in the Renaissance and Baroque eras, too. The champagne and sandwiches after the performance were the perfect alfresco addition. Woolsheds were often a venue for folk dancing in early colonial Australia.

I liked connecting with this tradition and thinking about the utterly opposite soundscape in a working shed full of shearers and their clippers, the sound of sheep hooves on the hardwood floors, and the lingering odour of lanolin.

∽

The plentiful performance work was a good thing because by this time, Ros and I had had our first child. Henceforth, I needed to secure a dependable income stream.

Emily Alexandra Atherton was born in Crown Street Women's Hospital on 3 March 1981. The pregnancy went well for Ros, but her labour was arduous, as Emily was in a posterior position. I did my best to comfort Ros in the birthing suite but felt useless. When I heard the obstetrician call for the forceps, I was fearful about what was going to happen. The procedure shocked me, but I stayed on my feet while our beautiful daughter came into the world and took her first breath. The look on Ros's face was one of relief and indescribable joy when a nurse put Emily in her arms. I cried with joy at becoming a father. Hours earlier, I had penned these lines:

You are coming (3 March 1981, 2:30 pm)

Music plays on the radio.
It's a warm, sunny day outside.
I watch your mother resting on the sofa.
You, my possum, are making your way into the world,
Your mother feels pain
And we are preparing for your arrival.
Love awaits you.

It was yesterday that your mother stopped working,
and I finished the music for a film.
And here we are, at the hour of anticipation.
If you are a girl, we will call you Emily.

The world you come into is a place of mysterious forces,
of inequality and contradictions.
But it will greet you with wonder
And ask you to look, to listen, and to learn,
As you journey through life.

Composing and writing

When asked if I have a particular approach to composition, I don't. Most of what I do is intuitive. The word 'comprovisation' is a better description for much of my output. I might have begun improvising sounds and gestures before selecting and notating for re-performance. And the recording studio and, more recently, the digital audio workstation have been part of my compositional process, particularly when writing music for the screen.

I admire the skills of the symphonic composer, but I am yet to explore this genre compositionally, probably because my music relies on shorter forms. Further, I didn't study composition. I did meet with Nigel Butterley a few times for comment on my scores.

Nigel was one of Australia's great composers and deserves wider recognition. He gave me copies of his scores to study and told me bluntly how to make my compositions more interesting, especially in the setting of words to music.

I explore different modes of thinking when composing music. I'm guided by my experience as a string player, percussionist and occasional wind player. Capturing rhythmic energy, the sublimity of the singing voice, and unusual instrumental timbres are my goals. My mantra is 'collaboration, connection and community'. My engaging with musicians from different cultures has been osmotic for me as a composer.

The freedom of improvisation was there when I picked up my first guitar on the way to becoming a self-taught musician. Mimicry, emulation, and adapting what I heard became a springboard for further exploration – like the birds themselves. It led to song writing and composing incidental music for theatrical productions, including musicals. This pathway led to composing music for film and television.

Nobody is an island. One is also what one hears. I aim to listen to something different every day. If asked about influences, I could be cheeky and say the entire world. The soundscape is also an ecology of sound, and its sound marks linger in the memory. Distinctive sounds mark most experiences, as described earlier in my childhood recollections of the soundscape of post-war Liverpool.

I can list such influences as singing in school assemblies, the popular music revolution of the 1960s, my 'troubadour' years exploring early music, and then hearing Bach, Beethoven, Stravinsky and Bartok, Ravi Shankar and Laurie Anderson. Similarly, the music of Java, the Balkans, the Middle East and many more. Trying to understand these composers helped me to grow and discover a personal voice.

My exploratory practices have resulted in musical hybridity

nurtured by collaborative work in a tolerant and plural Australian society. My work is also situated between Asia and the Pacific, where performer-composers, improvisers and multi-instrumentalists can steer away from European music hegemonies.

I honed my discoveries through research into musical instruments – their construction, function, and cultural significance. If I designed music that revealed diverse, disparate sound sources, it was not to produce musical syncretism for its own sake, rather to find and maintain personal music nurtured by osmosis.

∽

Once I settled into music as a career, writing about it presented no obstacles, and I could draw on literary and cultural frameworks. I'd written both BA Honours and MA Honours theses, plus essays and journal articles. My body of writing increased with scripts for television tutorials on early music, articles on music therapy, song lyrics, and program notes for concerts and recordings.

In 1981, ABC Books commissioned my first book, *The ABC Book of Musical Instruments*. I wrote this 88-page volume with young people in mind. Most books on musical instruments contained awkward stereotypes and bias towards a Eurocentric view of music. For example, stringed instruments implied the typical European concert orchestra. The harp was always in the hands of a woman. Men played the contrabass, trumpet, tuba or timpani. Such stereotypes propagated the view that women were not as strong as men and should be content to sit demurely at a piano. Similarly, this hegemonic position of western classical music was the arbiter of choice for deciding which instruments to include, who could play them, and how to classify them. I wrote my book to challenge such nonsense.

I opted to bring music, culture, and science together. Hence, the didjeridu and the trombone are described on the same page as other lip-vibrated aerophones because both compare acoustically, although their cultural significance sees them differently. The thing about musical instruments is to expect the unexpected. They are constantly emerging and evolving, something that I have witnessed many times. For example, children in the playground are a source of rhymes, chants and clapping games. But the children are capable of invention. Walking into a playground on my way to give a school concert, I was surrounded by a group of children, each blowing coloured plastic clothes pegs between their lips! They had discovered a new musical instrument by reversing the metal spring on the peg to work as a reed. They improvised a hocket-like fanfare. It underlined the inquisitiveness and ingenuity of humans, in this case, to transform a household object into a reed aerophone.

I engaged a technical drawing expert to produce line drawings of every instrument described in the book, to capture aspects of design, shape, and detail that are not always obvious in photographs. Using the taxonomy of aerophone, chordophone, idiophone, membranophone and electrophone helped to remove cultural bias in the classroom. For example, if a teacher asked the children to name an instrument in the string family and a child of Greek-Australian background said the bouzouki, they were likely to be corrected. The teacher expected to hear violin, viola, violoncello or contrabass.

The world of music, as reflected in multicultural Australia, demanded due care in school textbooks. Narrow views lead to supremacist views of cultural superiority. Selecting random pages from my book, such as pages 32 and 33 in the section on idiophones, one finds a drawing of a group of Melanesian people stamping on a board over a pit. Next to this are drawings of a tap dancer, clapsticks, bones, spoons and castanets. Each instrument includes a cultural reference and is of equal significance as a sound-making object. Pages 58 and 59 include the Hawaiian ukulele, Russian balalaika, Mexican guitarron, Japanese shamisen, the Middle Eastern oud and the European Renaissance lute. All are string instruments. Playing positions are shown.

Australian libraries, secondary and tertiary institutions and individuals ordered *The ABC Book of Musical Instruments*. Sales topped 30,000 copies, each at a modest price. This was possible because I opted to be paid a commission fee rather than royalties. It was a milestone for me to write the first book of its kind in Australia that acknowledged musical pluralism and encouraged young people to appreciate both the cultural phenomena and the science of acoustics. I learned how to use simple and unambiguous language.

Throughout my career, collaborations with others have been a potent vehicle for creativity. Some of them have involved actors and radio. In 1981, for example, I worked with actors, John Bell and his wife, Anna Volska, on a production of *King Ubu* by Alfred Jarry. It was a radio adaptation for which Ros and I played incidental music. Then in 1982, John encouraged me to present a short one-hander show at the Nimrod Theatre where he was director. I called it *The Art of the Minstrel*, in which I played a time-travelling medieval musician giving an extended performance. The script allowed me to play and introduce various musical works on original instruments. It was a first for me and different from a solo concert. Despite being nervous under the microscope of lights and the intimacy of the Nimrod, I pulled it off.

John and Anna loved the show, and I would have developed it into a season had not Sirocco become my mainstay. However, I was to work with John again in 1991. We devised a program together called *My Love is as a Fever*. John read love poetry and I wove in love songs and instrumentals. We performed it at the Independent Theatre at North Sydney as a fundraiser for the theatre. This was followed by a live-to-air performance on Valentine's Day for the

ABC in its old Arcadia Studio in Chatswood. I still have a copy of the program. It's a treasure, especially for John's fabulous interpretation of Shakespeare sonnets.

In 1982, I co-scripted an educational film with Ursula Kolbe, a lecturer at the Institute of Early Childhood in Waverley (formerly Sydney Kindergarten Teachers' College) and author of the book *Early Childhood Art*. We invited Tom Zubrycki, the doyen of documentary filmmakers, to direct for us. *I Can Make Music* was a 16 mm film funded by the Australia Council's Arts in Education program. It focused on the process in musical experiences: we showed the children delighting in the joy of exploring and playing instruments, as well as singing and dancing. The underlying premise of the film was that music comprises patterns of sound and that child-centred exploratory play develops skills and creativity. The film suggests a variety of ways of stimulating and developing children's innate musicality. It shows how musical concepts are learned indirectly.

We based each scene on a piece of different music and different instruments used to capture a variety of individual responses by children aged four to five years. I composed a skipping chant and a flamenco guitar sequence to encourage call and response behaviour. I created drum dialogues to develop highly patterned interplays. In addition, I introduced the children to unusual instruments chosen for their contrast in timbre, shape, and construction, including pre-recorded electronic music for dance improvisation. For the last scene, I created a sound sculpture in the outdoor play area for the children to explore patterns and timbre.

The late Richard Gill, the music education luminary, then a senior lecturer in music education at the NSW Conservatorium of Music, joined me in on-camera discussions after each scene. I put questions to Richard about children's interactions and he provided explanations. *I Can Make Music* was developed for pre-school, infant and primary teachers, students, parents and music educators. It was a successful and much sought-after resource. I saw a digital restoration recently and the freshness of the material and the rich colours of the cinematography hold up. Important for me was meeting Richard Gill. What an inspirational and passionate man he was. He left us too early. Richard made an indelible impression on my understanding of how music is essential to life. He carried an incredible commitment into every one of his projects and teaching roles, equally at home with people of all ages, whether it be working with infants, teaching tertiary students or conducting choral masterpieces and opera. Soon after working with him, I would ask myself, 'what would Richard think or say about this or that, what would he do?'

Setting words to music for songs and linking literature to music was another strand in my freelance work as a composer-performer. Rigby publishers had an education branch in the 1980s that provided me with regular composition work. They augmented their graded primary school reading books with cassettes containing readings and music. Sometimes, I set early reader books as songs or chants. I might also musically illustrate recorded readings with incidental music and songs. Where appropriate, I would write new songs based on the text. The aim was to involve children orally and aurally. The readers included actors such as Noni Hazlehurst, and ABC presenters, including Richard Moorecroft.

I recorded most of the material in the Sydney Opera House Broadwalk studio, with the benefit of excellent acoustics and first-class sound engineers. I amassed a lot of material including atmospheric music and songs about bunyips, fish, trees, places, and historical events. I covered styles from classical to jazz, folk to rock. It was a lot of fun doing vocal impersonations using my falsetto voice. One of the books was about the Australian gold rush in 1851. The song I wrote for a Rigby Reader book on this subject became my source for 'Gold Fever', recorded by Sirocco in 1982:

Going Freelance

The rush was on in '51
that set Australia on the run;
wild in the streets, shouting, 'It's gold,
we're gonna get rich before we grow old!

Put their lives on the line for an ounce of gain,
a tent in the mud and work in the rain,
loaded with shovels and guns and grog,
to live by the law of dog eat dog.

CHORUS: *They've got the fever, they've got the fever, to strike it rich before they grow old. They've got the fever, they've got the fever, to sell their souls to the devil for fools' gold.*

They worked like slaves from day to day.
They had no boss and no equal pay,
digging like madmen tortured by dreams
of the easy lives of kings and queens.

They'd kill for a quid or a patch of ground,
chase the big nugget that can't be found,
turn to bushranging or roaming the land,
and die in despair with an empty hand.

A man's life is short, and gold always shines.
The end of a rainbow, a few will find.
For the rest, there's the long walk home in the dust
cursing the price of gold or bust!

Nothing has changed; it's still the same;
It's stocks and shares in corporate gain,
while the Earth is scarred by the profit machine;
now, the miners wear ties and keep their hands clean!

More performing opportunities

Sirocco's popularity skyrocketed. It performed in most sectors of the music industry, including subscription concerts, television specials, commercial TV morning shows, ABC live broadcasts, folk festivals, and community events. It could lay claim to taking part in the Tanelorn Festival at Stroud in October 1981.

However, this mini-Woodstock event was a bit of a non-event for us because Sirocco was barely known then. Organisers listed us to perform in the afternoon heat on a minor stage. Most of the audience were half-naked hippies spreadeagled on the dusty paddocks. One photo shows Sirocco on stage in front of massive loudspeakers, with monitors and Marshall stacks used by Midnight Oil the night before. There were more speakers than audience when we played!

A festival that lingers in my memory was in Tasmania in January 1982. It was in the lovely Georgian-styled town of Longford, south of Launceston. The festival was ideal in scale and programming. It was also family-friendly, and Ros joined me, bringing almost-two-year-old Emily along too. We camped by a river, played in pubs, halls, and open-air stages. I treasure photos of Emily dancing under the trees to Bill's melodeon. The weather was dry and hot. Sirocco brought innovation to what we might construe as the Anglo-Celtic phase of the folk revival circa 1973 to 1986. Folk music had shifted from American folk and the protest movement to traditional British, Irish, and Australian music. We were on fire musically among the 7,000 festival-goers. Unfortunately, in the following years numbers grew rapidly, and the festival attracted increasing numbers of bikies. There was no violence, but the leather, the machines, and the alcoholic excess felt intimidating. Sadly, this contributed to the festival's demise.

Musica Viva and performing in schools

Andrew de Teliga's mother, Rae, worked for Musica Viva, a leading classical music presenter. Rae mentioned Sirocco to the manager, Philip Henry. He knew about my background in the Renaissance Players, which included performances in regional concerts and festivals in Sydney and Melbourne. Philip invited me to meet him for a chat about the prospects of including Sirocco in Musica Viva's Music in Schools Project.

In 1982 Musica Viva invited us to perform for infant, primary, and high school students throughout western Sydney. I devised a teaching kit to assist teachers at in-service workshops to prepare for our visit to their school. We had a lot of fun showing teachers our more unusual instruments and involving them in dancing. We encouraged them to have their students write tunes for us to play for them at the concert.

They programmed the concerts in blocks of three weeks. We performed three concerts per day, often in two or three different schools, five days a week. The schools were reasonably close together and the liaison teacher who attended the in-service course always hosted the concert at their school. It was a new and challenging experience for Bill, Andrew, and Guy. I had the advantage of both teaching and music therapy experience. But they caught on quickly and revelled in the spontaneity of young audiences with their often-humorous questions and comments about the music, the instruments, and our personal lives. For example, one kindergarten child renamed Bill's bagpipe a 'magpipe' after the bird. Common questions were 'Where do you sleep?' or, 'How much money do you make?'

We motored our way around most of sprawling Western Sydney in Guy's Volkswagen Kombi. Invariably, there were enthusiastic students sent to meet us at the school gate, to help carry our instruments and take us to the venue. It delighted us to see large drawings and paintings decorating the venue, with depictions of us holding our instruments. The concerts lasted fifty minutes and began with Sirocco walking in to play among the audience – a gesture I brought from the Renaissance Players. And late in each concert, we chose students to come forward to play percussion instruments. We concluded each concert with a question-and-answer session, aiming to be light-hearted and not too technical in our answers.

It surprised me to meet primary school children in the Western Suburbs who were experiencing live music performances for the first time, and some infants who were yet to see the ocean! Our music helped students from diverse backgrounds to feel included. This was possible because our repertoire might shift from a Macedonian dance to an Irish reel to a South American folk song and a Bulgarian dance in 7/8 or 9/8 time, as well as our original compositions. Andrew and I were the prime vocalists and able to sing in different languages.

Sometimes primary school children would write music and send it to us to play for them at their concert. I think we had a positive effect on the teaching staff too, especially when we spent an entire day in a school to play three concerts to cover all age groups. The place would be full of smiling teachers. I found this vignette of the band's school concert experience written in one of my early touring diaries:

> Sirocco was setting up inside a double classroom at Granville South public school. We displayed our instruments on stands and tables. We checked our tuning and ran through the order of the program. The effusive chattering of 250 expectant children surrounded us. I gazed at this microcosm of multicultural Australia. It included Aboriginal children and those of Greek, Italian, Chinese, Vietnamese, and Middle Eastern backgrounds. The school could boast children from twenty-six nationalities. We were looking at the future of Australia.
>
> The children were visibly excited and fidgeting with instruments they'd made a couple of weeks before our concert. There was a girl in a Lebanese costume, another girl wearing a Turkish scarf. Teachers probably selected both to dance. The

double classroom was now a dynamic meeting place for an exciting hour and I'm not sure who was the more privileged, the children or Sirocco.

We left the stage carrying two bombardes and two drums. And on a signal from a teacher, we strolled up and down the aisles and around the perimeter of the audience, playing tunes from the villages of Brittany. The children clapped in time as we slowly processed towards a makeshift stage. Granville South Primary was one of the high points during a three-month period in which Sirocco played to 9,000 children in 72 schools. Daunting and enervating, yes, but it was highly rewarding musically and culturally.

At Winmalee Primary School, the children had made a set of innovative musical instruments from recycled materials. At Grantham High School, we had the satisfaction of winning over a group of seemingly intractable and boisterous adolescents who were sitting at desks. We got them dancing and playing African drumming patterns. At Marsden Park Primary School, we went outside to teach the children the steps and patterns of a French farandole. They were dressed in many colours and were ducking and weaving in and out of each other. It was a joy to make a living entertaining children. Because we played acoustically, it was much easier to adapt to the conditions in the hall or the classroom. We could set up easily and move around more regularly than if we were behind microphones and amplifiers.

At Tregear Primary School, we had to play in the community hall behind the Post Office because the school hall had burnt down. This was in the morning in the middle of July. The hall was without heating, and it was freezing. I watched the children arrive in orderly lines and sit down on the floor. We re-ordered our program and started with an African drumming piece, with all the children and the staff involved in chanting a chorus. We danced as we moved in and around them, playing the percussion, adding some of the children to the band with extra instruments. Things got warmer from there on and we continued with the other pieces in our concert. It was our most aerobic concert! No one felt the cold after that.

Adaptability was very important. On another occasion, also in a Western Sydney primary school, we were on the second floor and had to enter a double classroom packed with 300 children. Just as we were going to stroll in and play in our usual manner, an imam from a local mosque arrived and called out to the teacher in charge and pointed out some children in the audience. He spoke politely, but he was determined that these children could only hear music in a religious context. It must only comprise the sound of a hand beating a drum in prayer. They shouldn't stay in the room. For us, it was a tense moment. We felt for the children as they sheepishly left the room. Satisfied, he left, but when he was out of sight, the children came back carrying some chairs to sit just outside the wide-open double doorway. They got to hear the entire concert in the comfort of their seats, and soon everyone forgot about the incident.

Playing in schools for Musica Viva stands out as an enriching experience in my career. It was life-changing – for us, as well as the young audiences – to be part of a 'Musical Fever' concert, as they were sometimes called. Playing in double classrooms, on basketball courts, in corridors and bike sheds was also part of the magic. Nothing stood in the way of up close and personal music-making.

Musica Viva developed a lasting partnership with Sirocco that would continue for many years. The school performances led to our being offered regional concert tours, festivals, and performances at the Sydney Opera House and the Melbourne Concert Hall. Our acoustic sound and originality crossed musical boundaries and appealed to diverse audiences. There were few groups able to present three school concerts in a day, play in a pub in the evening and follow up with a performance at a classical music festival for clientele who also liked string quartets and piano trios.

Once we were established as a group with a national profile, I led the charge to make records, without which the marketing of the group would be limited. I devised a schedule for the group to rehearse for our debut album, *Paths of the Wind* (1982). Drawing on my studio recording experience from making several albums with the Renaissance Players, I took on the role of producer. I booked the Recording Hall at the Sydney Opera House, which I knew well. It had excellent acoustics and came with tip-top engineers in Max Harding and Dave Connor.

After a few meals and more than a few beers, we came up with a program. The critical production question was how to capture on an LP record the energy and spontaneity of Sirocco's live performances. The obvious approach would have been to record a live album with audience involvement, but it was too difficult to find a suitable venue with favourable acoustics and good recording gear, and an audience to make this work. Our instruments required many microphones to capture their varied timbres and dynamic levels.

I booked the group into the studio for several four-hour recording sessions, which we fitted in after school concerts or the day after an evening concert. We were well-rehearsed and aimed to stay teetotal! It would have been anathema to the great Keith Richards caressing a bourbon bottle. To capture the energy of the band, we did whole takes, with no overdubbing and editing. This demanded the careful balancing of our diverse instruments against voices. I asked the engineers to listen carefully, and close to each instrument, before they selected and positioned a microphone. Happily, we completed the recording in just a few weeks. Guy found us a photographer to shoot black-and-white photographs at Glebe Point Park, under the Moreton Bay fig trees. I collected and edited the group's biographical material and wrote a narrative around the musical sources to include as liner notes. We were new on the scene and the recording would attract broad interest, so I tried to combine ethnography and hype to lay the trail of our innovation. It was still in the days of the LP, and I used every bit of space to tell the Sirocco story both on the record sleeve and the cover. Success! We had an album and a stream of reviews in print.

My friend and music critic, Roger Covell, shared with me that he felt Sirocco communicated rock-and-roll energy with the improvisation of jazz and the musicianship of classically trained musicians. Like others, he saw us as groundbreaking with our combination of diverse instrumental forces, and even when comparing us with the famous Irish group The Chieftains, was astute. I wasn't surprised when 'O'Keefe's slide', an Irish slip jig that I arranged in a quasi-medieval style for two tin whistles and two bodhrans, turned up on a wide range of radio programs, both folk and classical.

Australian music in pubs was legendary throughout the 1970s and 1980s, until poker machines led to a massive reduction in live music venues. Acoustic bands such as Sirocco were part of a thriving live music scene that was great for audiences and a living for musicians. It's often said that Australian rock bands who extended their careers in England and the USA were more potently professional and had greater touring stamina due to their experience at home. Pub venues became the breeding ground for such groups as Midnight Oil, INXS and AC/DC. These bands encouraged an increasing demand for music in pubs. Publicans were confident of good business, and folk-rock groups such as the Bushwhackers, Redgum, Sirocco and Raglan Road were beneficiaries of a vibrant industry. I found a page in one of my diaries listing some of the pub gigs in 1983:

Saturday 12–14: Port Fairy Folk Festival
Wednesday 16: Renown Hotel in Fitzroy
Thursday 17 March: New Lincoln Inn
Friday 18 March: Collingwood Town Hall
Saturday 19 March: Blush and Stutter in Carlton
Sunday 20 March: Montsalvat in Eltham
Monday & Tuesday 21–22: Renown Hotel in Fitzroy
Thursday 24 March: Dan O'Connell in Carlton
1 April Easter: National Folk Festival in Adelaide with Eric Bogle and Redgum

This is evidence that the band could fill a pub every night of the week in nearby suburbs. Melbourne was such a vital scene, and in the halcyon days of the pub gig, nothing rivalled our regular Saturday night at the 'Three Weeds' (the Rose, Shamrock & Thistle Hotel) in Rozelle, Sydney. We built a loyal following, in part because of an enthusiastic promoter and fixer in John Gallagher, who delighted in organising gigs for us. John arranged the handbills and the posters that emphasised our wild folk music. He set up poster runs around Balmain, Rozelle, and the inner west. It was a buzz to see the band name and our mugshots or silhouettes in vibrantly fluorescent-coloured posters wrapped around telegraph poles or posted on hoardings.

From the publican's perspective, it was about filling the 'Weeds' and boosting the drink sales. For us, it was simple: the more paying at the door, the bigger our share between John and the four of us. The overheads were but few: the cost of posters, money for the poster-hangers, a couple of ads in the newspapers and a sound engineer for the night. It was a good earner because we always played in a packed house. There were tables for those who came to eat as well as listen, chairs for those wanting a drink, and space in the centre for calling dances.

The crowd's dance favourite was 'The Horses' Brawl'. Bill taught the steps and called the moves of this exuberant French folk dance, first mentioned in a sixteenth-century treatise on dancing. Like dances in most cultures, it celebrated separate male and female roles. Being liberated and switched on to social change, we dared to make them gender neutral. Mares could be stallions and vice versa. Bill, a great spruiker, called for participants to get up to dance: 'Right ho, come on you lot. You've paid your money. Put your drinks down and up you get. First, you form two lines opposite each other about three metres apart, the wild stallions and the wild mares.'

The dance comprised three sections. In the first two, lines of dancers moved in opposite directions and eyed each other off. Take seven steps and a horse kick. In the second section, the 'wild stallions' stamped a hoof and turned around to show their hindquarters. The 'wild mares' reciprocated by trying to do better than the stallions. In the third section, the lines come together, and each wild mare and stallion swung around their opposite number in a movement that is universally known as 'do-si-do'. I called this symbolic mating.

This movement could become chaotic depending on the level of intoxication of the audience, and it was a hoot while playing from the relative safety of the stage to see people falling over each other until we got them back into line for the repeat of the dance. Our aim was not to be authentic in steps and deportment but to emphasise the joy of participation in dances with simple steps and movements.

Some Sirocco dances sent the participants wild. Such was 'Rada Pere', a Macedonian line dance in which we gradually increased the tempo until it became impossible to keep up, only then to slow down and gradually build up again. As in many of these village dances, there is an opportunity for the participants to call out to each other. We were on a winner with a formula that saw us begin with a concert set that ended with a couple of dances, then a break, followed by the same for the second half. We ended with more energetic dances. A bonus for us was being able to include family, children, friends, and paramours in our gigs. They were safe. No bouncers, no glass throwing, just wild folk music. The 'Three Weeds' felt like a permanent landmark, and I wish we had recorded and filmed some of the nights, for these performances could never be captured in a studio.

Sometimes it fell to me to call the farandole, a French dance. I would leap off the stage and organise the crowd into four or five long lines, everyone holding hands. There are four movements. In the first movement, everyone skips or walks behind a leader tracing a snake pattern on the floor. This movement alternates with subsequent movements leading to the threading of the needle. After herding people into lines – and it was certainly 'herding' when the crowd was sozzled – I would grab the hand of a leader of one of the lines. Guy and Andrew used to tease Bill and me for favouring the hand of attractive young maidens, but we chose both males and females and swore we were strictly impartial. I took the hand of Catherine Kagan one night in the Three Weeds, not knowing that years later fate would bring us together again after I performed at her pre-school around late 2000. Thanks to Bill, I owe his teaching me to call the farandole for meeting my Catherine.

Pubs were great venues as were town halls, community arts centres and church halls. Most venues were ideal for folk dancing, although the house public address system (PA) and lighting were often below par. We carried our own PA for venues up to 350 people. It provided enough volume for most venues, including Balmain Town Hall. We ran a couple of dances there. I disliked the high stage, preferring to be connected more closely with our audience. The hall had a noise-limiting system. Attached high on the back was a strip of three lights – green, yellow and red. The lights changed according to how loud the band played. Green was 'go' and yellow 'be aware,' but if the red came on for three seconds, the power to the stage would simply cut out. I found the lights distracting when they flickered between the colours. Their purpose was to protect nearby residents from rock bands.

We were never short of work. However, we could occasionally end up in the wrong place. Our then manager, Greg Coulton, a mate whom we nicknamed 'Squirrel' because of his ginger hair and freckles, booked us a gig at the Wentworthville Hotel near Parramatta. We arrived at the venue to discover that it was a country and western pub, not our style. Squirrel had got it all wrong, so we had to fudge it and hope that patrons would not throw bottles at the musicians (as in the Blues Brothers movie!). I suggested the rapid deployment of 'Botany Bay', 'Click go the Shears', 'The Road to Gundagai' 'South Australia', and 'A Pub with No Beer'. Well, we 'winged' it, but there was little applause. During our break, a suntanned gent came up to the stage with a schooner in one hand and a 'roll-your-own' cigarette in his mouth. He drawled, 'Youse blokes are okay, don't get me wrong, but your music's up the shit!' He said this without malice, only the freedom that intoxication delivers. We laughed because he was speaking the truth. We weren't playing country and western, only pretending. At the end of the gig, we sat down together and shouted him drinks.

Sirocco made many forays to Melbourne and back. We were able to fit our gear into Guy's Kombi, and Guy devised the travel plan. We would load the Kombi and leave Sydney at noon to drive to Yackandandah, a small town off the Hume Highway just across the Victorian border. What a musical name! It reminded me of kookaburras. At Yackandandah, there was a billabong in a picnic ground, and that was where we used to set up our basic camp. We would light a fire, cook steak, drink a few bottles of Cooper's and sleep on the ground in our bags. Come dawn we'd hit the road again, aiming to be in Melbourne around 10 am. The return leg was usually in one go, driving from Melbourne to Sydney non-stop through the night.

I loved playing in Melbourne and living there for a couple of weeks at a time, although I missed my family. But that's where we got most of our paid gigs. Some of the pubs gave us accommodation. I declined the pub food in favour of the Italian coffee shops and restaurants in Lygon Street, and that became my stamping ground. The publicans were mostly good to work for, with one exception. Strangely, his pub burned down a year after we performed there. The word went around that he hired a couple of scoundrels to set his pub on fire to claim an insurance payout. It didn't surprise me because having complained to him about the air conditioning, I discovered that he would set the air cycle to 'heat'. 'The crowd will buy more spirits when they're hot,' he explained. Spirits sales were more lucrative than beer. And this was on hot summer evenings in Melbourne.

The reputation of the group expanded in 1983 with the increased support of Musica Viva, and there was a demand for us to appear at festivals and for political and charitable causes. There were concerts for the Total Environment Centre, Earth Day, Anti-Nuclear rally and more. Sometimes we shared the bill with the Bushwackers and Redgum, who were attracting big crowds in venues including the Sydney Town Hall and Birkenhead Point.

When supporting these bands, we had a twenty-minute set to get the audience fired up. Typically, we jumped off the stage at the end of our set, with Bill and I playing bombardes and Andrew and Guy playing side drums. The magic of this combination connects the Celtic music of Scotland and Brittany with the pipe sounds of the villages of Bulgaria and the Middle East. It was wild, acoustic, and charged with the energy of dance.

I liked the big gigs supporting the Bushwackers. We were an ideal support band for them. My only reservation was their PA. Their sound guys struggled regularly to prevent feedback from our close-mic'd stringed instruments, including the bouzouki and the oud. They didn't pay much attention to the balance. Their use of six Bose speakers for onstage monitors was anathema to our requirements. When we asked for balance, their engineers just turned up the Bose speakers until they were dangerously loud. My preference was to support acoustic headline acts such as Eric Bogle.

Eric was a friend of the band. We supported him frequently. At one gig in Melbourne, I asked Eric for his thoughts on our style of music. He said he loved it and added, 'but please don't get the audience too excited before I come on with only my voice and guitar.' Eric had witnessed our dragging the audience into the aisles to dance.

Turning poems into songs
One night in 1983 at a 'Three Weeds' gig with Sirocco, a short, bespectacled man in a flat cap bailed me up at the bar when I was on a break between sets. It was the journalist and teacher Denis Kevans (1939–2005). I saw the fire in his eyes as he handed me his paperback book. I loved its title, *The Great Prawn War and Other Poems* (1982). In just a few minutes, I discovered that he was known affectionately as Australia's 'poet lorikeet' and that he was a committed champion of workers, Aboriginal causes, and the environment. We continued to bump into each other at festivals and rallies where he sang and recited his poems, and we became good friends. He often sent me poems written on scraps of paper folded up in recycled envelopes. They were often reworkings of earlier poems. After he moved to live in a shack in Wentworth Falls in the Blue Mountains, we continued a conversation about the birds and the threats to species, including 'Wyeela', the black cockatoo.

Denis's poem 'Albert Namatjira' impressed me. I set it to music and recorded it in 1984 with the help of Sirocco. Namatjira, the great Aboriginal painter, was a man caught between two worlds, as reflected in his style. He achieved nationwide fame with sell-out exhibitions in 1951. All he wanted in his later years was to build a house in Alice Springs. However, being an Aboriginal, and a ward of the state and not a citizen of the Commonwealth, Namatjira had no right to acquire property in the town. Following a public outcry, he was granted Commonwealth citizenship. This meant that for legal purposes, he was non-aboriginal. But the locals blocked his aspirations to acquire real estate. Blatantly racist stereotypes about multitudinous relatives and dependants and drunken parties were behind each plot to thwart his aspirations.

Denis picked up all this and more in his poem about Namatjira. I premiered the song with Sirocco at our concert at the Araluen Arts Centre in Alice Springs. We played outdoors on a cold evening, under the desert sky. It became an eerie experience, singing the song, when a wind blew up on what was a quiet night. I thought about Namatjira's presence among the ghost gums that he painted, the same that were deemed banal by the State Galleries of Victoria and NSW, not worthy of their collections. Denis's song captures the psyche of Albert Namatjira in this verse:

> Desert winds are scratching dust,
> And whirling vapours from the sand,
> Colours sift into my mind,
> Australia grips my shaking hand,
> Down desert tracks my memory tramps,
> And in the heat of desert noon,
> I see the dead in blackened camps,
> I hear them chant a people's doom.

William 'Bill' Porter-Young was a Uniting Church Missionary who came to Australia from Scotland. Bill was a friend of Ros's parents. We met over dinner in 1983. We talked about the poetry of Robbie Burns, and Bill told me he wrote poems about his Scottish heritage. A week later, I received a few typed pages of poems about Scotland, Celtic folklore, Henry Lawson, and life in the bush. I was immediately interested in his poem, 'Askival'. It celebrates a mountain with an old Norse name, the highest mountain on the island of Rùm in the Inner Hebrides of Scotland. Bill was thrilled with my desire to set his poem to music and agreed that I include repeats of the word 'Askival' to suggest long horns calling across the sea. The poem made a fine Sirocco song with voice, pipes and fiddle and drums.

> Askival stands by the sound of Rhum
> And he scans from Coll to Skye,
> As he did a thousand years ago
> When the Viking ships went by.
> And the tide was tinged with a darker red
> Than the scad of a sunset sky.
>
> Askival stands by the sound of Rhum
> And he scans from Coll to Skye,
> While the gentle doe rests by his foot
> Where the old sea-raiders lie.
> For the island of deer is a haven of rest,
> As the hurrying years go by.
>
> Askival stands by the sound of Rhum,
> And he scans from Coll to Skye
> Where the men and the ships of the world pass by,
> On their wearisome ways they ply.
> But here we joy in the Tir Nan Og,
> However, the years go by.

The Northern Territory, 1984

In September 1984 Sirocco toured the Northern Territory, leaving a rainy day in Sydney for the tropical heat of Darwin. After checking into our hotel around midday, we relaxed for the rest of the day. The sunset at Darwin's Mandil Beach was spectacular. People were draped around a swimming pool, listening to jazz and sipping gin & tonic. We had the evening off to enjoy a swim and a drink before meeting our tour manager. After a good sleep, we drove early to the airport to meet our pilot, Dave Fylde, an easy-going man with a sense of fun. We found him on the apron of the airfield, testing the props of an Air North twin-engine Cessna 340. The Arts Council had chartered the plane to help us manage the distances involved in touring the Territory. We loaded our instruments into the nose storage compartment and in the cabin's rear. It was full by the time we took our seats and departed for Groote Eylandt.

After an hour's flying, Dave gave us a view of spectacular Kakadu. We flew over flood plains and through Death Adder Gorge and other ancient landscapes that were too hot and eroded to explore on foot. Flying further, we saw the waterfalls of Kakadu. Then we crossed lush green areas with many water buffaloes in the waterholes and rivers. I thought of crocodiles and tried to recall the difference between the 'salties' and the 'freshies'.

We reached Groote Eylandt and, circling, looked down at the mining operations below. Large machines were tearing manganese ore from the earth. We touched down on a bare-bones airstrip and Dave parked the plane and accompanied Sirocco to the local hotel. After settling in, we went to a beach that was supposedly free of crocs and stingers. The water was incredibly warm and welcoming.

Our major performance was in the miners' mess in the late afternoon next day. Beers in hand, they were a rowdy but appreciative audience. Their responses ranged from 'it's fantastic' to 'yeah, okay, and 'different stuff' and 'weird'. The Irish reels and jigs plus a couple of Australian bush songs carried the day.

Our next stop was Nhulunbuy (Gove) in Northeast Arnhem Land. We flew there in blue skies, enjoying wonderful views from our Cessna cruising at 15,000 feet. We saw the scale of the Nabalco mining operation and the extraction of bauxite in this remote location. There was also an alumina refinery that is now closed.

The small but appreciative audience included people of many nationalities. They switched on to our music with its blend of

Balkan, Middle Eastern, Hungarian, and Irish tunes. Afterwards, we went to an all-night party, which included a risky ocean swim in the dark amongst glowing blue-purple bioluminescent creatures that glinted on our skin.

At first light, I went walking alone along the beach. I met a Yolgnu man dressed in football shorts and guernsey. He asked me for a cigarette, but I had none to offer him as I didn't smoke. I wanted to chat, but he moved on. I knew I was on traditional Yolgnu land, and that Indigenous people had tried unsuccessfully to block Nabalco. This encounter made me acutely aware of the cultural distance between the Yolgnu people and the multinational company ripping up the ground for mega profit. It made me uncomfortable that I couldn't even give him a cigarette, only a polite hello.

The Land Council gave us permission to visit Yirrkala, 18 kilometres southeast of Nhulunbuy. Here we saw how the community lived, in low houses close to the white sand beach and the turquoise sea. Many children were playing in the water. Men, young and old, were fishing with nets and spears. It was so peaceful. I bought a pair of bilma (paired hardwood sticks). We left Nhulunbuy and flew back to Darwin over the North Coast on the Arafura Sea, and over the Eastern Alligator River. This was especially memorable because our pilot, Dave, invited Guy to pull the yoke back for our take-off. Later in the flight, I sat at the controls for fifteen minutes.

After touching down in Darwin and loading our instruments into a minibus, we said farewell to the Cessna and Dave, who said he'd had a great time touring with musos. The next day, we drove to Katherine. The temperature was 36 degrees Celsius when we arrived. We performed in the evening to a small audience at the local roller-skating rink, where we had rehearsed in the afternoon before having a go at skating. We followed up with a school the next morning and then visited Mimi Aboriginal Arts and Crafts, an Indigenous art gallery run by Chips Mackinolty, where we looked at wonderful bark, oil and watercolour paintings produced by the Jawoyn, Dagoman, and Wardaman people.

I hired a canoe and paddled and swam along the freshwater Katherine River, a tributary of the Daly River. The weather was perfect. Lush tropical vegetation, mangroves, many birdcalls, little jumping fish, and the odd small freshwater croc. So quiet, still, and warm, with the smell of the tropics, perhaps mixed with the scent of the desert further down the track via Tennant Creek to Alice Springs. This peaceful timelessness is only interrupted by the first storm of the wet season when the desert turns into puddles of mud.

Before heading off to Tennant Creek we took a detour to visit the Barunga community, about 80 kilometres southeast from Katherine. We performed for a small community with about 150 Aboriginal children in the local school. I included two Indigenous songs that I'd learned from a friend, the songwriter and bush poet, Ted Egan.

At the end of the concert, the children responded by singing a song about bush tucker, 'Ai laikim idimbat bush daga'. The headteacher had helped encourage children to create lyrics in Kriol to an existing melody for 'The Wheels on the Bus Go Round and Round'. The children sang several verses, and Sirocco gradually joined in. That day it was overcast and humid at Barunga, as it had been for weeks. Just after we'd finished, the oppressive skies opened, signalling the start of the wet season. The children were so excited. They ran outside to play football in the teeming rain and to slide through the mud. They jumped around, performing cartwheels and rubbing mud into their hair and daubing their faces. Once the rain had eased, we packed up and drove southeast to Tennant Creek, a 650-kilometre drive. As usual, on such long drives, we took turns at the wheel, except for Bill, who didn't drive. He could sit in the back and play his melodeon!

Tennant Creek was mostly flat and flanked with low granite outcrops that shimmered in the sunset. They appeared to be dropped onto the flat desert landscape. Spinifex and mulga abounded. The flows of red mud after rain, and a few mining shaft headers, punctuated the horizon. The pace was slow. Booze was on everyone's mind – the perfect escape in a place with little or nothing to do.

We played at Tennant Creek Primary, followed by an afternoon concert at the high school. The audiences were mostly Indigenous children and adults of diverse backgrounds including British, Irish, German, Indian, Thai, and Filipino. They worked in either mining or the cattle industry. A highlight of the concert was the audience of parents and community members all getting up to dance, including teachers.

I did some sightseeing in Tennant Creek, using a borrowed bike to ride out of town to look at derelict mine sites. The area had once had a hundred mines, and I discovered scenes of twisted metal and rotting wood surrounding a deep open shaft. A rusty headframe poked out from behind hills of excavated rocks and soil, with the ground covered by jagged quartz, ironstone, and clay. I found a broken drill bit. An old, corrugated shelter flapped in the wind. Perhaps it was the ghost of Tommy Bevan, the dead owner, trudging around the header. It was unnerving. The sky grew heavy, a sign of an afternoon storm moving in. I threw a pebble down the black hole. It pinged from side to side, falling deeper and fainter, towards oblivion. Stumbling over the rocky rim of a ventilation shaft, I saw the desiccated remains of a rock wallaby, its entrails marking the finite, utter end of it all. Only the stone remains.

Back in town, I ended my day in a large tin shed, dancing with new friends to the reggae-influenced music of the South Australian Indigenous band Coloured Stone. There were many characters in the dance, including an eccentric Irish guitar-playing miner from Nhulunbuy, a sun-baked German leathercraft worker and a supermarket manager in her fifties dressed like Cleopatra with a headband. She was the archetypal femme fatale perched at the bar waiting to swoop on any well-heeled miner.

The next morning we drove to Ali Curung, a small, remote Aboriginal settlement. Its name comes from traditional sites connected with Dingo Dreaming. It's an area of red sandy plains and low ridges. We gave an impromptu school concert, playing on the grass adjacent to a covered area. The teachers were non-indigenous. They relied on Indigenous teaching assistants.

Some families sat separately, with their babies in coolamons. A coolamon is a dish with curved sides, from 30 to 70 centimetres long, similar in shape to a canoe. Women can use it to carry water, fruit, nuts, as well as to cradle their babies. Young men sat on the edges, and four Indigenous language groups were represented. The young children were excited by our music and thrilled to play percussion instruments with us. We taught them a farandole. As they performed in lines like the conga and moved into circles or bound the line into a snail's shape, the children created a new movement by leapfrogging over one another.

One of the teachers gave me a coolamon made by a local woman. It was for my daughter, Emily, to carry her doll. I bought two pairs of mulga clapsticks decorated with dream motifs. Sadly, we only had enough time to spend a morning at Ali Curung because we had to make the 370-kilometre drive to Alice Springs before sundown. Our Toyota Tarago was not equipped with bull bars to cope with collisions with kangaroos and other wildlife that can occur as the light fades, so we needed to use as much daylight as possible.

We arrived in Alice Springs as the stars emerged, one by one, and what a show that was. The air was clear, and the night skies were brilliantly lit with the Milky Way, or 'amiwarre' in the Arrernte languages of Central Australia.

Back in Alice, the local Arts Council manager, Clive Scollay, invited us to his house, where we sat around a large campfire and gazed at the glorious night sky and ate well and drank good wine. It was only 3 degrees Celsius, so the crackling fire was very comforting. Clive told about his work in the Northern Territory, about the special powers of Aboriginal desert people, with their navigational skills, their ceremonies, and how they blended ancient lore and ancestry with a modern lifestyle. He also reminded us of our proximity to Pine Gap, the secretive, US-funded military tracking station. I shuddered to think of a missile strike being ordered and monitored from the centre of Australia. Already, there had been British atomic weapons testing at Maralinga in South Australia, almost coinciding with our involvement in the Vietnam war. CIA operatives likely worked at Pine Gap, and US marines were stationed in Darwin. These activities continue to see our near neighbours question our sense of an Asia-Pacific identity.

While in Alice, I also caught up with Ted Egan, the quintessential bush storyteller, outback song man and writer. He had just finished building a new house. It was rendered with a cement made from myriad anthills, which Ted reckoned had to be the toughest and environmentally relevant material. It looked great. Much of the house was underground, especially the bar, a room fitted out like the snug of an English pub. It had timber, stained glass and pint posts. Naturally Ted called his house 'Sinkatinny Downs' – a perfect name from a great bloke who was always ready to share a tinny with you and accompany himself by drumming on an empty beer carton. And yes, he called this his 'Foster fone'! It's worth adding that Ted and his wife, Nerys, built a swimming pool in the shape of Australia, without forgetting to include Tasmania – it's the spa.

Mittagong

Sirocco's busy year continued. We achieved new status in music by being the first non-classical group invited to perform at the prestigious Mittagong Easter Festival. Mittagong is a major township in the Southern Highlands of NSW and is located 110 kilometres southwest of Sydney via the Hume Highway. The town's name derives from the Aboriginal word 'marragon', possibly meaning 'little mountain' in the language of the Dharawal people. The typical patrons of the festival were well-off and well-educated aficionados of classical music. While quite used to concert halls and black ties, patrons flocked to the intimate, informal atmosphere and the high level of music-making of the Mittagong Easter Festival, which had begun in 1960.

The patrons would have experienced some early music-making and exotic instruments before, but nothing like Sirocco. When they filled the seats and looked at the stage, they beheld instruments resting on chairs, including bagpipes, Middle Eastern and Irish drums, a bouzouki, a melodeon, a didjeridu, seedpods, and rattles. They were either intrigued or quietly apprehensive. We didn't walk out onto a stage. We possessed it, entering as always with the shrill skirling of bombardes and drums. To some, it must have been a marauding party of Jacobites, to others the sounds of the devil. I looked into their eyes as we crossed the stage, and I encountered surprise and delight. We had broken through a cultural barrier.

To preserve the suspense, we took a modest bow and remained standing, to go straight into the first item, 'The Hunter'. This was, by then, one of our signature songs. Andrew wrote the melody. I came up with the words, including a quote from the iconic genius, actor, artist and song man, David Gulpilil. We sang them in the Yolgnu language. The arrangement began with a slow prelude in 3/4 followed by a fast 2/4 section. Instruments included tin whistle, bouzouki, cittern, drums, and seedpods used as beaters. The procession and the song lasted for ten minutes. We finished the song. The audience, including other musicians due to play later in the festival, clapped and stamped their approval. We'd passed the test, and the festival was off to the proverbial flying start, just like the Southern Aurora train rushing through Mittagong.

From July 1984, Sirocco undertook tours to New Zealand, The People's Republic of China, and Hong Kong.

China and Hong Kong

The China tour from 3 to 25 October was under the auspices of the Chinese People's Association for Friendship with Foreign Countries and Australia's Department of Foreign Affairs and Trade. The Friendship Association covered costs within China (accommodation, meals, local and domestic transport); Musica Viva covered the international airfares; and the Australia-China Council covered the group's fees.

I hadn't been to Asia for ten years since the Renaissance Players tour. We travelled from Sydney to Hong Kong, stopped over, and flew on to Beijing, to commence a tour that included concerts in Beijing, Xi'an, Ürümqi, and Shanghai.

The arrival lounge at Beijing was adorned with many red stars and duck-egg blue paint. Soldiers were visible. Two young delegates from the Friendship Association greeted us, along with the driver of a spotless blue and white Toyota commuter bus. Tree-lined roads took us from the outer precinct into the sprawling capital, competing with bicycles, buses, donkeys, and many jaywalking pedestrians.

Our accommodation was in the Beijing Hotel, an old building in three parts, reflecting its development from the 1930s, 1950s and 1960s. It had a grand entrance, like its counterpart in an American movie. Bellhops were in abundance. There were desks for money, enquiries, and Chinese medicine. Eight lifts conveyed passengers and luggage up and downstairs. Each one had a differently pitched bell, and when several doors opened near-simultaneously, it sounded like a carillon.

There was a posse of valets on every floor ready to welcome visitors with '*Ni hao*'. My room was grand, in the old style. It had curtains draped from high ceilings to the floor. There were views on the side streets enabling me to observe bicycles weaving between pedestrians.

Our hosts allowed us time to rest before escorting us to our welcoming banquet. It was a formal occasion. We were VIPs. The venue was a restaurant called the 'Sick Duck', so nicknamed because it was near a hospital. This made me laugh because the inference resonated with Australian humour.

The first concert in Beijing was unforgettable. A full house of 2,000 turned up to hear us play at the Zhongshan Music Hall in the Forbidden City. First bell, second bell – Chinese announcements, and the curtains were up. The audience cheered us on stage. They were so animated that some talked while we played, apparently fascinated by our instruments and eclectic repertoire.

There was a song added to our repertoire for this tour, the traditional Australian folk song, 'Click Go the Shears'. The rationale for its inclusion was to do with its popularity since the landmark visit to China by Gough and Margaret Whitlam in 1971. Young and old learnt the song and it became a mark of the friendship with China advanced by Whitlam. His initiative heralded a new era of respect and understanding between Australia and China, the antithesis of what is happening today.

Sirocco's first China concert, 1984, in the Forbidden City, Beijing. *l-r*: William (Bill) O'Toole; Andrew de Teliga; Michael Atherton; and Guy Madigan. Photo: Peta Williams

Towards the end of the interval break, we met Madam Yun En Feng, a famous Chinese soprano who specialised in folk music. She had attended the concert as a guest of the Australian Embassy. She heard us perform my arrangement of 'Pao ma liu de shan shang (On Galloping Horse Mountain) for flute, violin, guitar, and percussion. This is a famous Chinese song, and she requested we perform it again with both of us sharing the verses. We had five minutes for a rehearsal and divided up the verses ready to spring them on the audience during the second half.

The audience rose to their feet as we processed back into the theatre. It was a thrilling moment to be supported by 2,000 people in the Forbidden City clapping in unison to our music. Stage and audience became one – the spirit of folk or people's music was alive. They went into raptures when Madam Yun joined us onstage and explained what we had prepared during the interval. They knew every word and joined in. The Australian Embassy staff in the audience viewed it as 'diplomacy friendship' on steroids, especially when Madam Yun offered to meet us in Xi'an and perform with us again. Jokingly, I told her we could get it right next time.

Ürümqi

The flight to Ürümqi was uncomfortable and noisy in a rather old-looking Russian Tupolev twinjet. We were seated up the back next to the engines. Breakfast came in a small blue cardboard box, holding a boiled egg, a brand-new empty salt cellar, and abundant green tea. We would be cruising one minute, then suddenly, without warning, we might ascend 500 metres or bank steeply to the left or right. They likely used the flight for pilot training or instrument testing. It got worse when we flew into a snowstorm half an hour out of Ürümqi. I'm a white-knuckle flyer and was prone to panic, thinking of Ros and Emily back home and the possible news of my disappearance over the Tian Shan mountains. Anyway, we bashed through the clouds and into the bright sunshine out of the turbulence, and the pilots guided us to our landing in Ürümqi, hoping our instruments would be okay.

The imprint of Islam was potently visible in Ürümqi. This was Central Asia, on the Silk Road and close to the Middle East. There were mosques, bicycles, and street butchers preparing kebabs. Sides of sheep and dogs hung down on hooks, expertly butchered and ready for sale. There were mounds of fresh vegetables on the sidewalks. I thought it might resemble a European town in the Middle Ages. There were mud-brick dwellings, donkeys, Uyghur hats, Uzbek hats, Russian hats, and flat caps like those in Turkish Anatolia. The people were sun-weathered, fine-featured with big smiles. We must have been an equally rare sight for the locals as we ambled along the streets, looking in the markets for arts and crafts. Sheep and goats wandered freely in the streets and many old men chatted in small groups. As well as butchers, there were bakers, knife sellers and textile makers. Many were herdsmen who were coming down from the high pastures as winter closed in. Meanwhile, barbers were working on the sidewalks, giving 'short back and sides' or 'all off', but always leaving the beards. We were an anomaly with our longish hair, jeans and leather or denim jackets.

Concerts and cultural exchange

There were two concerts at the People's Theatre, both of which were sold out. Our tour bus pulled up, and we saw a huge banner outside the theatre that publicised our concerts. Someone had painted it beautifully in Uyghur script and Chinese characters. In the foyer, men were finishing another bi-lingual banner with an Australian flag in the top left-hand corner.

Half an hour before the curtain, I was in my dressing room, dressed only in my jocks, about to iron my shirt when a female attendant burst in and took the iron out of my hands. I was embarrassed, but impressed with her ironing! Indeed, I rarely ironed my shirts. I would take the shirt out of the suitcase and wear it, hoping the wrinkles would smooth out with body heat.

The audience identified immediately with the sound of the oud (Turkish lute), Bill's bagpipes, Andrew's bouzouki, and Guy's hourglass drum. These are relatives of traditional Central Asian musical instruments. They gave us a standing ovation when we played these instruments in our post-interval procession from the back of the hall to the stage.

On our last day in Ürümqi, we met the Xinjiang-Uyghur Song and Dance Ensemble. We sat down to a sumptuous afternoon tea and were welcomed by our host, the director, Rabi Ya Muhammat. His ensemble presented a concert just for the four of us. It comprised two *rewap*s (long lutes), two *ejik*s (spike fiddles), one *yangqin* (trapezoidal struck zither), one cello, one bamboo flute, and one *dap* (frame drum). There was also dancing. The music was pulsing and energetic – Turkish and Balkan in flavour and yet with a Chinese character. The women wore colourful dresses as they sang and danced. The dancing seemed to mix flamenco and *raq sharki* (middle eastern dance). The musicians, all men, wore black suits and Uyghur caps.

Following the concert, we mingled with our hosts and swapped ideas. We played a Greek item, 'Omorfoula' which we thought resembled the spirit of Uyghur music. It fascinated them as did our instruments, especially the bouzouki, gemshorn, darbuka (Turkish goblet drum) and transverse flutes. Our meeting was all too short. We had just made friends only to say goodbye.

We visited the Xinjiang national instrument factory for a guided tour. The walls were festooned with finished and partly finished instruments, the main ones being the rewap and *dutar* (two-stringed long lute), which derive originally from Persia. To our delight, the visit developed into an impromptu jam session. The friendly boss and staff leapt up and danced, sang Uyghur songs, and played instruments taken down from the wall. They were excellent makers and musicians and knew exactly how to set instruments up for playing.

Shanghai

The Shanghai leg of the tour was memorable, not only for our enthusiastic audiences but also for a visit to the Shanghai Conservatorium of Music. Students studied both Chinese traditional and western music. Now, I knew that in the 1960s Cultural Revolution, the Red Guards smashed as many violins and pianos as they could find. Instrument making, we were told, was flourishing again, even in the conservatorium since 1980. I was surprised to discover that every student at this elite institution had to attempt making a violin during their first year of studies. Also, since composers and performers were keen to assimilate Western performance practice and styles into their playing, the instrument factories were adding keywork to Chinese oboes, bamboo flutes and others. A radical development in the yangqin saw a new string layout, devised to make the instrument fully chromatic and playable at lightning speed.

The hospitality extended to Sirocco throughout the tour of China was overwhelming. The various branches of the Friendship Association set up the perfect itinerary, with a mix of concerts by local musicians, sightseeing, visits to factories and welcoming banquets. Everywhere we travelled, people were consistently friendly and generous. It was a privilege to be involved in cultural exchange and to promote goodwill and friendship between our two countries.

7

RIDICULOUSLY BUSY

Listening to a change of rhythm.

I left Sirocco in October 1985. I was restless and needed a break from touring. Emily was four. Ros and I wanted more time together as a family; I had spent much of Emily's early childhood on the road. Also, my musical interests were broadening to include film music and solo projects. I had enjoyed five exciting years with the band and been part of its dynamic development. I was ready to study again and enrolled in two years of Ethnomusicology subjects at the University of New England from 1986 to 1987. The teachers were inspirational: Professor Catherine Ellis, a leading scholar of Indigenous music research and preservation, and Dr David Goldsworthy, an expert in Pacific music cultures. I attended residential schools and workshops where I could again enjoy the camaraderie of student life, this time with mature-age students. One of my buddies was ABC music producer Ivan Lloyd. And the wine flowed in the evenings.

I chose ethnomusicology as a field of enquiry to enhance my theoretical understanding of music in culture and society. Its overlap with anthropology and investigation of music-making materials – instruments and sound objects – helped me to contextualise my performing and composing career. Further, the study consolidated my academic trajectory, securing a major in music to add to my degrees from UNSW and subjects at Sydney University.

From a practical standpoint, distance education allowed me to spend more time with family. However, the home time was not to last. With another child on the way and a reduction in income since leaving Sirocco, I was reluctant to turn down work. It flowed, and like a freelancer, I jumped at it. I soon had a new band going and was focused on performing and composing, while also doing more film composition. There was touring, too. Indeed, looking back, 1986 became a ridiculously busy year, as if I was on the rebound after a long-standing relationship with Sirocco.

Atherton Tableband

After a few months' respite from performing, Musica Viva invited me to form a trio to perform in schools. I was a fan of Synergy Percussion and knew Michael Askill, a founding member. Michael had recently resigned as the principal timpanist with the Sydney Symphony Orchestra to go freelance. I called Michael, and he was keen to join me. We approached John Napier, an improvising, classically trained cellist and singer who played with the Mambologists. I came up with the name 'The Atherton Tableband'. This name invoked Tafelmusik – a Renaissance term for feast or banquet music – as well as the Atherton Tablelands in North Queensland. Musica Viva liked the name because it maintained my profile for publicity.

The Atherton Tableband began school tours for Musica Viva in April 1986. The repertoire differed from Sirocco, with a focus on cello, synthesizers, orchestral percussion and my wind and stringed instruments. We blended medieval songs, African drumming, and Renaissance ground basses with jazz and original compositions. Adding a sequencer and small keyboard amplifier enabled us to use through-composed electronic loops and harmonic constructs to enrich the texture. John's fine tenor voice was featured, with me singing baritone accompaniments. We included a collapsible vibraphone, congas, crotales and African bells and rattles. The effect of this eclectic instrumental combination led one reviewer to call our style ethno-classical, a term I much preferred to the often-used 'world music'.

Korea

The school concerts made an immediate impact. Musica Viva sent us to Korea for the Department of Foreign Affairs and Trade (DFAT). Once again, I was playing for Australia but in another group. Our mission in Korea was to perform lunchtime concerts in five major universities, to entertain and encourage students to ask questions about Australia and its universities. We were part of soft diplomacy aiming to see Asian students choose Australia over the USA as a place to study.

Our staging requirements were minimal: three chairs, a table and a power outlet. However, this had clearly not been successfully communicated to our hosts. As we were climbing the stairs to go to the venue of our first concert in Seoul National University, we had to step aside to allow eight men, huffing and puffing, to struggle past us with a full size concert grand piano and set it on the stage. We didn't use a piano in our concerts. I had not included it in our list of requirements. But we didn't want to seem ungrateful, so we rolled the piano upstage. I lifted its lid and put a sandbag on the sostenuto pedal. This enabled the strings to vibrate sympathetically with the sounds of our instruments, especially the percussion. It captivated the audience, which revelled in our music and instruments and my explanation about the position of the piano and its sympathetic resonance.

It was my first visit to Korea, a country largely unknown by Australians, who knew more about Japan and China. The Korean audiences and our hosts were most welcoming, the older ones reminding us of Australia's contribution to the Republic in the Korean War. During the tour, we purchased Korean percussion instruments that soon featured in our concerts. I became a fan of Korean classical music, later going on to establish a university Korean percussion ensemble at my university.

Winds of Solstice

Not long after I left Sirocco, in October 1985, Vanessa Chalker, Education Director at Opera Australia, invited me to discuss an idea she was putting forward to the management. Opera Australia was in season with *Lucia di Lammermoor*, starring Joan Sutherland. They had devised the production for the Concert Hall with spectacle in mind and with much larger audiences than the opera hall. On the nights when Joan wasn't performing there to enthral the audiences, the set of *Lucia* was available, and Vanessa had the inspired idea to use it to develop a youth opera workshop.

It excited me when Vanessa said I was the right person for the project, given my composing, performing and music therapy experience.

The brief was to develop the musical concept for a 50-minute music piece with secondary students in a two-week workshop in January 1986. After the framework was developed in consultation with the director, assistant director, and design consultant, the students' ideas would also be incorporated. I was to aim for an operatic style, with a chorus, integration of music and drama, and a certain grandeur of scale. It was my job to coach the students in musical skills and improvisation, rehearse the music, and conduct the performances in February.

I accepted the role and suggested Guy Sherbourne as the stage director. I had first met Guy at UNSW in 1980 when he was the director of two productions that I worked on as a composer: Rolf Lauckner's *Cry in the Street*; and in 1983, *Between the Worlds*, a group-devised play. Vanessa appointed him as my stage director. We would use improvisation and role-play to encourage the performance skills of a cast with different levels of experience. Guy suggested we employ Annelise Smith to take on the dramaturg's role and stage management.

The project began with a publicity drive to attract young performers willing to give up their summer vacation for an opera workshop. Our working title, 'Medieval to Mad Max!', aimed to stimulate interest. The response was overwhelming.

In early December, at the Opera Centre, we auditioned 300 students aged 15 to 19, paying attention to the diversity of talents. The successful applicants would work collaboratively on the libretto, music, dance, and action sequences. 'Medieval to Mad Max!' would be an innovative project in music theatre in education. We selected seventy students and contacted them by letter, also advising them that there was a small workshop fee of just $30.

There were two intensive, week-long workshops at the Sydney Conservatorium from January 13 to 24, 10 am to 4 pm each day. I coached and rehearsed the vocalists and instrumentalists and an ensemble together. Guy worked with the actors and dancers, and Annelise led a group of students to write story text. We expected input from everyone on the story, the music, costuming and choreography.

At the end of each day, we met as a company to discuss the day's work, assessing the development of the production and tossing around suggestions. Within a week, we had a story. From this, the dramaturg and her group created dialogue for the actors and lyrics for the singers. I compiled the music from the collective composers and assigned students with overnight tasks to compose recitatives, arias, and choruses. We used ancient Greek drama and Australian poetry as guides to establish a style for the libretto.

The energy of the seventy outstanding students was unforgettable. They travelled from as far afield as Emu Plains and Gosford. Most could sight-read music. Many could play several instruments. Each workshop day was exhilarating, with an atmosphere of improvisation, writing text, developing action, and sketching musical drafts. Following the company meetings, Guy and I would retire to the Ship Inn at Circular Quay to reflect on the process and devise a plan for the following day.

I went home to stitch the composition fragments together and arrange interludes. Within two weeks 'Medieval to Mad Max' morphed into *Winds of Solstice*, a one-act opera. It was in a classical style with a fusion of nineteenth-century romanticism and twentieth-century harmonies. There were epic entrances and fanfares. The pastiche approach encouraged drawing on the musical gestures from opera. I recall asking the sixteen-year-old Stuart Skelton, now a world-famous *heldentenor* (a term for a strong and sonorous tenor voice covering baritone to high tenor) to sing the role of Chronos and to write an aria, which he produced overnight. Incidentally, he could also play four instruments if required.

The plot called for the jesters to dance for Chronos. Chryssotemis Tintner, the daughter of Maestro Georg Tintner, produced a fabulous composition that was fully arranged for the orchestra. I encouraged students to draw on their backgrounds and interests. The first violin, Heather Bakopoulos, knew Greek music from her parents' background. She responded to a suggestion to compose a ballet segment in the style of a Greek *kalamatiano* dance in 7/8 time. It was her first exploration of her Greek musical heritage, and the ensemble thoroughly enjoyed it. Today's artistic director of Sydney Philharmonia Choirs, Brett Weymark, also contributed as a student composer, as did Lanneke Jones, whose career included singing with the Song Company.

We set the emerging libretto to music each day. The excitement of the first run-through was unforgettable. *Winds of Solstice*, a one-act opera, was ready to rehearse and transfer to the Sydney Opera House. This was the synopsis:

> Two opposing clans are summoned to the court of King Chronos, a figure that holds supernatural power, whose ageing has led him to the necessity of divesting his power to a suitable leader. Jesters in his court supply a subtext of parody and conscience for the kingdom of Chronos, against the two clans.
>
> The two clans have different styles of action and thought. The Peladions consider themselves highly cultured and ethically advanced, with the assumption of leadership considered a right. The Morranors show discipline. They are heroic warriors who live by the code of the sword, believing that they deserve to rule. They revere battle, through which they bring order to chaos.
>
> The principals of both clans strut and debate, presenting their credentials for leadership to Chronos. Dissatisfied, he banishes them all for a year. During this time, they battle each other for ascendancy and return for his decision. Chronos must decide between the Peladions and Morranors or an alternate source.

Guy and I took a small group of writers and composers to view the set of *Lucia di Lammermoor* at the Sydney Opera House. Its stage manager ushered us into the empty concert hall. He called out to the lighting technician to bring up full light on the dark stage where 'La Stupenda' was already in mid-season delivering her stratospheric notes. Everyone gasped in awe. The set looked just like the model he brought with him. This would help us to transfer *Winds of Solstice* to this stage, albeit a different story from Donizetti's tragedy set in a forbidding Scottish castle.

No stage machinery or changes were necessary because the set was fixed. So was the lighting rig. Fortunately, we were able to access cues from the current opera that worked for us.

The Australian Opera advertised our performances for 15, 17 and 18 February. When school recommenced, we would have to rely on the commitment of the cast to attend rehearsals at the Opera Centre and then at the Sydney Opera House.

Vanessa invited Opera staff to a rehearsal. It caught them by surprise. They had only imagined a couple of scenes in a concert format, not a one-act opera. Guy and I sensed they didn't know what to do with the outcome. Opera management's interest was elsewhere. It was nervous about the reception of its forthcoming world premiere production of *Voss*, Richard Meale's opera based on the Patrick White novel.

Opera Australia is patronised by mostly a culturally conservative clientele that is not interested in new Australian work. There was, and still is, a fetish for European repertoire from 'dead white male' composers. One only need ask Moya Henderson about the struggle she endured trying to have her opera *Lindy* produced, or the difficulty composers have in obtaining a second season of their work. Opera Australia has sucked up eye-watering sums of taxpayer subsidy for years but is yet to show a sustained interest in homegrown opera.

For example, in 2012–13, the taxpayer subsidy of the company used up 43 per cent of funds available to all art forms in Australia. I can speak with authority because I have served on the Performing Arts Board of the Australia Council for the Arts and was also Chair of the NSW Arts Ministry's Music Committee. Peer review committees I chaired favoured less subsidy to Opera Australia, but people in high places treated it like a 'sacred cow'. Today, we have an opera house that has become a major catalyst for a variety of artistic forms – music, theatre, and dance – yet we can say that a commitment to new Australian opera remains stifled by a repertoire of repeat productions of *Carmen*, *Madama Butterfly*, *La Traviata*, *Turandot* and *La Bohème*.

As a landmark for music theatre in education, *Winds of Solstice* was ready to go. We 'bumped in' to the Concert Hall and performed for audiences of fifteen hundred, eight hundred, and nine hundred, respectively. Chairman Charles Berg came to two performances. He waxed lyrical. But his organisation neither filmed nor recorded *Winds of Solstice*. They focused their publicity machine on promoting *Voss*, as expected given the financial risk of a new three-act opera. But Opera Australia lost an opportunity to showcase how to workshop, teach, enthuse, and build practitioners and audience in a novel way. They never repeated a project such as *Winds of Solstice*.

Marionette Theatre

I could not find a follow-up to *Winds of Solstice*, but an opportunity to work in a different genre fell into my lap. The Marionette Theatre of Australia commissioned me to write a score for their adaptation of Carlo Collodi's *Pinocchio*. It proved to be a joy from start to finish. I met the director and producer, Michael Creighton, at the Marionette Theatre in the Old Sailor's Home in 'The Rocks'. He introduced me to the puppeteers, including the immensely talented Slabacu sisters from Romania.

I drew on a lingering interest in the Italian folk music of Naples and Sicily, the tarantella, and the saltarello. I discovered, in a recording of a group called Il Nuova Compagnia di Canto Populari, resonances of my Renaissance Players and Sirocco days in its combination of wire-strung plucked instruments, flutes, violin, bagpipes, tambourine, and castanets. My *Pinocchio* score used similar instruments plus an accordion. I composed, performed, and recorded the entire score at home on an 8-track tape recorder. The production was very successful, and the Marionette Theatre asked me to compose more scores for *Kakadu Man* (1988); *Little Darlings* (1989); and an adaptation of Rudyard Kipling's *The Jungle Book* (1990).

Composing for film and television

While working on *Pinocchio,* I was also branching out into music for film and television. It would provide steady employment for a few years.

I enjoyed working collaboratively, approaching music very much from the heart rather than the head, and becoming involved in the complete sound design. A film composer must be versatile. One day requires a composer to write music for a string quartet. The next day, a project might require a rap-attack bass riff, or a score for a jazz band appearing in a movie scene, or some bush music for a documentary about colonial Australia.

The film composer emerged in the silent movie era, when a pianist, organist or small orchestra accompanied the pictures while the projectors motored away in the background. The composer became an 'alchemist' creating the invisible character for the film, adding that final dimension in the collaboration. Music implies a psychological dimension. The music works in several ways; it helps create an atmosphere of time and place, exploiting strong associative values of instruments, genres, and styles. Film composition is a complex creative process that involves understanding all aspects of production from the script to the final cut. The composer 'spots' the film with the director, deciding where music should go. Film music helps to realise the meaning of the film.

To compose for moving images means appreciating and understanding how films are made. Directors are just as important as film composers in their influence on my work. Stanley Kubrick, Akira Kurosawa, Peter Weir, Joel and Ethan Coen, Martin Scorcese and Ridley Scott all stood out for me, especially for the way they incorporate music and sound. The composers who helped me understand something of the craft include Eric Korngold, Bernard Hermann, Ennio Morricone, Vangelis and Australians Chris Neal and Brian May. I enjoyed the rare experience of performing with Sirocco as a bush band in *Archer* (1985), directed by Denny Lawrence. Chris

Neal created the score for this telemovie based on a true story of the first horse to win the Melbourne Cup. I studied Chris's approach to each cue, his instrumentation, the multi-tracking technique, the contiguity between sound effects, dialogue, and music. Chris's work was masterly for starting and ending a cue. There were few, if any, women working in film music other than Moneta Eagles and, later, Jan Preston, but today, there are excellent active composers including Nerida-Tyson Chew, Amanda Brown, and Jessica Wells.

The second source of inspiration came from my contacts with the music of many cultures and luminaries, including Ravi Shankar, the great Indian sitar player and composer. I read his book in the 1970s and still remember his profound description of *raga*, the basis of Indian classical music:

> There is a saying in Sanskrit – 'Ranjayathi iti Ragah' – which means, 'that which colours the mind is a raga.' For a raga to truly colour the mind of the listener, its effect must be created not only through the notes and the embellishments but also by the presentation of the specific emotion or mood characteristic of each raga.

I viewed this as a mantra for exploring how music can convey feelings and values when synchronised with images.

Kalash: the Last Pagans

Most of my scores were for documentaries involving a socio-historical perspective. *Kalash: the Last Pagans* enabled me to reference the sounds of central Asian folk music as a source of material for the composition. The film celebrated a small, non-Muslim minority living in the Hindu Kush Mountains, near Chitral, North Pakistan. The Kalash, who are blue-eyed people, unlike their Pakistani brothers and sisters, consider themselves descendants of Alexander the Great.

DNA researchers suspect they originated in Afghanistan, but the Kalash cling to their story, saying they are of Western and European appearance. Unlike Muslims, they make and drink wine. They are polytheists and guard their traditional ways. Hence, they are seen by their Islamic neighbours as pagans.

The film director, David O'Brien, included footage of *buskajee*. This is a game on horseback. The aim is to wrest a lamb's carcass from members of the opposing team. I used flutes made by the Kalash that were collected by David for me when he was on location. He recorded songs for me. I drew on this and wrote music for the *buskajee* scene using the Turkish *bağlama*, oud, transverse flute, and a Uyghur frame drum from Ürümqi. In contrasting scenes about winemaking and the worship of deities, I added electronic samples and synthesizers to underscore feelings of mystery and otherworldliness.

Composing on a hired Fairlight Computer Music Instrument, 1988.
Photo: Rosalind Atherton

Kids and Traffic

The NSW Traffic Authority commissioned me to compose and record songs and chants for use by children, parents, and teachers to teach road safety. There were two projects: *Kids and Traffic: Song and Rhythm* (1985), which was co-composed with educator, Margaret Weeks; and *Streetsense* (1986), which I composed myself. The music was for use by teachers at infant and primary schools. It presented the road safety information in the most natural, entertaining and informal way possible, relying on catchy rhythms of jingle-like songs, for example, 'Click, clack, front and back' and 'I am a seatbelt'.

> Click, clack, front and back
> When you close the door
> Click, clack, front and back
> Hear the engine roar
>
> I am a seatbelt front and back,
> Buckle me up, Buckle me up
> Buckle me up, I go
> Click, clack!

Music for children

I had worked in many schools with Sirocco and the Atherton Tableband, so it was natural for me to accept offers to present interactive solo performances in pre-schools. I had a swag of children's songs and selected instruments and sound-producing objects to engage the four- and five-year-olds. The program included songs and dances. The children sat on the floor in a semi-circle, usually forty at a time. I placed my instruments on a circular red velvet mat: classical guitar, psaltery, accordion, didjeridu, 3-holed pipe and tabor, flute and bagpipe. Red is a standout colour and helped to accentuate the colours of the instruments. My show required children to handclap a flamenco sequence and join me in call and response songs.

I used to dismantle my bagpipe completely in front of the children. I would reassemble it by blowing the double reed detached from the chanter and then the single reeds from the drone pipes.

I would re-connect the pipes and ask one child to squeeze the bag as I inflated it. When it functioned again, I asked a second child to come forward and hold the drone while the bag was being squeezed. I played 'Twinkle, Twinkle Little Star' with their help. After much laughter, I pretended to run out of breath and keel over, leaving the bagpipe in the hands of the children. Then I would spring up, thank the children, inflate the bag and play a lively jig.

Singing at Caloola

My itinerant teaching took me to some remote places in NSW, such as a residential workshop south of Canberra. I remember driving my mother-in-law's 1967 white Holden along a dusty bush track to a homestead of an extensive property. The first gate was open. I drove on and shut the second gate, then the third gate, and forded the river twice. I made my way up the valley in the still of morning. The foothills of the Snowy Mountains looked wild and inviting through my car's windows. I wanted to stop there and take in the splendour, but I was due at the farm. Round the last bend, I saw the sign 'Caloola' and drove in the last gate. I switched off the engine. Silence, except for the chink of cutlery and clatter of crockery coming from inside the house. I walked into a large room and saw thirty young people chattering over lunch.

They were members of a choir called Gaudeamus or 'Let's rejoice' – a perfect name for this delightful group of people. Judy Clingan, their director, stood up and called out 'Welcome, Michael', at which point the choir broke into a welcome song. What a treat.

I came to Caloola to run a workshop in early music and here were enthusiastic kids ready to sing, play instruments, and dance. After lunch, they encouraged me to play an 'echo' singing game. Half the group went up a steep hill behind the farmhouse, taking me with them. The other group stayed just outside the house. They sang call and response songs up and down the hill, followed by a Hungarian song using counterpoint and sung with high-voltage energy. I knew immediately that I would not underestimate their talents in my classes. I spent the next two days with them exploring medieval songs and dances, showing them how to embellish the music.

Playschool

Word got around about my show. I never advertised but took regular bookings. I performed all around Sydney. ABC *Playschool* took an interest and filmed me in 1985 for a segment with Noni Hazlehurst, a prominent Australian actor and *Playschool* presenter. The educational values of the program were unsurpassed. A team of early childhood experts devised the activities according to key learning and development areas. There was a buzz in the studio as the crew prepared to shoot the scenes while in-house pianist, Warren Carr, limbered up. Noni and I shared a scene in which I played on a Mongolian horse-head violin, and she told the story of its origins. The ABC filmed me playing pipe and tabor and leading twenty-five pre-schoolers in a dance procession around Osborne Park Pre-School in Lane Cove.

ABC Television has been a constant companion for me since I migrated to Australia in 1965. My first recollection is the black-and-white test pattern of ABN 2, before and after transmission. I came to rely upon the ABC's informed, concise and comprehensive news and weather reports. News readers from James Dibble until those of today are the faces of a quintessential ABC style more welcome than ever in this era of hyper-saturated media excess and government funding cuts.

ABC outside broadcast vans continue to bring the world into our homes – from suburban rugby grounds, the mulching of gardens, and jazz clubs to a cornucopia of stuff for kids. *Playschool* is surely the most iconic – brilliantly researched and produced, and always fresh. I watched it years ago with my now grown-up children and watch it again with my grandchildren. *Playschool* nurtures early childhood learning without being didactic. I appeared in several programs, performing in preschools and recording under the shadow of the transmitter at the Gore Hill studio.

Touring again

Working with young audiences led to more bookings to perform for children at the Sydney Opera House and then at Melbourne's Victorian Arts Centre. I could adapt to any age from infants to high-school-aged audiences.

My performances in the Sydney Opera House were held in one of my favourite spaces, the carpeted northern foyer in front of John Olsen's mural based on Kenneth Slessor's great poem 'Five Bells'. The stairs and vaulted ceiling are like an amphitheatre. It was glorious performing in the late morning or early afternoon. I could work close to the audience, bathed in the light streaming through windows, with vistas beyond of the Harbour Bridge, Fort Denison and Kirribilli.

Canada

In June 1986 also, Musica Viva sent the Atherton Tableband to Vancouver to represent Australia in the Asia-Pacific Festival. We appeared as a 'world music' group because of our instruments – voices, didjeridu, oceanic flutes and reeds, guitar, cello, medieval guitar, hurdy-gurdy, accordion, vibraphone, African/Asian percussion, and synthesizer.

The first performance was on the Asian Courtyard stage and shared with the local Musqueam Indian Sundancers and our new friends, Tamatea Ariki Nui, a Māori group from Hawkes Bay, New Zealand. The organisers dubbed it a 'tribal exchange', the festival director implying we represented Aboriginal Australia, most likely because

I played the didjeridu in one of our compositions, 'Nullarbor Train'. We insisted it would be extremely disrespectful to present ourselves this way, as none of us was an Indigenous Australian. Once sorted, we enjoyed being part of a splendid concert in a glorious space.

Following a request from David Coombe, formerly Secretary of the Australian Labor Party, then Senior Trade Commissioner, we performed at Southland Elementary School, which was attended by his son. It is in Musqueam Indian Territory in an outlying suburb near the University of British Columbia. About 70 per cent of the children were Musqueam. The contact teacher, Ron Romak, was delighted with the response to our music. We connected the Musica Viva school concerts in Australia with Southland Elementary by sharing poems written by Year 5 and 6 students from Sylvania Primary School (NSW). We read the poems to improvised music suggesting the Australian outback. At that time Sylvania Primary had engaged Indigenous teachers to teach Aboriginal studies. They divided the school population into twelve dreaming groups of the specially named Kilikintori tribe. Groups were assigned a sacred site to manage and the responsibility of creating a story. All lessons and transmission were oral. Each group passed their 'sacred stones' onto the subsequent year. We presented a copy of a poem to the children of Southlands Elementary School:

> We are the red people,
> The people of the sun.
> The sun warms our bodies
> and our souls.
> It strikes the shimmering sands
> and burning plains with spears of light.
> Flowers the colour of fire bloom in our desert,
> The land is our mother
> and we, her children,
> care for her.
> (Children of Sylvania Public School, NSW)

We enjoyed the luxury of ten days in Vancouver and environs and only five performances. This gave us time to mix with other artists, take trips on ferries, walk on Whistler Mountain, and enjoy the multicultural culinary delights of this friendly city. Following our stay in Vancouver, Musica Viva had us booked to perform in Washington State, USA. We collected a large black Buick rental van and drove south to the Canada–US border, where our arrival led to frustration.

As we approached the Customs barrier, we were flanked by two heavily armed guards, one of them a woman carrying a silver 44-Magnum Smith and Wesson in a holster. She took our passports and documents from us, ordering us tersely to stay put. She returned fifteen minutes later to tell us we weren't allowed to enter the USA. I remonstrated that we were guests of honour at a reception in Renton (near Seattle) that evening. We had a letter of invitation from the Mayor of Renton. That we were long-haired musicians in a van, with Aussie accents, wearing T-shirts, two of us with beards, may have aroused suspicion.

We waited for two hours before we were grudgingly allowed into the USA but only with visas valid for four days. Surprisingly, our van wasn't searched. Unfortunately, we were too late for the reception and missed out on performing in Renton, a place I knew as the birthplace of my guitar hero, Jimi Hendrix. We did make it to Longacres Racecourse the next day, the next date on our itinerary. But this was a let-down. On arrival, we were ushered to stand near the paddock fence and tersely instructed to 'do our thing'. There was no sound system and no real announcement. So we played a few items and just slipped away quietly. Such are the vicissitudes of touring that teach one to rein in expectations!

An even sillier scenario occurred after our successful appearance at the prestigious Asian Arts Festival in Hong Kong. An employee of the Australian Consular Office drove us to a supermarket to play as a promotion for Australia! I was furious because I had assumed it was to be a trade promotion opportunity at a convention hall or similar. But Michael Askill broke me up with his comment: 'This is the first time I've had to play standing next to the celery.' We were in fact in the greengrocery section of a supermarket and completely ignored by the trolley-pushing Hong Kong citizens.

Edinburgh

Despite leaving Sirocco in October 1985, I continued to maintain an occasional connection with the 'Three Weeds' pub in Rozelle. I sometimes shared the stage with the fabulous folk singer Margret RoadKnight. The publicity included the words about me as 'formerly of Sirocco'. Margret is one of Australia's great folk/blues/jazz singers, described somewhere as 'virtually a walking, talking, singing folk festival in her own right – 6 feet 4 inches of musical history with a South Pacific Flavour'. I accompanied some of her songs. She had excellent stage rapport and was never short of a word. I recall her response to a couple of women in a mostly female audience in a Sydney gig. When I came out to accompany Margret, the women, hidden by the dimmed houselights, hissed as I walked on stage. Males, it seems, were unwelcome. Margret quipped: 'I think someone's leaking out there!' They said no more.

Margret and I accepted an invitation to appear at the Commonwealth Arts Festival in Edinburgh. This festival was an adjunct of the Commonwealth Games, the one that was subject to a boycott. We performed in an 'Australian Spectacular' on the last night of the festival, sharing the stage with the cast of *Honey Spot*, a play by Aboriginal poet Jack Davis. I performed a solo bracket and teamed up with sound artist Colin Offord to improvise together.

There was more in Edinburgh for me. I was also a guest member of Warren Fahey's Larrikins. Warren, a doyen of the preservation of Australian colonial folk music through authentic performances, recordings and books, ran the group as a family, choosing people for particular jobs. The Larrikins had presented many line-ups since their formation in 1972. They invited me to play alongside harp and voice specialist Cathie O'Sullivan; violist Cleis Pearce; and Dave de Hugard, vocalist, accordion, banjo and fiddle specialist. I contributed guitar, cittern, bodhran, and percussion. Warren, the chief Larrikin, played the concertina, which he referred to in a typically Australian play on words as his 'constant screamer'.

We put the show together in just two rehearsals at Warren's Eastern Suburbs pad and gave a concert at the Belvoir Theatre and then at the Basement in Sydney. The ABC recorded the performance, and Warren released it as double album, *A Larrikin History of Australia*. What I enjoyed most about the Larrikins was playing traditional Australian folk music from its Anglo-Celtic roots. My comrades in the Larrikins were superb musicians, and I learned a lot from Dave de Hugard. He could play anything and play it with style. He had an impressive stage presence.

Musica Viva and DFAT approached Warren to send us to play some concerts in Kuala Lumpur, Malaysia, before heading to Scotland. They also billed me as a solo performer and shared the performances. Unfortunately, following the first Larrikins gig, I had a meal at the English Club and contracted a gastric illness. Somehow, I managed, with medication, to keep on performing on boiling outdoor stages. But I was dreading the eleven-hour economy class flight to London plus the five-hour train journey to Edinburgh. Tired, I could only take fluids. Fortunately, the cabin crew on the flight allowed me to stretch out on blankets next to an exit row door. Sleep helped, but I felt washed out.

On my arrival in Edinburgh, a festival guide sent me to see the nurse. An angel appeared, a delightfully animated Scottish nurse in her sixties. She looked at me, asked me about my symptoms and had me glug a big dose of Kaomagma. It fixed me up in a couple of hours. I wanted to hug my rotund Florence Nightingale. A day later, Edinburgh beckoned, and I wandered around this lovely city, visiting the castle and taking a hill-walk out of town.

Many Commonwealth nations withdrew from the Games. The boycott was in response to the Thatcher government's policy of keeping Britain's sporting links with apartheid South Africa in preference to taking part in the general sporting boycott of that country. Of the fifty-nine countries eligible to compete, thirty-two African, Asian and Caribbean nations boycotted. The Games went ahead looking like 'whites-only' games. Prime Minister Bob Hawke urged Britain on two occasions to revise its position statement on South Africa, but to no avail. The games included Australia. Our first Larrikin concert was co-billed with the Scottish band, Boys of the Lough. We followed this with a bush dance, Australia's version of the *ceilidh*. The last performance was the 'Australian Spectacular', a presentation of Australian classical, folk, jazz and Aboriginal music and dance.

Unfortunately, musicians from Sri Lanka, India, Mauritius and Caribbean countries had already arrived for the festival. They stayed in their accommodation as their teams had withdrawn. We agreed unanimously that all apartheid was abhorrent and commiserated with these musicians by sharing music in impromptu after-dinner jam sessions.

After recovering from my gastric bug, I travelled twenty miles to East Lothian to climb a mountain called North Berwick Law. This is a 180-metre-high remnant of an ancient volcano. On top there was an installation – a pair of whale jawbones formed an arch. The first whalebones appeared on top of the Law in 1709. They were originally a beacon for homecoming sailors and came to be a symbol of North Berwick. I walked to the top of the Law with just enough puff to play a pibroch-styled improvisation on my pipes. It was my homage to Scotland, its sailors and the majesty of whales.

Southern Crossings tours

The Atherton Tableband's engagements increased steadily from 1987, and being freelancers, we were able to do our projects simultaneously without too many clashes. Musica Viva engaged us to present evening concerts in Canberra, Alice Springs and up the east coast of Queensland to Cairns, as well as school tours. We became instantly successful, but on returning to Sydney, I felt we needed to change the group name. The Atherton Tableband was unworkable as a long-term option. Queensland newspaper editors were unaware of the pun and changed our name to The Atherton Tableland in concert reviews! We needed a more expansive name with an Australian connection. I was working with superbly professional, classically trained musicians in Michael and John, both skilled in a range of ensembles and many styles of music, superb improvisers, each a composer in his own right. Something collective-sounding was required. Ros came up with the name Southern Crossings. It drew attention to our 'crossing' musical styles and boundaries. It identified us with the southern hemisphere and constellation on the national flag. We changed the T-shirts, the letterhead and the publicity shots.

Musica Viva sent Southern Crossings on school and regional tours throughout NSW. We arranged the diaries around other commitments. Touring was also about juggling home and family. Both Michael Askill and I had families to consider. Going back to August 1987: Southern Crossings was booked on a school tour in western NSW from August through September. Ros was pregnant with our second child and overdue when I left Sydney. I was hoping the birth might coincide with my being at home. But no such luck. Two days into the tour, I received a call at Millthorpe Primary School during a lunch break between performances. It was the obstetrician. He felt it was time to induce Ros and asked where I was. I told him I was in the small town of Millthorpe, 220 kilometres west of Sydney and 22 kilometres from Orange. He made me a deal: he would 'play a round of golf in the afternoon and induce Ros around 9 pm', and I would get a flight home and be at the maternity ward by then.

My heart pounded with excitement throughout the 1 pm concert, the third of the day. The moment we finished, John and Michael packed my instruments and I bolted to the staff room to book a seat on any plane. I was in luck. There was a single seat available on the evening flight to Sydney. I planned to attend the birth and return to the tour the next day. A teacher drove me to Orange airport, where a six-seater plane was ready for boarding. I walked across the tarmac wondering if the doctor could make everything run to schedule, also hoping that I could return to the tour and not leave John and Michael with the burden of rearranging the program.

We took off and flew over the magnificent Blue Mountains. It was a sublime sunset as we flew over the Sydney basin towards Mascot, where the lights of Sydney were beautiful and welcoming. After touchdown and a canter across the tarmac, I dashed for a cab to take me to the (now demolished) Royal Women's Hospital in Paddington. I gowned up and arrived in the birthing room, with time to spare. The avuncular doctor walked in and boasted that he'd won at golf and said to Ros and me, 'It's time to greet your baby.' Marc Edward Atherton was born. I was overcome with joy and teared up, especially relieved for Ros, that it was a routine birth compared with Emily's. Once again, I was given the opportunity to cut the umbilical cord, which I did proudly. We confirmed the names for our newborn, and both of us were keen on the French spelling, Marc. I could only stay with Ros for an hour before I went home for some sleep, knowing that I had to rise early to make a 7 am flight to Orange and re join the Southern Crossings tour.

Next morning, I recall grabbing a banana and black coffee at the airport and boarding my plane, tired but elated from the birth, hoping that Ros and Marc would manage without me for a few days (Emily was staying with her aunt Leone). The Sydney weather was fine. The flight was on time; I should make the first concert at

9:30 am – but the weather had the last say. We began our descent towards Orange, but it was too foggy. The pilot circled a few times, looking for a clear approach, before telling us we had to land in Bathurst, which was fog-free.

From Bathurst, I took a taxi for a half-hour dash to where John and Michael were already performing. I arrived halfway through the second show of the morning, entering the auditorium carrying an overnight bag. Michael and John, who had done a great job as a duo, stopped playing, and everyone clapped me onto the stage. It was a lovely moment, but I couldn't help thinking about leaving Ros behind to deal with exhaustion and feeding Marc. She deserved the accolade more than I did. Bleary-eyed and wobbly from lack of sleep and circling an airport several times, I tuned up and took my place on stage. The show went on.

Indonesia and the Philippines

In 1988, Musica Viva sent Southern Crossings on a tour of Indonesia and the Philippines. This was also for DFAT. There were opportunities for cultural visits and sightseeing. Playing in Jakarta included a concert at a public venue and an appearance at the Boomerang Bar at the Australian Embassy. We incorporated some jigs and reels plus Australian bush ballads and sea shanties. The melodeon, lagerphone and clapsticks came in handy for such occasions, as did my feral baritone for singing 'The Ryebuck Shearer', 'Flash Jack from Gundagai', and 'The Overlander'.

For diversion, Southern Crossings agreed to do something out of its comfort zone. Bob Hewitt, an expatriate Australian working for the Petro Indo Corporation, signed us up to join in a Hash House Harriers 'Fun Run' near a golf course off the Cibinong Road. It was 70 kilometres from Jakarta. The Hash House Harriers is an international group of non-competitive running social clubs. It was started in 1938 by a group of British military officers and expats in Malaysia, who met every Monday afternoon to exercise after the excesses from the weekend before. They ceased to meet during World War II, as Malaysia was invaded, but started up again after the war was over, and the meetings have continued to this day. The reason they are called the Hash House Harriers is that in Malaysia, many of them ate at a local diner called the Hash House, dubbed 'a drinking club with a running problem'.

We arrived at the course to find umbrellas, a beer wagon and over a hundred runners, some looking seriously kitted out. We were the motley crew in board shorts and borrowed runners. The aim was to run 7 kilometres through the jungle surrounding the golf course. We started at 5 pm, running to different points, named after Australian capital cities, where we collected a card to show that we had arrived.

It was hard going for us, running up and down hills and along the edges of rice paddies, dragging our feet through clay and dense undergrowth. Sometimes we ran around the houses of startled villagers. We pounded over bamboo and wire suspension bridges stretched over tributaries of the river.

I felt like an escaped fugitive in a war movie. The skies looked angry with heaving grey clouds. Heavy rain threatened. John and I made it back to base before dusk, but Michael Askill hobbled back after dark. I had never seen Michael in shorts and a singlet. I joked with John that we could see Michael's white legs running out of the dark.

Race over, cards counted, winners declared, we stood under umbrellas, worshipping the beer wagon. Some runners sat on bags of ice to cool down. It became the archetypal 'six o'clock swill', with English, American, New Zealand and Dutch accents added to the mix. Beer was tossed around, and they threw pies into the air as it rained steadily. We played a bit of music while His Excellency Bill Morrison, the Australian ambassador, beer in hand, recited a couple of poems about Kiwis and 'Septic tanks' (Yanks).

Another break from performing was an offer to get out of the hectic, sweltering streets of Jakarta for two nights in a calmer and cooler place called Puncak, 100 kilometres southwest of Jakarta. The Embassy offered a house to staff and families on a roster basis. We jumped at the opportunity to breathe some fresh air.

Yogyakarta
It was a lovely surprise to meet Julian Purwanto and his wife, Aysha Gani, on our next leg in Yogyakarta. Their hospitality and preparation for our visit were overwhelming. Julian met us at the airport with a fifteen-strong entourage of helpful people. I remembered Julian and Aysha from Medan in 1974 when I had toured with the Renaissance Players. Their daughter, Luluk, (now a jazz musician in Europe) was studying classical violin in Indonesia and at the Sydney Conservatorium. The crew loaded our instruments and bags into an enormous truck and took them to our venue. Julian drove us in his Volkswagen Kombi to the guesthouse at Gadjah Mada University, which was comfortable and old-fashioned accommodation overflowing with friendly people and staff. We met in the lobby for radio and press photos and to discuss our stage program.

The rector arranged a treat for us – an *adong*, a horse-drawn carriage to take us on a campus tour. We ended up at our performance venue, a *pendhapa*, which is a large pavilion-like structure built on columns and open at the sides to the sun and the rain. We found everything was prepared for our concert in the evening. There was an attractive stage backdrop plus a huge 1,000-watt sound system. The crew gave us T-shirts, labels, banners and posters used in the promotion. Nine hundred people attended. The atmosphere in the pendhapa was unforgettable.

On a subsequent trip to Indonesia, I could satisfy my curiosity about the making of bronze instruments. Jennifer Lindsey, a cultural counsellor at the Australian Embassy and author of a book on Javanese gamelan, arranged a visit for me to a village near Bogor, to see how the bronze was poured, shaped and tuned. Jenny led me through a doorway into a collection of single-storey dwellings around a courtyard. We went into a building with an earthen floor and introduced ourselves to the men working inside. They were illuminated by several fire pits of glowing coals. The blowing of bellows created flecks of fire like shooting stars dropping into the dirt. I saw molten bronze and moulds for gongs. Children were playing outside, teasing their chickens, oblivious to the foundry work. Back inside, red-faced men pulled a pot of molten bronze from a fire, poured it into a flat dish and left it to cool while the men talked animatedly. In another room, a young man took a hammer and struck a warm bronze ingot to test it for shaping but it cracked, and it had to be recycled. The quality of the bronze is critical to enable it to be beaten into the shape of a small gong. Once again, I responded with some verse:

Javanese Gamelan

A sultry afternoon in Jogja.
Children are playing outside,
chasing chickens and teasing dogs.

Men sit in the shade,
hammering new-moulded gongs,
tuning their sacred tones.

Inside the foundry, faces shine.
Squatting men work bellows
pumping sparks into the air
and over the dirt floor.

White-hot bronze is pulled from the fire
and poured into rectangular dishes,
to strike and shape into metal bars.

> Cooled and filed,
> Some will be tuned in *pelog*, some in *slendro*
> and carried to a room of carpenters,
> waiting to fashion the frames and stands,
> then to painters
> poised to guild dragon motifs.

I was most excited about the tuning of the largest gong, *gong agung*, which is considered to have the most 'sacred' sound in Javanese gamelan. This one was a metre in diameter. It had been made and filed a week earlier. One of the makers threw a lump of clay mixed with straw to enable it to stick on the surface. He used a rubber-covered wooden hammer to tap the gong to tune its harmonics. I was astounded to find out that this process can go on for several days until it resonates satisfactorily. It was a rare insight for me to see such a combination of high-level metalwork skills and acoustics used to achieve the resonance and tunings of all the gongs.

Philippines
We flew back to Jakarta on Garuda Air and departed for the Philippines for the next leg of the tour. We landed in Manila where we gave our first concert in the impressive Cultural Centre. I remembered it well from my time in the Renaissance Players. Unfortunately, the hall was less than half full, but the audience made up for this in their wild enthusiasm.

This leg of the tour included a surprising range of venues and occasions. The formal concert in the Cultural Centre was preceded by our playing in Rizal Park amphitheatre for Valentine's Day celebrations. We performed two one-hour sets and were filmed for a telecast by PTV-4. There were 4,000 people watching. They clapped along, but I felt they were expecting something more schmaltzy than we could offer, perhaps Andre Rieu! That said, they loved our bush songs and the rhythms of our African-influenced repertoire. And they joined in our call and response songs.

We travelled to Baguio City in a 22-seater bus, which we boarded through the back window. It was a seven-hour drive with no air conditioning. Leaving Manila, we drove through dense clusters of dwellings where the poverty was like that on the outskirts of Jakarta. This gave way to rice, sugarcane and banana plantations highlighted with tall Coca-Cola signs and many Catholic churches. We passed flamboyantly decorated Jeepneys, the most popular means of public transportation in the Philippines, originally made from US military jeeps left over from World War II. The first hour of our journey had the distinctive smell of burning cane as we coped with the heat of our engine in the airless cabin. But the skies were clearing as we drove through the Province of Tarlac and left behind the dense, flame-tinged clouds blowing through the cane fields. The car interior cooled a bit when we neared the mountains, but it was a hell-raising drive. Our driver had to dodge the maniacal drivers in the always-speeding red Rabbit buses that transported the locals. They were paid according to the number of trips they made. The rule of thumb was to overtake at every opportunity.

The drive through the mountains, however, was spectacular, and the sky was a pristine blue. We arrived at 4:30 pm in Baguio, a city 1,500 metres above sea level. We went for a walk through the markets where traders were selling bamboo, wooden and shell artefacts, children were begging, and other villagers were selling corn crops. We ate *bubingka* – a local rice cake from the Igorot tribe – and watched a magnificent sunset. We met our hosts from the local Arts Council and were immediately provided with tea and taken to see street theatre performances, including fire breathing, dancing and kulintang – music played by striking tuned gongs arranged in a rack.

At a dinner party with our hosts, we met musicians, writers, and filmmakers. We joined in a jam session. I got the chance to play a *frolong*, a Mindanao lute, also a *tongali* – a nose flute – and a bamboo stamping pole. Our new friends included Dave Baradas, an intellectual devoted to what he called 'earth points and consciousness'. There was Shant Verdun, a composer, and Jesse Boy Garrovillom, who played the *faglong*. His friend, Jerry, specialised in playing the *kubing* (jew's harp). He helped me find a maker in the market. I purchased some *bilbil*, a split bamboo instrument played by the Kalinga people, and a tongali. The latter is found in some Pacific islands and has a similar name. Michael Askill was especially interested in the *pakkung* or 'devil chaser'. Women traditionally played this instrument while they walked through fields, to ward off evil spirits and, presumably, snakes.

A documentary crew filmed our concert at the University of the Philippines in Baguio, including an informal interaction with local musicians. Once again, we were overwhelmed with the generosity of our hosts. Unfortunately such connections, like many made through Musica Viva/DFAT tours, were fleeting. The likelihood of meeting again was always slim. Sadly, Baguio was ravaged in the Luzon earthquake of 1990, which registered 7.8 on the Richter scale. The earthquake caused damage within an area of about 20,000 square kilometres. Many buildings collapsed in Baguio, and it killed hundreds, possibly some of the people we met on tour.

Back in Manila and alone after the last concert, I began to feel the 'touring blues' again. I missed my family – Ros, Emily, and Marc, who was just six months old. It was also the eve of my thirty-eighth birthday. However, the next day, John and Michael and a couple of embassy staff raised my spirits by surprising me with a cake and champagne.

Norfolk Island

Our next tour, in June 1988, was to Norfolk Island – something I arranged outside Musica Viva. Unfortunately, Michael Askill wasn't available because of commitments with his group, Synergy. So, John and I adapted some of the repertoire, to present as the

Southern Crossings Duo. This tour was especially enjoyable because Ros, Emily and Marc came with me for a holiday.

Norfolk Island is an external territory of the Commonwealth of Australia and a duty-free port, so we had to pass through Customs and Immigration. Departure for Norfolk was unusual: our body weights were also required at check-in, as well as weights for baggage and instruments. This was to determine how much fuel was needed to carry as much cargo as possible to serve the locals and have enough to return should the weather prevent a safe landing.

Arriving was magical, like landing on a jewel in the Pacific Ocean. The island is approximately 1,700 kilometres northeast of Sydney and parallel with Evans Head, NSW. It's the largest of three small islands, including Philip and Nepean, collectively known as the Territory of Norfolk Island. The territory uses the native pine tree symbol as its flag, and there are around 1,700 residents today. Eastern Polynesians first inhabited Norfolk, but they had gone by 1788, when the island became a penal colony of Great Britain.

Our hosts were Ned Lenthall, a former Australian naval rating, and his wife, Elaine. I had met both on my previous visit to Norfolk Island with Sirocco. We stayed at Fletcher Christian Lodge, owned by an eponymous descendant of the infamous mutineer. Many locals are descendants of the Bounty mutineers who first sought refuge on Pitcairn Island, coming to Norfolk on 8 June 1856. Their language or patois, called Norfolk, combines eighteenth-century sailors' English with some Tahitian words, from the Tahitian women who went with the mutineers to Pitcairn Island.

John and I gave three performances on Norfolk: one in the Pacific Hotel, a second in the Adventist Hall, and a third in the central school, which combined infant, primary and high schools. Ros and Emily came to the concerts and Emily joined in the dancing. We went swimming and snorkelling at the picturesque Emily Bay – a safe beach fringed by Norfok pines, with clear water and white sands.

Our week on Norfolk Island coincided with a traditional annual event called Bounty Day, held on June 8. This began with a gathering of local people and tourists, followed by a walk to the cemetery to pay respects to the graves of descendants. I met locals with surnames Christian, Quintal and Buffet – descendants of the mutineers. The service at the cemetery included 'God Save the Queen', not 'Advance Australia Fair'. And the picnic that followed on the grounds of now ruined colonial buildings featured local dishes with Tahitian influence, including *pilhi*, made from bananas.

John and I joined officers from the National Parks and Wildlife Service for a working bee on nearby Phillip Island, a place that was ravaged environmentally in the nineteenth century by introduced pigs, goats and rabbits. We departed Kingston jetty at 8:30 am in a small motorboat. The landing on Phillip Island was tricky. There were strong currents, with only rocks and coral undergrowth. John and I, along with eight other volunteers, had to jump onto basalt rocks to get ashore.

After scaling a gap in the cliff, we spent the rest of the day carrying

Sitting in an old fishing boat near Kingston jetty during my earlier trip to Norfolk Island, 1986.
Photo: Pastor Keith Jackson

backpacks heavy with seeds. The island looked like a Martian landscape of pitted red clay. There was little vegetation other than a few pockets of native hibiscus. We saw birds of a type called 'Masked Booby'. They are large gannets. I saw many nests while walking up Jacky Jacky, the highest peak on the island. From the knife-edged top I looked over a sheer 280-metre drop on the other side whilst marvelling at the boobies dive-bombing the turquoise waters for fish.

Eastern Australia

We returned to Sydney and joined up with Michael for a tour of western NSW and rural Victoria. This tour typified the professional musician's life in Australia, which often requires travelling long distances by road in diverse conditions and circumstances. The prime mode of transport for us was a minibus loaded to the roof with instruments. Every night, we would unload it and take the instruments with us to our motel rooms, however tired we might be: we never wanted to risk a theft on tour. Many of our handmade instruments, our tools of the trade, were irreplaceable.

Our first concert was in Coffs Harbour. We performed to a full house. The audience was so appreciative to see us in Coffs Harbour that they bought a lot of our records before the show! After three encores, we packed up and were whisked away to the house of the local music society president. We enjoyed a sumptuous seafood feast and premium Hunter Valley wine shared with committee members. Back at the motel, we unloaded the van to take the instruments into our rooms.

We started early the next day for the drive back to Sydney. It was evening by the time we all got home. For me, it was a chance to catch up with the family before heading west the next morning. The round trip to Coffs Harbour clocked 1,150 kilometres. The trip from Sydney to Dubbo, Nyngan, Cobar and Broken Hill added 1,270 kilometres. Travelling west away from Sydney traffic and smog was always a good time to slow down, tell stories, and share a joke.

After an overnight stay in Dubbo, we drove on to Nyngan. We always looked for good coffee first of all, but this time we were doomed to the haute cuisine of a flyblown greasy apron joint, the only place open and reeking with the smell of old chip fat. And when I dared ask for a cappuccino, I was put in my place with a few grunted monosyllables: 'Don't have none of that fancy-pantsy stuff ere mate.' We were starving and had to rely on a vending machine with potato chips. However, after the concert, our hosts treated us to an impressive spread of country cuisine and conviviality. Where would we be without the legendary hospitality of country folk?

When arriving at motels, usually in T-shirts and jeans and carrying musical instruments, we often got a cool welcome at Reception. Just another mob of musos – the type that puts a glass of beer on the piano at the 'bowlo' (bowling club) or 'rissole' (Returned Services League club). Tradies in utes (utility vehicles) and pickups were deemed to be higher up the phylogenetic scale. We didn't spend up big at the bar or restaurant. Indeed, we never ate in a motel because we needed to be at the concert venue before dinner. We were usually late to check-in and probably aroused suspicion that we were just dole bludgers in disguise.

We presented our concert to families at Nyngan Primary School before leaving for Wilcannia. There was time for a detour via Cobar, to visit cave painting sites at Mt Grenfell, about forty minutes out of town. It was remote and unspoilt. The Ngiyampaa people have inhabited the area for tens of thousands of years. The white ochre figures and hand stencils are among the finest examples of rock art in Australia.

We drove on to Wilcannia for an overnight stop en route to Broken Hill. Our first day in Broken Hill was a rest day, and we visited two mines and looked at Silverton to see where Mad Max and other Australian outback movies were filmed. To the north of Silverton is the Mundi Mundi, a vast plain that inspired one of our compositions, 'Edge of the Desert'. The view from the lookout on the top of the hill conjured a feeling of eternity. The Sturt's desert pea flowers were in bloom and made a gloriously woven carpet at sunset.

Touring Australia by road has provided access to many unique landscapes and events that became unforgettable. I recall driving through a mouse plague in the Riverina region where we gave concerts in Finley, Deniliquin and Tooleybuc. The roads at dusk were overrun with waves of mice. It was impossible to avoid them.

Following our concert at Broken Hill Civic Centre, which was attended by many families and children, we loaded the Tarago and headed 300 kilometres south to Mildura. We left the vehicle at the airport and loaded our instruments into a Metroliner 19-seater turboprop and took off in bright sunlight.

After touching down at Tullamarine Airport in Melbourne, we collected another Tarago and drove to Geelong for a concert. Once again, we performed to a full house (in Morrison Hall, Geelong College). We had travelled 1,300 kilometres by road and air from Broken Hill and enjoyed wonderful hospitality and relaxation after the concert. The next stop was Warrnambool for a concert at the Regional Performing Arts Centre. Warrnambool became a special place for me. I discovered its maritime museum at Flagstaff Hill, where I first heard about shipwrecks along the southern coast. I collected a lot of information that would contribute to a future composition, *The Mahogany Ship*.

The itinerary sent to us to Hamilton next, where we played to a discerning audience of prosperous landowners. The venue was the art gallery, which boasted an exquisite collection of Asian art. The local art society, which hosted our concert, got our prize for the most posters we'd ever seen to promote a regional concert. It was sold out weeks before we arrived.

In January 1989, ABC Radio invited Southern Crossings to present a national live one-hour concert from the Broadwalk Studio in the Sydney Opera House. This allowed us to introduce a new member of the group, the versatile Jess Ciampa. Jess added percussion, singing and bass guitar. The bass playing added depth to our sound and gave Michael the opportunity to play vibraphone and marimba. Jess could also play a bit of trumpet, and his singing meant we could include three-part vocal texture. This primed us for our first tour to Europe.

Southern Crossings Sunday Live, ABC Radio, from the Broadwalk studio, Sydney Opera House, 1989. *l-r*: John Napier (cello, vocals, synthesizer); Michael Atherton (wind synthesizer, vocals, bouzouki, guitar, flutes, didjeridu); Jess Ciampa (bass, vocals, percussion); and Michael Askill (marimba, vibraphone, timbales, congas. Photo: Lasallian Ciampa

Italy

Robert 'Bomber' Perrier, a cultural advisor in the Victorian Arts Ministry, invited us to participate in Settimana Australiana in Italia, a July festival in Northern Italy. It aimed to celebrate and promote relations between Italy and Australia. The line-up included a contingent from the Flying Fruit Fly Circus, a national performing group of young acrobats; Bungul, an Aboriginal dance troupe; street theatre groups Stalker and Chrome; the Binneas String Quartet; the Bachelors from Prague, a jazz-funk group; and Stefano di Piero, the Victorian minister for ethnic affairs.

We spent two weeks based in Vicenza, a splendid city located between Venice and Verona, where twenty-six buildings and surrounds are attributed to Andrea Palladio, considered the most influential western architect in history. I loved the echoes of voices and footsteps in the streets and around the piazzas, especially the Piazza dei Signori, where a large stage awaited us. It was summer, and performing al fresco was magical in such a venue. We would repeat this experience in other towns including Asiago, Treviso and Schio.

We travelled by bus to Asiago. It is situated on a plateau in north-eastern Italy and was the site of a counter-offensive by the Austro-Hungarians in World War I. The writer Ernest Hemingway saw action at the Battle of Asiago. The town is famous for cheese made from unpasteurised goat's milk. We weren't expected to play at Asiago but to meet local people and enjoy a photographic exhibition about Italians living in Australia.

They listed our first performance for 9:15 pm in Vincenza the next day. We were to share the stage with the Fruit Flies. But as we waited to go on stage, it began to rain heavily. The large crowd that had seen the first set from Bungul and the Bachelors of Prague had to leave disappointed.

Day 3 of the tour included the gala opening of Settimana Australiana in Italia. The venue was indoors at the Teatro Olimpico designed by Palladio. This magnificent building was completed in 1585, five years after his death. Vincenzo Scamozzi, a contemporary of Palladio, designed the stage scenery to give the illusion of real streets. The Teatro is a masterwork assimilating Roman design, especially the work of Vitruvius. Given the small stage and the heritage status of the Teatro, the launch included only the Australian pianist Stephen McIntyre following a reading in Italian from Manning Clark's *A History of Australia*.

Southern Crossings' next concert was in Vittorio Veneto, surrounded by the Little Dolomites and Mount Pasubio and known since the twelfth century for its wool manufacturing. People also called it the Manchester of Italy for its busy textile industry. They set our pyramid stage up in front of a fountain in the Piazza del Populo. We played one music set and accompanied the Flying Fruit Flies. It was an unforgettable opportunity to collaborate with these dynamic circus performers and meet Stalker and Crome. The night finished with the Bachelors of Prague.

The itinerary then took us to the small town of Schio. The stage was in an amphitheatre in a park surrounded by trees. We shared the stage with a local choir, Coro Monte Pasubio, and our Indigenous touring colleagues, Bungul. It had been a hot day in Schio, but despite some threatening drops of rain we took the stage at 9 pm and gave an excellent concert. The choir enjoyed themselves so much that, after the concert, they invited audience members, friends and organisers on stage. We sang for each other and shared supper.

Our final performance for Settimana Australiana in Italia was in the Piazza Matteotti, the main square of Vicenza. The program would last three hours with the full Australian line-up of performers. But with so many genres – circus, actors, dancers, and a band –the afternoon sound and lighting check had to be meticulous. There was a lot of waiting around in the heat of a July afternoon. The rain held off, and the cooler evening air added to the comfort of the sizeable crowd and the performers. The Piazza was full of people. We relished using a powerful sound projection system for our set, and we enjoyed hearing an Italian reviewer referring to 'Le calde musiche Southern Crossings' (The hot music of Southern Crossings).

India

Musica Viva continued to promote Southern Crossings. We performed in schools and presented regional and capital city concerts, and undertook four more international tours: to the USA, Jamaica and Mexico (October 1991); India (January 1992); Japan (November 1993); and a second tour to Korea (July 1994).

Following a second successful broadcast on ABC Live in January 1992, Southern Crossings embarked on a tour of India for Musica Viva and the Department of Foreign Affairs. The itinerary included concerts and workshops planned for New Delhi, Hyderabad, Bangalore, Goa and Mumbai. The group was excited to make this trip. Michael and I had a keen interest in Indian classical music. John's then fiancée, Shanti Raman, inspired his deep cultural interest in the country, and Jess couldn't wait to get his hands on more percussion instruments for his already extensive collection.

After we arrived in Delhi, the tour all but stalled. I was to meet a tour manager, Mr Devarajan (Mr D) who worked for the Australian High Commission. Well, expectation flummoxed me. Southern Crossings sat in the arrival lounge and watched people departing but no sign of Mr D, or so we thought. I kept a lookout, wondering if the Delhi traffic had held him up. Thirty minutes elapsed and few people were left in the lounge. I looked around and checked my documents and contacts. This had never happened on previous tours.

I went to the Air India counter at the other end of the terminal lounge for information and as I did, a well-dressed, older grey-haired gentleman with fair skin stood up. He politely asked, was I Michael? I realised instantly that despite his being fair skinned, he looked Indian. We shook hands and apologised to each other for not meeting earlier. Mr D was genetically albino. It embarrassed me not to have found him first.

However, he laughed and so did I. There was an instant rapport. He was the most efficient, interesting, reliable tour manager and cultural guide we had ever met. It made such a difference having someone who knew the system and understood our Australian background, given his years of service at the Australian Embassy. We kept him very busy with copious questions. Mr D shared his profound knowledge and wisdom on many subjects. We became great friends on the tour.

We gave our first concert to fifteen hundred people in Siri Fort Auditorium, New Delhi. It coincided with Republic Day, when most Indians were watching the colourful parade in person and on their television. Southern Crossings spent the day settling its instruments, tuning and rehearsing. The concert began with a welcome by Mr B R Muthu Kumar, Deputy Director of the Indian Council for Cultural Relations (ICCR). He welcomed the VIP guests and Southern Crossings and acknowledged the Australian High Commissioner, Mr David Evans, inviting him to speak a few words. As it was both Indian Republic Day and Australia Day, David Evans emphasised the significance of 26 January in the lives of both Indians and Australians and said that visits of artists such as Southern Crossings promoted amity and goodwill among both nations.

The Indian audience grasped the connection between the improvisatory element in our music and that of Indian classical music. Indeed, we would soon discover on this tour a sophistication extending to European classical, jazz and music of many cultures. We were 'garlanded' afterwards with red roses and high praise from our hosts, who told us that it was a record attendance for a Republic Day event in the venue auditorium. We scored great reviews in the local newspapers.

Wishing to say more than 'hello' or 'g'day', I felt that trying to address audiences in the local language showed respect, especially in New Delhi on Republic Day. Mr D obliged when I asked him, just 30 minutes before the concert, to translate and teach me how to pronounce a few words of introduction in Hindi.

> *Namaskaar, aaj aap logon kay samney yeh kaaryakram prastath kartthey hoovay hamay bahooth kooshi hoe rahee hai. Yeh kaaryakram hum Australia waasiyonko tharafsay bharat – Australia mitrathaa kay liyae smarpith karthay hai hamaari mitrata amar rahay.*

[Good evening and welcome to the music of Southern Crossings. We come from Australia to perform in the name of friendship between Australia and India and we bring a big hello from all at home, especially our fellow artists.]

Hyderabad was next on the itinerary. It's the fourth most populous city after Bangalore, Delhi and Mumbai. The city is located on the Deccan Plateau in the northern part of South India. It is the capital of Andhra Pradesh and is situated on hilly terrain. It's a fascinating city demographically. The population is around 60 per cent Hindu and 30 per cent Muslim, the remainder comprising people of other religious communities including French-speaking Christian, Sikh, Jain, Buddhist and Parsi. There are iconic temples, mosques, and churches throughout the city. Hyderabad's dynamic cultural diversity is featured in its ancient and modern architecture. There are fine examples of Indo-Persian, Moorish, even European Art Deco architectural styles.

We visited a mosque in the noonday sun, where I pointed my camera upwards to view the architectural features. The Makkah Masjid, built in 1694, is one of the largest congregational mosques in India. It can hold 20,000 people. Its central arch includes bricks made from soil that came from Mecca. Inside, the slightest sounds contributed to a murmuring ambience, like a large indoor stadium or convention hall. Attendants wearing off-white cottons ushered us to view a large, solid gold prayer plate.

From the Makkah Masjid we climbed a steep road to the Hindu temple, Birla Mandir. It is more than 200 feet high and was constructed in the nineteenth century from 2,000 tons of white marble. It was an exciting moment to arrive during a ceremony in progress. There were skirling sounds of two *nagasawaram* (Indian double-reed instruments). The players were waking the gods. There were men in loincloths leading the chants. Everywhere flowers, colour and the scent of oils, as if the body and the senses were being celebrated – the opposite of the quiet austerity of the mosque earlier on. John showed his respect by prostrating himself. I admired his commitment, born no doubt from his acculturation through his meeting Shanti and her family.

We completed our sightseeing in Hyderabad by visiting one of the best markets I've seen, the Laad Bazaar. It is a narrow street located on the west face of Charminar and perpetually busy. The bazaar is still considered the best place in India to purchase bangles, precious stones, jewellery, pearls, gifts, velvet and gold embroidered fabrics.

Our concert later that night was held in the Ravindra Bharathi auditorium. This popular space is the hub for all cultural and drama-related activities. It was built to commemorate its centenary celebrations in honour of poet Sri Rabindranath Tagore. I asked the sound technician to play a recording, 'Kakadu Billabong', by Les Gilbert, to create an Australian ambience while the audience took their seats. As in previous concerts, my didjeridu was a source of great fascination to the sophisticated and inquisitive audience, and I contextualised it in a description of the landscape as inspiration for 'Nullarbor Train'. More than 900 people listened to the music enthusiastically, even boisterously towards the end of the concert, when we played our version of West African drumming.

Mr D was equally exuberant. On this occasion, Mr Jesu Das, the regional director from the Bangalore ICCR, who flew up to Hyderabad to see us play, joined him. He was late for our planned meeting at breakfast before our departure from Bangalore. He arrived at our table and explained his lateness. 'Michael, last night I sent my luggage on ahead to the airport, but when I looked for my trousers, I remembered they were in my suitcase. Michael,' he added, slightly embarrassed but with a sense of humour, 'you will laugh your guts out when I tell what happened next. I had to send a porter to buy some new trousers for me because my one pair has gone to Bangalore without me!' We roared with laughter.

We concluded the tour of India with concerts in Bangalore and Mumbai. One of the many concert reviews waxed lyrical:

> The waves of music brought from Australia to India by 'Southern Crossings' touched Delhi, crossed the Vindhyas southwards into Hyderabad and Bangalore and joined the Arabian Sea at Goa after washing the Bombay coast. All along the course the strains of the vibrant music enthralled the audiences and raised them to new heights of joy.

8

CONSOLIDATION: WRITING AND RECORDING

No boundaries, no borders.

It seems that I had gained experience in just a few years working in many areas of the music industry. I was described as a multi-instrumentalist, composer in diverse styles, and educator. I continued to perform at pre-schools, and given requests from teachers for my songs, I produced a CD, *Radum Scadum*, published in 1990 by the *ABC for Kids* music label. I could sell copies at my pre-school performances and give them out to every child in my extended family and among my friends. The painting featured on the cover design was by my daughter, Emily, created when she was just four years old. My musical horizons continued expanding in many directions at once, including collaborative composition and performance, audio production, screen music and ethnographic writing.

Recording

The didjeridu is played in diverse contexts, and it features in many contemporary music styles, in films, car commercials and tourist promotions. Its sacred ritual status in the culture of specific tribal groups is blurred by the perception that the didjeridu has become a global musical tool. It is just as likely to be heard in the jazz cellar or through a headset on a Qantas flight as in traditional ceremonies. It seems to be one of the most popular souvenirs for young visitors to Australia. And in Europe and the USA, it is assuming a role in 'new age' alternative healing.

The performing arts, especially music, remain central to Indigenous culture. Singing is a powerful means of expressing and preserving beliefs. Traditional ceremony continues on Aboriginal lands, missions and settlements, but today, Aboriginal people enjoy increasing prominence in the mainstream of the performing arts as singer-songwriters, didjeridu players, and rock groups. Dance and theatre companies command a world stage.

In 1989, Natural Symphonies, a small independent record label, invited me to work with Alan Dargin (1967–2008). Natural Symphonies was new in the music industry. The company consisted of two brothers, Ian and Neil O'Hare, from Camden, NSW. They emerged on the scene after teaming up with Les Gilbert, a Melbourne sound ecologist who spent most of his time doing audio recordings of wildlife. Natural Symphonies produced the CD *Kakadu Billabong*, a soundscape of superb recordings packaged beautifully in an informative glossy booklet illustrated with photographs. The brothers got into every corner of the market through their greenhorn doggedness. They fronted shops repeatedly until the proprietors caved in to let them display CDs on their counters. They also got onto radio stations across the country. In modern parlance, the CD went viral. People who hadn't been to Kakadu could go there via their hearing. Next, Ian and Neil wanted to do the same for the didjeridu, and I think they first heard Alan Dargin busking in Kings Cross and were won over by his performance and communication skills and patter.

I met Alan at The Rocks in Sydney. He wanted to show the world that his instrument should be taken as seriously as classical musical instruments were. We both believed in the principle that it should be 'modern didj', an instrument influenced by tradition but embracing contemporary styles and genres. Alan's rationale for a contemporary expression was, 'Who am I to make such a choice about playing traditional tribal music? I respect the elders. It wouldn't be right because I'm only this little speck. I would never record traditional patterns or songs.'

Alan and I had a great time experimenting with different approaches. I recorded him busking, and I asked him to experiment playing a 3-metre piece of conduit over riffs on a drum kit. And, to extend the environmental theme in Natural Symphonies recordings, I asked Alan to improvise to a recording of humpbacked whales. One of my compositions, called 'Storm Warning', concluded with thunder recorded in outback NSW. I wrote the track for didjeridu, slide guitar, bass, drum kit and synthesised strings. Its bluesy feel and expansive didjeridu sounds became a listener favourite on radio.

My contribution was my experience in music production, and I co-composed and produced the recordings. We explored fresh sounds and techniques for the didjeridu through improvisation in a range of styles of contemporary music styles. Players have often remarked that the didjeridu is over-used as a drone tone colour; that its complexity as an instrument capable of rich timbres and endless rhythmic articulations is not understood; that the producers consign it to the musical background as a programmatic evocation of the outback. In this project and others, I have addressed this issue during the composition, production and recording of music for this instrument.

The unsung hero in the project was the immensely skilled audio engineer Michael Gissing, mentioned earlier. He is like a water diviner who knows where to look, feel and listen. The rich hi-fidelity sound was peerless as was Alan's. Alan played an instrument made and painted by his grandfather, made from a now-extinct species of the bloodwood tree (*Corymbia opaca*). He made it sing. It had a unique tone because it was a heavy log. What he could do with breathing and articulation on a termite-hollowed tree branch was sublime.

Recording with Alan Dargin in an adjustable reverberation room at the National Acoustic Laboratories, 1989.
Photo: Michael Gissing

The opening track, 'Virtuoso Didj', was an exhilaratingly virtuosic improvisation. I became annoyed with detractors who said it was impossible to play as Alan did, that it was a multi-tracked or sped-up performance. As a producer and participant observer, I stood my ground and challenged them to come and watch him play. Once he appeared on television to promote *Bloodwood*, he soon silenced those who did not believe he could produce such extraordinary sounds.

His appearance on the CD included improvisations made in the National Acoustic Laboratories, as well as a location recording of busking in front of a small crowd in Kings Cross, Sydney. Alan called it 'The Hitchhiker's Nightmare'. He mimics the sound of a road train and its horn while talking about a hitchhiker trying to get home. Its inclusion was criticised by one reviewer as disrespectful to Alan's cultural background. This person failed to understand that busking is a common source of income for most Aboriginal didjeridu players and singers. Alan was no exception. He loved drawing a big crowd around him and maintained it was his job. Including it on the CD was in keeping with his often-stated aim of making 'modern didj' a respected instrument.

Alan played with the London Philharmonic and with jazz trumpeter James Morrison. He appeared at hundreds of festivals throughout North America and Europe. So, to reflect his career, we combined recordings made in an acoustics laboratory, in the street, and the studio. We included the sounds of insects and birds to create a mosaic approach to shared musical interests.

Bloodwood: the art of the didjeridu was recorded in six sessions, the entire album produced for $6,000, from the first coffee in a Darlinghurst café to the finished master recording. It sold over 25,000 copies – a lot by Australian standards for a non-mainstream independent recording. It catapulted Alan onto the world stage.

Alan was never vocal about politics and sometimes drew criticism from some of his 'brothers' who insisted that he should use his status to condemn white Australia. He struggled to grow up in a white man's world. He knew the history of the stolen generations, the dispossession of land and the mortality rate of his predecessors. As an artist he preferred the subtle, subliminally healing messages in his music, his collaborations, and his teaching of young and old. He cared deeply for all his brothers and sisters, whatever their race. He believed that he could talk through the didjeridu and give joy, healing and help to others.

Natural Symphonies eventually folded, but Alan and I made another recording, *Crosshatch*, in 1998. This collaboration used mallet percussion, guitars and electronic sounds to accompany the didjeridu, combined with *pejogedan* gamelan instruments from Java, as well as drums and bells from West Africa. Sound effects from the natural world were again combined with these diverse instrumental timbres. This project explored the role of the didjeridu in a range of musical contexts, enhancing the didjeridu's status as a solo instrument in contemporary music. The music critic, Lynden Barber, acknowledged its 'atmospheric musical journey full of unexpected turns ... constantly fresh and stimulating'.

Alan's career took off, but we always kept in touch. Indeed, we performed in London as part of a trio with Indigenous storyteller, Pauline Wright. Alan gave us our name, Yidaki Dreaming. We performed in Queen Elizabeth Hall. This was an extraordinary time for me because I was the only non-Indigenous performer in the Corroboree Festival at the South Bank Centre. I was invited to my former homeland to play on the same stage as Archie Roach, Ruby Hunter, Kev Carmody, and the Tiddas. Alan's premature death in 2008, from a ruptured blood vessel in his throat and a cerebral haemorrhage, was a great loss to me and my family. My son Marc loved him as an uncle. When I last saw Alan in hospital, he was running through his plans for a new album, discussing his idea for a national didjeridu competition. I can still hear him holding court in the cafés of Bondi Beach, see him wearing Jimmy Pike T-shirts, Indian 'happy' pants and greeting me with 'G'day Mr A', to which I invariably replied, 'G'day Mr D!'

I recorded *Windshift* in 1990. It was an essay on intercultural music. Notated and improvised compositions were multi-tracked using an array of Asia-Pacific instruments. On the album, I explored combinations of instruments from diverse music cultures and in the process looked for fresh sounds, for example, a composition for hurdy-gurdy, tuned gongs from the Philippines and an orchestral bass drum. These works drew inspiration from my touring experiences and interactions with several musicians who introduced me to their sound worlds. The album, therefore, represented a process of discovery rather than an emulation of other musical cultures.

Film

There is a divide between the film composer and the composer writing for the concert hall. Very few composers do both well; the exceptions in Australia include Nigel Westlake, Christopher Gordon, Felicity Wilcox, and Jessica Wells. The division is mainly due to background. To be a successful feature film composer means being able to understand all aspects of film production, in effect being a filmmaker, and being confident in collaboration with and subservient to several masters, including the producer, the director and the sound editor.

Documentaries

In 1990, I took part in another educational film through my connections as a composer, creating documentary scores for Film Australia. The organisation approached me to be the subject of a film that looked at musicians involved in composing, performing, conducting, and educating. The film aimed to show young people how music is conceived, created and presented and to give them an opportunity for enjoyment and participation.

Initially, the plan was to focus on my career. But I preferred to focus on group discovery of music-making in diverse acoustic environments. I proposed the title, *Bending the Beat*. Film Australia liked it and appointed Pip Karmel, a dynamic recent graduate of the Film and Television School, to direct the film. Pip and I agreed on a sequence of different musical activities. Film Australia budgeted for a 35 mm format with full stereo sound. I wanted the film to look and sound natural in outdoor settings. There would be no voice-over on the film and no post-synchronised sound, no overdubs or miming to a soundtrack. Pip supported this, and we steamed ahead on a script.

The film examines the responses of young people to creative challenges in music. It shows young people working with me, experimenting with materials from the natural and built environment to discover how resonant objects can be musical instruments or sound-makers. I created music based on a variety of approaches to improvisation. The film is also about the potential of space in shaping sound. One scene takes place in a circular concrete stairwell of the former Convention Centre in Darling Harbour. I lead young performers, improvising drones and harmonies in a highly resonant acoustic. There was also a scene that used the coastal walk from Bondi to Tamarama for a musical procession. We then made plastic pipe 'whirlies' to create a polyphonic texture to accompany rolling waves as we walked towards Tamarama.

Another scene was shot in the bushland behind Film Australia's superb building in Lindfield. I asked the group to gather fallen pieces of timber, leaves and seedpods. We made simple xylophones by laying tree branches across each other, and cut up some branches to make mallets. We improvised patterns that drew on Pacific Island drumming. I didn't want to talk in this film, preferring to allow the location, the music and the players to do the talking.

The film *Kula: Ring of Power* (1991), set in the Trobriand Islands, Papua New Guinea, introduced me to Melanesian culture through the story of Chief Nalabutau, a traditional and ageing Kula master. Nalabutau led voyages for the ritual exchange of Kula shell necklaces and armbands. The inherent value of the shell pieces determined the status of the player in the community. The film, directed by

Mike Balson, created a captivating glimpse of an ancient bartering system under threat from modernity.

For the opening title theme, I composed and performed the music on an 8-track reel-to-reel tape recorder. I provided music for the preparation of the outrigger canoes for inter-island journeys, as well as music for the witches on Dobu island. I delivered most of the music as primary and secondary themes, linking sections and reprises. Each cue included different instruments and timings. Such a flexible approach enabled the film's editor to cut most of the pictures to music.

On reflection, my interest in ethnography was also complemented by working on polemical and political documentaries. Three titles to mention are: *Who Killed Malcolm Smith?* (1992), *Admission Impossible* (1992) and *Colonists for a Day* (1993).

The death of Malcolm Charles Smith on 29 December 1982 shocked Australians. Ripped away from his family as a child, he lived a life of institutionalisation and deprivation and took his own life while he was in prison in NSW. Ten years later, Richard Frankland helped investigate Malcolm's death for the Royal Commission into Aboriginal Deaths in Custody and was deeply critical of the state government for not taking the investigation seriously. He tried to make sense of the man's tragic passing in a documentary. The film includes Richard's visits to see Malcolm's family and friends. There is also a scene in which Richard runs a workshop with police recruits to challenge racial profiling stereotypes of young Aboriginal men and boys.

The opening scene is a dramatisation of Malcolm's suicide in Long Bay Gaol. The camera is tracking along a corridor towards a toilet block as we see a paintbrush stirring water, so it looks like blood. Melody was impossible. I accompanied the action with a wash of sampled and synthesised electronic sounds gradually building towards a blood-curdling scream, the point at which Malcolm stabbed himself with a paintbrush, the very tool he had learned to use later in his short life to express himself in art therapy.

This music cue set the tone of the film underscoring the voice-over as it described Malcolm's childhood. For the rest of the music, I relied on piano and string samples to accompany Richard's narration. My role was to add the invisible character, to intensify feeling and value in the film. It was hard not to feel grief about Malcolm's tragic life.

The documentary *Admission Impossible* (1992), was produced by Film Australia and the BBC and directed by Alec Morgan. It's a documentary about the behind-the-scenes political forces and propaganda campaigns of the 'white Australia policy' before the rise and leadership of Gough Whitlam in 1972. I composed a score that aimed to unify the diverse materials – newsreel footage, still photography, dramatised segments, and narration. The instrumentation, apart from the oboe played by Ros, was piano and sampled orchestral string programs because the modest budget didn't permit engaging more musicians. The film achieved a 'Best Film Score' and 'Best Film Theme' at the Australian Performing Rights Association Awards.

Colonists for a Day (1993), co-produced by ABC TV and Film Australia, was a critical account of Australia's colonisation of Papua New Guinea. The score included location sound and music. It employed a combination of instrumental timbres from flutes and rattles of the Eastern Highlands, Papua New Guinea, and western instruments such as the cello, piano, muted trumpet and percussion. The resulting intercultural music makes a narrative statement about the cultural difference between the propaganda music of Australian newsreel footage and the indigenous voices of Papua New Guinea.

༄

Documentaries are usually single films. Being offered a series to score is a financial boon to the film composer. Two titles to mention were *Riding the Tiger* (1990) and *Plagued* (1992). *Riding the Tiger* was a three-part documentary series directed by Curtis Levy for the ABC. The film is an exposition of the rise of modern Indonesia. I composed music for the series by drawing on my experience performing Indonesian gamelan and music of the Middle East and India, to reflect the diverse cultural influences. *Riding the Tiger* achieved 'Best Music for a Documentary' by the Australian Guild of Screen Composers (1992).

Plagued (1992), also known as *Invisible Armies*, was a four-part documentary written and narrated by Walkley Award–winning broadcaster Dr Norman Swan. The film investigated the relationship between history, destiny, and disease. Every era has its new diseases. Norman, who trained as a medical practitioner, turned to journalism. He became a popular voice on ABC television as the fount of information on Covid-19.

Part I investigated, through various case studies, how epidemics break out, and covered environmental ailments such as carpal tunnel syndrome, post-traumatic stress disorder, and heart disease. Part II concentrated on bubonic plague (Black Death) and cholera, recounting the spread of these diseases via exploration and trade. Part III explored the relationship between the immune system and history. Part IV showed the interaction between the epidemics of HIV and syphilis, both fostered by drug use and prostitution.

It gave me free rein to develop common themes and compose a library of music cues for use in each episode. I used an anonymous Italian medieval dance, 'Lamento di Tristano', as the source for the signature opening and closing theme.

A director's readiness to say a blunt 'yes' or 'no' to what the composer delivers would deeply offend many famous symphonists. I have experienced directors who changed their mind after I had recorded the music. They wanted changes despite cost and regardless of an exhausted composer. There were directors who knew little about making and recording music for their picture. Sometimes they were obsessed with using temporary tracks to edit their picture. One producer I worked with was so obsessed with the tune 'Danny Boy', it became his cliché for nostalgia.

There was a first-time director who had such an antipathy to a cello that she distrusted me when I delivered music that featured a solo cello passage. She thought it was too heavy. I spent a lot of time explaining the range of the cello and what it could sound like when played by an outstanding musician. Most directors, however, are great communicators. You know this when they have simple ideas about where to synchronise the music. I have great respect for the many I have worked with, including Peter Weir, David O'Brien, Curtis Levy, Alec Morgan, Mike Balson, Pip Karmel and Gary Steer.

My worst experience occurred when I walked out of a job. It came after a falling out with a director. We had a fabulous rapport on an earlier film project. But the second film didn't move me. I couldn't get into the material. I tried different approaches, going back and forwards to the director with many sketches. He couldn't say what he wanted, except it wasn't right for him. This went on for a couple of weeks before I picked up the phone and told them I was withdrawing. I've never regretted my decision because there will be a time when even the hungriest composer knows they don't fit the project. Time to walk away.

Fortunately, my few excursions into television music and channel themes were always a joy. David O'Brien, mentioned above, invited me to work with him on a Ten Network series called *Down to Earth* (1989). This coincided with a time when I was realising the crisis of global warming. The series was for prime time viewing, and delivered a powerful message about the risk to humanity from climate change.

I composed the main theme to introduce each program and then a variety of other pieces using a theme and variation approach to enable similar material to be used throughout the series. Geraldine Doogue, a long-time stalwart of the ABC, introduced each program.

David O'Brien, who wrote the script, asked me to compose a long piece in response to his rushes plus library footage. The sequence included a meeting with a tribe in Brazil who were losing their habitat because of encroaching deforestation. David delivered a coup by persuading Sting to narrate this scene. He flew to London and filmed Sting narrating a sobering montage underscored by my music, to describe on the screen the environmental catastrophe facing us. I composed a slow processional piece as if for a cortège. We aimed to have viewers feel as if the planet was dying. The message in *Down to Earth* was given in 1989. It showed then what we are still doing to destroy our planet.

Dogwatch

Honing my craft in music for documentary films made me curious about the big step towards working on a feature film. The major difference for me would be a question of scale. I composed, performed, and recorded most of my documentary scores in my home studio, including, where required, a soloist to play instruments that were not part of my skill set. Ros played the oboe in a couple of films and my friends, the percussionist Jess Ciampa and the cellist John Napier, helped me out as well.

Feature films require more work than a documentary and an appropriate budget. I found that a documentary averaged twenty to thirty minutes of original music, whereas the feature film might require up to sixty minutes, depending on the subject and the director. Devolving a feature film budget demands careful planning and costing once studio hire and musicians are considered. Typically, the recording process may not be linear. There was never any point recording anything for the credit roll until late in the project. It was imperative to have confidence in the director's wishes and communications. One might record sequences that get rejected and drain one's budget.

I went into my first feature film, *Dogwatch* (1997), thrilled to be chosen but also apprehensive about making the budget fit the project. Its producer, Richard Brennan, had heard my documentary scores and my music for Sirocco and Southern Crossings. He set up a meeting with the writer/director of *Dogwatch*, Laurie McInnes, a high-profile art film director, writer, and cinematographer. Her work is like that of Jim Jarmusch. Her short film *Palisade* had won the top prize at the Cannes Film Festival in 1987.

Dogwatch was set on a run-down merchant ship. The story begins in an Asian port. The ship's captain, William, is a ruined man. He has a shady past, a drinking problem, and a dirty job to do. He has agreed to sink the *Arabella* for an insurance scam. The film is about the crew's battle for survival. The sea and the ship are significant parts of the atmosphere, with a surreal quality, partly delivered through imagery and lighting. Sometimes, it's like watching moving stills. The script is minimal, and delivered by top actors, including Joel Edgerton, Richard Carter, and Steven Vidler.

The compositional task was to complement the sound effects with a score that blended with the sounds of the ship and the sea, that established locations and intensified reflective and dramatic moments. Resonances of Chinese music using the yangqin were both contrasted and blended with western instruments such as strings, timpani, woodwinds, and electronic sounds.

Sadly for everyone involved, *Dogwatch* never scored a theatrical release. After completing and delivering the music, the film was supposed to be on its way to the Cannes Film Festival. However, because of a dispute between the financiers and the producers, possibly the director too, the film sat on a desk somewhere. This was frustrating because I had been expecting to use some of the film for a showreel to find more work. I'd fantasised that this would be the beginning of a career in features. I had toiled for six weeks to deliver the music on time, but the film disappeared. Even the producer couldn't divulge what had happened. I was, of course, paid, and the producer told me the music was great. I was doubly pleased because I had engaged long-term friend and musical engineering luminary Michael Gissing and his Darlinghurst studio for orchestral musicians to do overdubs on the score. My wonderful professional friends helped me out: Philip South played the timpani; his wife, Vanessa, played the violin. Christine Draeger played flutes. Ros Dunlop played bass clarinet.

The next time I heard of *Dogwatch* was in 1999. One of my students saw a DVD in the window of a Parramatta video store. Behold, *Dogwatch*. I bought a copy and used it for teaching screen composition.

∽

Film music offered me scope to compose eclectic scores and play diverse instruments. It helped me develop and maintain a home recording studio to use this as an instrument of composition. After starting with a 4-track cassette recorder, I moved up to an 8-track reel-to-reel and on to 16-track. I kept adding new keyboard synthesizers. My first was a Juno 6 monophonic, then a Korg Polysix, before I turned to electronics with a Roland Jupiter, and many more, including sampling synthesizers. Like many film composers, I was buying new stuff to incorporate in my soundtracks as soon as it came onto the shelf.

I involved myself in supporting the profession by joining the Australian Guild of Screen Composers to help run seminars. Sometimes, I wrote articles about the issues faced by film composers. For example, I said in 'Synchronous Sounds: the film composer' (1990):

> Spare a thought for the Australian film composer. The curtain has opened and closed for the last time; the audience has hissed the international jet-setter ads. Then comes the surround sound

fanfare from the self-congratulatory multi-national distributor, and now ladies and gentlemen, the main feature will begin, all $10.50 worth. Spare a thought for the composer if you are watching an Australian film.

These words refer to my concern about the tendency of producers not to trust and indeed to overlook Australian composers. There was a tendency to avoid risking a decent budget on a local: evidence, once again, of the cultural cringe.

Studies into sound and space

One of the musical activities I do just for myself is to find remote places to play. I inhabit these acoustic spaces with joy. I like wide-open spaces and sites of natural beauty or historical significance. Once, while on a Southern Crossings tour in Alice Springs, I travelled west to Stanley Chasm to sound this space by playing my didjeridu. This is a geological formation in Tjoritja / West MacDonnell National Park. The Western Arrernte people, its traditional owners, call the chasm Angkerle Atwatye, meaning the Gap of Water. It's a natural wonder that cuts through the quartzite rock. Floodwaters created the narrow gap thousands of years ago. It made an alleyway through walls of rock that reach up to 80 metres in height. The red rock contrasted with lush green cycads, plants with stout woody trunks. The didjeridu, one of my low-pitched instruments with a B fundamental, seemed to fill the chasm when I played.

However, I learned after leaving Alice Springs that Angkerle Atwatye is sacred to Women's Rock Wallaby Dreaming. While nobody had ever told me not to play music there, I now acknowledge and apologise for my lack of awareness.

Much later, in 2011, I drove to a remote place on the saltpans near Burketown on the Gulf of Carpentaria. It was flat there and quiet, without sounds of insects, just a very light breeze. I could look in any direction and see the plains disappearing on every horizon. I imagined I was a speck on the curvature of the Earth. I succumbed to the stillness and solitude and played a Chinese bamboo flute to accompany the sun setting in the happiest of skies. I was hearing empty stillness, as in the Japanese aesthetic principle of *ma*. This describes the pauses between the sound and flow of the notes. I wanted to stay there in the moment beyond dusk, but there were no roads, only my tyre marks, and I had no signal on my phone. I left vowing that I would go back there again.

Back in 1986, I experimented with acoustic spaces regularly. I enjoyed improvising in crypts, stairwells, carparks, caves and tunnels. I liked long decaying sounds and echoes as a call and response musical dialogue.

∽

Spaces condition us. We talk in a hush just as a performance is about to begin, making the space feel special in our minds. Most musicians like reverberant acoustic spaces. I enjoy 'playing the space' with an instrument or sound-producing object. Musicians in recording studios ask for some reverberation in their headphones. An Irish musician once asked me, 'Mick, might I be having a little touch o' magic on me whistle now?' He had heard the recordings of Paul Horn in the Taj Mahal. I patched to his headphones a program called 'Münster Cathedral'. This is a simulation of the cathedral's reverberation mapped and stored in a rack-mount unit designed by Yamaha audio engineers. The whistle player was happy to play 'inside the box', playing the simulated space. But I could hear the electronic noise in the digital signal-processing technology. What the situation lacked was the freedom to move around within an actual space and to play it.

There is, therefore, a compromise made to reconcile the imbalance between the recording studio and the resonant space. Studio work can be claustrophobic when close-microphone, multi-track methods and a forest of stands and encroaching leads restrict the physical space. I wanted to play in recording environments that permitted more freedom.

I called my first solo recording *Solo with Instruments* (1986). Originally released as a vinyl LP, it comprises improvisations in a highly resonant space, the fourteen-storey fire escape of a Library Tower building at the University of New South Wales. My friend Michael Gissing helped me. Michael was the first engineer in Australia to switch from analogue to digital in the location recording of film sound. We talked about my desire to record a solo album. He suggested we use a Sony PCM F1 recorder, a pair of Schoeps flat response Collette Series Omni-capsule microphones and a Sennheiser dummy head that he nicknamed Sir Richard (Dick) Head! Michael changed 'Dick' to fit the capsules, and we spent many stimulating hours filling up Betamax cassettes with recordings of instruments, including flutes, pipes, strings, oud, lute, hurdy-gurdy, psaltery, wooden and plastic objects, and my voice.

We experimented with endless microphone locations on every floor. One problem working close to parallel concrete walls was the inevitability of standing waves caused by early sound reflections. These became most audible at high frequencies when playing the whistles and transverse flutes. They sounded akin to digital glitching.

For one stairwell improvisation, I played a Macedonian bagpipe on the top-floor landing of the stairwell. I kept playing while descending the stairs, moving towards 'Dick', who was on the ninth floor. In my walking downstairs, passing 'Dick', Michael and I were hoping to capture a sense of vertical movement in the recording, as well as the gradual crescendo and decrescendo effect. Every item recorded was an improvisation. There were no edits, overdubs or signal processing on the custom LP, released a few months later. I left a few playing slips in, including overblown notes on the flute, guitar fret noise, and footsteps.

My aesthetic approach differed from my work as a film composer, which relied heavily on multi-track recording and processing. I wasn't against machines. It was more the multi-dimensional approach to audio quality and real-time human playing that was important. I once saw an advertisement on the wall of a music shop that said *Wanted – live drummer to replace a machine*. This was gratifying because the world was talking about artificial intelligence and the likelihood of cyborgs. The originality of *Solo with Instruments* was making music sound the entire space to provide the listener with a rich and authentic sound.

Most concert hall musicians will clap their hands or sing a few notes when they enter a performance hall for the first time. How often have I heard comments on acoustic spaces such as, 'it's not very kind'; or 'it should be good for the voice', or 'it's too dry'; or, 'too wet'. Musicians know what they want from an acoustic space but must often settle for second best in a world where architects mostly address noise abatement over sound design. But it is also a world which is both enhanced and restricted by the projection of stereo speakers, a world that offers the insidiously clinical perfection of digital production.

However, in 1991, I was jubilant after attending a concert by The World Saxophone Quartet that played in the first Brisbane Biennial. The quartet performed acoustically in the main concert hall of the Queensland Performing Arts Centre. They played mostly centre stage, occasionally moving to different parts and carefully pointing their instruments at the walls and roof surfaces to manipulate their sound. There wasn't a microphone in sight. Their music ranged from homophonic-styled arrangements of standards through to multiple melodic lines of effortless improvisation. The audience delighted in WSQs 'playing the space', visually as well as aurally.

I shared my interest in highly resonant spaces with Melbourne sound artist Ros Bandt. Like me, Ros has a background in early music. She said on the sleeve of *Stargazer* (1985), 'Every place has its sound ambience and its qualities of dimension, mass, contour, context and climatic conditions. These qualities will affect and play a part in your work.' Her improvisations in disused silos in the Victorian wheat belt were inspirational. I sensed a kindred spirit committed to experimentation with sculpted and found sound-producing objects in unusual places.

I contacted the National Acoustic Laboratories, one of the quietest and best-equipped facilities of its kind in the world. The facility was on Commonwealth land in a quiet suburban setting in Chatswood, backing on to national parkland. It was operationally unique in being the only single group of test rooms in the world specifically designed to undertake acoustical measurements spanning the full frequency response, dynamic range, and perceptive characteristics of human hearing. For reasons I am yet to fathom, the government decommissioned the laboratory and sold it off. The buildings are now owned by the Church of Scientology.

Working with Michael Gissing, I played in the Reverberation Rooms, the Anechoic Rooms, the large Quiet Room and the large Horizontal Plane-Wave Tube. Both Reverberation Rooms provided twelve seconds of uniform decay. It was fabulous to hear the natural resonances of an instrument enhanced in these spaces. By using cheap foam rubber mattresses, I could also vary decay times, which is useful when improvising with percussion.

I recorded Australian-made instruments in the anechoic spaces. I did this to collect control data for future research into the unenhanced timbres of the instruments. The large Anechoic Room had an absorption frequency of 50 hertz inside 300 mm thick concrete walls. Access was via a heavy door onto a suspended wire mesh floor. I could maintain control over each recording by using the same microphone and pre-amp, and the same volume settings. The distance of each instrument from the microphone was measured and noted. No equalisation or effects were added. Single notes, scales, and characteristic passages, as well as new compositions and fragments of existing works, were recorded for each instrument.

I can say that there is a connection between playing the space and my appreciation of the Renaissance lute, with its highly resonant, bowl-shaped body and multiple strings. I used to practise on a sandstone stairway off the Quadrangle at Sydney University; I loved the sustain and amplification of the lute's sound.

Recording Australian-made musical instruments at the National Acoustic Laboratories, 1989. *l-r*: Guitar, Kevin Johnson; portative organ, Ron Sharpe; psaltery, Peter Kempster; wooden tongue drum, Jonathan Chance; tapan drum, Risto Todoroski; tabor drum and bodhran, Martin and Catherine Healy; melodeon, Peter Hyde; and a didjeridu from the Northern Territory.
Photo: Michael Gissing

Australian Made, Australian Played

I was always curious about the unique acoustic properties of Australian-made musical instruments. Fortuitously, I was invited to write the book *Australian Made… Australian Played…. Handcrafted musical instruments from the didjeridu to the synthesizer* (1990). This book, unlike *The ABC Book of Musical Instruments*, focused on the making and building of instruments. I hoped to fill a gap in our knowledge about local makers and their lives, about their use of local materials and innovations.

The material culture of music in Australia began with the production of music and sound instruments by Aboriginal and Torres Strait Islander people, but since European occupation and settlement, new musical tools have entered the sound scape. New instrument production has been haphazard because of the difficulties of adapting to a new country and the harshness of environments. Distance has imposed further serious restrictions and required resourcefulness and ingenuity in devising solutions.

Aboriginal and Torres Strait Islander people likely settled in Australia over 60,000 years ago. Their traditional musical instruments are mostly idiophones and aerophones. The idiophones include paired boomerangs (rhythm clappers), paired sticks, rasps, and seedpods. The aerophones include the bullroarer and didjeridu. Hourglass-shaped membranophones are played in the Torres Strait, as well as panpipes and notched end-blown flutes.

The didjeridu is a natural trumpet, unique in the world of musical instruments for its playing technique. The first stage of its construction is a natural process. White ants hatch from eggs under the tree bark. They grow by eating their way through the hard timber to the core of the tree and turn its branches into pipes. The didjeridu maker selects a piped branch, strips off the bark, smooths the surface and clears the inside bore with a pointed stick and water. Cracks are sealed with mud or with sugar bag – a resinous paste made from native bees.

Traditionally, didjeridus were handcrafted for a particular ceremony. Some say that instruments made by Larrtjanga (Melville Bay, NT), George Jangawanga (Maningrida, NT) and David Blanatji (Arnhem Land, NT) are the best playing instruments available. The didjeridu is also an evolving instrument. Yamitji man, Mark Atkins, has included a 'diatonic didjeridu' that permits a range of fundamentals and overtones due to adapted bassoon key mechanisms. Players such as Tjuparrula Wongi and Charlie McMahon have experimented successfully with telescopic slide instruments made from PVC fitted with radio microphones. So the didjeridu has been given new life and continues to develop in contemporary contexts.

Instrument making in Australia is still carried out by a small number of individual crafts persons. There is no longer a music manufacturing industry since the demise of three large piano manufacturers: Beale, Wertheim, and Davies. The atelier studio is where handcrafted instruments are made, ranging from the didjeridu to digital sound producers.

Australian instrument makers are multi-skilled, idealistic, even reclusive. Their philosophies range from a conservative adherence to tradition, to iconoclastic methods and daring innovations. Many makers began as musicians and came to instrument making either to repair or to improve upon their instrument. Many have come as immigrants, bringing not only an increasingly diverse range of musical backgrounds but also an ability and a wish to make the most out of their new environment.

In addition to the instruments of European folk traditions, the orchestra, and the Early Music revival, there are the instruments of post–World War II immigrants from around the world, which contribute to a dynamic, pluralistic music environment.

The second half of the nineteenth century was a time when migrants came seeking their fortunes either in the gold rushes or post-goldrush boom. A few migrants turned to making musical instruments, some drawing on prior experiences of the craft, some beginning as repairers. The necessity of 'making do' enforced by the lifestyle of the goldfields or adapting to a new country is reflected in inventiveness. Distance from Europe imposed its restrictions and required resourcefulness and ingenuity in devising solutions.

The commission for *Australian Made, Australian Played* came from UNSW Press. I expected that a leading ethnomusicologist would write a book on the subject. However, I recall Roger Covell and his wife Patricia put in a word for me, knowing that my early music experience, my work in Sirocco and my ABC book were the backgrounds for the book. They supported my expanding expertise in organology. Also, composers, especially those working in film, often asked me to play on their film scores or to advise them on the availability of just about any acoustic object that could make a sound. I soon became a conduit for information on local players of non-western music.

After my drawing attention to Australian instrument making in this book, I hoped performers would readily seek out local makers and commission their instruments. It was essential that the music industry and the public place a greater value on the diversity and quality of Australian instrument making.

My research interest led to more book commissions as well as performances, lectures, and demonstrations. Even now, I am still regularly contacted to advise musicians and curators from around the world seeking an Australian-made instrument. For example, representatives from a new world music museum in Arizona came to the University of Western Sydney for advice on procuring Australian instruments. I pointed them toward some didjeridu makers and some luthiers making guitars, violins and percussion instruments. Several makers, as a result, were commissioned to contribute to the Australian collection.

Once contracted, I revised the publisher's book proposal to ensure the inclusion of many photographs of makers and their craft. UNSW Press invested in lavish book design in landscape format. It was strikingly attractive throughout. I contacted my friend Peter Sculthorpe. He was very excited that such a book was to be written. Peter secured his publisher's agreement for me to use an excerpt of notation from his work, 'Nourlangie', for the inside cover design. It was serendipitous because Peter, who composed this music for solo guitar, strings and percussion, dedicated it to the virtuoso Australian guitarist John Williams. Peter offered to contact John with an invitation to launch the book if in Australia. Unfortunately, the timing wasn't good, but John wrote a lovely foreword. Importantly, John was a champion of Australian-made guitars by Greg Smallman.

I had an absorbing time travelling to the workshops of instrument makers, interviewing them about their lives and work and taking photographs. They gave me press clips, as well as copies of their photos and brochures. I amassed enough material for two books in just a few months. They were enthusiastic about my choice of title, *Australian Made, Australian Played*. This became a regular appropriation in program notes and on record sleeves. Musicians and their promoters were noticeably forthcoming in mentioning the provenance of an instrument made in Australia.

Australian Made, Australian Played also led to a companion recording project, funded by the Performing Arts Board of the Australia Council for the Arts.

I chose instruments based on availability and whether I could play them, inviting some friends in to help. Most of the instruments recorded were from my collection. Others were kindly loaned to the project by their makers and/or owners. I am grateful to Carey Beebe for transporting, tuning, and playing his harpsichord; Ian Mackenzie for playing his uilleann pipes; Howard Oberg for playing his flutes and recorders; and Ceska Baret for playing the viola and a violin by Harry Vatiliotis, and John Napier for playing his Norman Miller cello.

I aimed to produce the highest quality recordings for deposit in the National Film and Sound Archives. The secondary aim was to produce an independent program of pieces suitable for a commercially released compact disc recording. Naturally, the research would not have been possible without the support of the National Acoustic Laboratories and two of its leaders in hearing research and ultrasonics – Bruce Gore, the Chief Engineer and Test Facilities Manager, and Peter Alway, the Senior Technical Officer.

I recorded the instruments in two simultaneous stages. Stage 1 utilised the medium anechoic room. We used a DAT (digital audio recorder), which was located outside the room. A Breul & Kjaer microphone and a pre-amplifier were supplied by the laboratory.

In Stage 2, I recorded many rare instruments, either completely inside Reverberation Room 1 or in the open doorway leading into the airlock, or even in the open area of the Sound Shell. This enhanced the natural resonances of the musical instruments. I included two items to indicate my commitment to improvisation with unusual combinations: 'Urban Gamelan' for Holden Kingswood hubcaps, brake drums, terra cotta flowerpots and glassware, and 'Ayers Barock' combining harpsichord, didjeridu and paired sticks.

I am grateful to The Australian Music Centre, which helped me in 1991 to release a CD on its Sounds Australian label. I named it *Australian Made, Australian Played*. It was the first recording to present an all-Australian program of original music on locally made musical instruments. There were many reviews. The book made an impact at home and overseas, encouraging the public and institutions to recognise and commission Australian-made instruments.

The Australian Museum and the sounds of Oceania

In 1993, I joined the Australian Museum for a short time as an artist-in-residence. My role was to develop public performances relating to the Pacific Collections. The staff provided me with objects with no provenance details: conch shells and bamboo instruments and stones, to which I added tuned PVC stamping tubes, seedpods and rattles. I teamed up occasionally with sound artists, including

Rod Berry and Victor Monasterio, to improvise with visitors to the museum. During my residency, the museum invited me to inspect the entire musical instrument collections of the museum and share my findings with the Anthropology Department. There were musical instruments and sound-producing objects from Aboriginal and Torres Strait Islander communities, Southeast Asia, and Africa, as well as Oceania. I noticed that no one had previously paid scholarly attention to the collection. This provided the impetus for my wish to remedy the situation.

There are thousands of objects in the stores, many of which are weapons such as spears, clubs and shields. This begged the question, 'Why did we collect so many?' Is it our museum mindset to crave artefacts of the past because we cannot develop them ourselves? Housing objects in a museum is a particularly Western habit born from a colonial past, and the process of decolonisation has led to the objects having assumed political importance for their cultural context, unrecognised at their time of removal. My search of the museum's registers, which date back to the 1880s, revealed that objects were collected by 'traders, missionaries, plantation owners, government officers/explorers and museum staff, who may have been natural scientists or non-specialists'.

All contact with objects required wearing cotton gloves to avoid potential damage from perspiration. This is difficult for a musician like me. I wanted to blow flutes, which meant contacting finger holes as well as blowing moist air into the bamboo. Another problem confronted me. The methods used to clean and preserve these objects had involved toxic chemicals, including arsenic. I wore cotton gloves. I inspected a small, raft-shaped panpipe collected by one of Cook's sailors in 1774 on the island of Erromango, Vanuatu, the fourth-largest island of what we formerly knew as the New Hebrides. I believe the panpipe is neither made nor played by the people of Erromango. It became silent and removed from the highways and byways of cultural exchange.

Fortunately, the Australian Museum began a policy of repatriating material from beyond Australia's national boundaries to institutions overseas when cultural ownership of the material is identifiable and those institutions can show their ability to preserve and maintain the items. Repatriation of material is ongoing. For example, in 1981, the Australian Museum returned a large slit drum to the Vanuatu Cultural Centre because the centre did not have one.

The Mahogany Ship

Music's links with history and literature have always been abiding interests in my composition. It gave me a connection with the Sydney Children's Choir in 1993, one that I treasure deeply. The choir is one of Australia's intangible assets, founded by its dynamic artistic director, Lyn Williams. I have composed several works for the Sydney Children's Choir and even experienced the joy of hearing my son Jared singing music I composed when he joined as a six-year-old in 2011. He became a bass in the Young Men's Choir.

Lyn commissioned me to compose an extended song cycle to fire the imagination of her singers. I thought immediately of the stories of shipwrecks on the southern coast of Australia that had aroused my curiosity while I was on a Musica Viva tour with Southern Crossings.

A mahogany ship, either a relic or a legend, is something that stirs the imagination of Australians. Captain John Mason, of Port Fairy, Victoria, accidentally discovered one in 1846. He was riding his horse along the beach at Warrnambool when he sighted a shipwreck. His written account of the incident has led to almost 150 years of speculation over its origin and disappearance:

> My attention was attracted to the hull of a vessel embedded high and dry in the Hummocks, far above the reach of any tide. It appeared to have been that of a vessel about 100 tons burden, and from its bleached and weather-beaten appearance, must

have remained there many years. The spars and deck were gone, and the hull was full of drift sand.

He described the timber of the wreck as having 'the appearance of mahogany or cedar'. A story began to develop: the Warrnambool wreck (perhaps a more appropriate name than 'Mahogany Ship') could have been one of a flotilla of Portuguese or Spanish discovery ships. However, by 1876 the wreck had disappeared. No one knows where it went. Since then, there have been several searches for material evidence. Was the wreck buried deep in the sands of what is a regularly changing coastline at the mercy of the swell of the entire Southern Ocean? Or was the wreck burned as firewood by the Gunditjmara people living there? If its timber was mahogany, then the ship-building technology involved in its construction was more likely that of the sixteenth century, some 250 years before Cook!

Perhaps we will never know the truth. But there was a wreck, and Mason's account will remain interesting enough to continue the search for the ship and knowledge about its crew and purpose. Were Portuguese explorers – at the time well known in the Straits of Malacca – the first Europeans to chart Australia's east coast, indeed set foot on the land called Jave la Grande on a map dated between 1530 and 1536? Was it a Portuguese caravel, secretly trespassing in the Spanish hemisphere, wrecked off Warrnambool? Were there survivors? One historical event prompts these questions. The papal Treaty of Tordesillas of 1514 divided the discoverable world into two halves: one for Spain, the other for Portugal. Warrnambool is geographically located in what was Spanish 'territory'. The presence of a Portuguese caravel by intent or accident adds to the intrigue.

Lyn was excited when I suggested this subject. It had history, recognition of Indigenous people, conflict, and lots of scope for lighting and staging the performances. I outlined a story that began with diviners, historians, and scientists searching the sands of

Warrnambool for clues. I wanted to set up a cultural confrontation between Captain Cristovão de Mendonça, a celebrated Portuguese navigator, and the Gunditjmara people, living sustainably in their own place. The scene is a fragment of what might have been, or of what may yet become a chapter in the history of the exploration of Australia.

I read accounts of sixteenth-century European explorers. I walked up and down the beaches of Warrnambool and surrounds and spent hours in the local maritime museum at Flagstaff Hill. Next, I investigated the history of the Gunditjmara people and met with an elder to discover their connection to Warrnambool and their spiritual beliefs. I incorporated Mason's account of 1876 and drew on words and phrases from early sixteenth-century maps. I included research on the Portuguese in Timor. I collaborated again with Amy McGrath to create the text. She had a fine ear for a good line and could précis research material in an instant to turn it into prose or poetry.

We created a narrative exploring the opposing worldviews of Europeans and Indigenous Australians. Whereas the Portuguese were seeking gold and trade, the Gunditjmara people were living off and managing the land, with no need for European concepts of wealth. My story included an imaginary but peaceful confrontation between Portuguese explorers and Gunditjmara people. Inevitably, I called it *The Mahogany Ship*. I chose to include a string quartet with percussion rather than a piano to accompany the choir. This was to shape the song cycle into an oratorio. Here is the synopsis:

> In 1521, Captain-general Cristovão de Mendonça sailed south from Malacca in search of the Ilhas de Ouro, the Isles of Gold; down past Timor, through the Straits of Torres, riding the road of stranger coasts and unknown winds; ridden with squalls, three caravels in search of Terra Australis.

Terra Australis, a different land, a great south land like an ancient castle defended by barricades of reef, by pounding seas on walls of cliffs and moats of swamp, around its hidden gates. The Portuguese explorer Mendonça and his men sailed down the east coast into Bass Strait, and the winds blew them towards Warrnambool in search of the Western way to the Indian Ocean. They came ashore under the watchful eyes of the local people, the Gunditjmara.

The Portuguese landed on the sands and later shared food with the Gunditjmara. The sailors asked about gold, but the Gunditjmara replied by singing and telling stories about the spirits: Bunjil, the creator; Pirnmeheeal, the good one; Muurup, the bad one who brings storms and tidal waves.

The music includes directions for mimicking the sounds of the ocean, seabirds, and storms. One song, 'Gi-ri-gi-ri-gi-a', uses meaningless vocables sung to mimic the vocalisations used in playing the didjeridu. The words of the song 'Abra Olhos', invoke the Abrolhos Islands and coral reefs off the West Australian coast, thought to be named after their discoverer, Dutchman Frederik de Houtman. *Abre os olhos* is Portuguese for 'open your eyes'. This is also appropriate for the southern Victorian coast, which is littered with shipwrecks. The song 'Shall We Dream', composed for soloists joined by an ever-increasing number of chorus singers, is wavelike and meditative, suggesting the ship rolling towards a distant horizon of peace and tranquillity, something that is so poignant in the uncertainties of our time. Repeated phrases build towards a close canon performed by individual voices, like the foaming of waves after they break. It is the calm before or after a storm.

There have been several recordings of 'Shall we dream?' In one radio broadcast, the announcer introduced me as a British-Australian composer. I've never used such a descriptor. Maybe it was an attempt to separate me from the former test cricketer? The song emerged as a last-minute request from Lyn to add to *The Mahogany Ship*. I penned a single melody line, with instructions, in the subfloor 'studio' at 15 Streatfield Road, Bellevue Hill. Ironically, the song is the popular standalone go-to from *The Mahogany Ship*. Simplicity and texture triumph, it seems. Youth choirs from Canada to Finland have taken it up.

Youth choirs have performed *The Mahogany Ship* around the world. It adds to the presentation and recognition of Australia's Indigenous and maritime history. The combination of English and Portuguese text and the acknowledgement of the Gunditjmara and Kirrae Whurrong peoples is an intercultural response to shared histories. It is innovative in the choral canon as a work lending itself to choreography and staged performance. It contributed significantly to the development of the Sydney Children's Choir and Gondwana Voices.

9

MOVING INTO THE ACADEMY

Joining hands in a farandole.

It was in April 1993 that I was reading *Sonics*, a music technology magazine, and noticed an advertisement with University of Western Sydney (UWS) branding. The advertisement described a search for a person to create a music department at the Nepean campus. I skimmed over it and thought it was unusual to see such an advertisement in a trade magazine. I had just returned from a Southern Crossings tour and composing a film score.

I mentioned it to Ros. She reacted immediately: 'You love teaching. Put your hat in the ring! Apply for the job. You have a lot of experience and nothing to lose!' I ruminated on this while Ros, as ever the confident optimist and with an established academic track record, encouraged me to apply. She talked me through the application criteria and helped me revise my curriculum vitae. I wrote a narrative on my broad experience in the music industry as a composer–performer, adult educator, music therapist, and author.

I outlined my community service with the Australia Council and the NSW Ministry for the Arts.

However, looking from a traditional perspective on professorial positions in the tertiary sector, I felt that my application was limited because I was neither the holder of a PhD nor a pianist or orchestral player, all traditional hallmarks of a professor of music. But Ros reassured me that the job description was more inclusive in looking for background and experience that someone like me could bring to the role. Founding a department was much more than teaching and research.

I asked three friends and colleagues to referee my application: Ross Edwards, composer and lecturer; Max Bourke, general manager of the Australia Council; and Ian and Neil O'Hare, the directors of Natural Symphonies Recordings. There were three supplementary referees: Trish Ludgate, the international officer at Musica Viva; Alec Morgan, filmmaker; and Norman Swan, journalist and head of ABC Radio.

Once I had submitted my application, I went back to working on a film score that was due for delivery. I might be offered an interview. There would need to be flexibility by the selection committee. One of my referees said the committee would need to focus on my 'capacity to cross easily between composition, music performance, music therapy, audio-visual performance and ethnomusicology ... and a strong commitment to all shades of contemporary music expression [as] a many-faceted arts practitioner'.

On 26 May, it surprised me to receive a phone call and a letter to confirm my short-listing for an interview. This was a recognition of my contribution to music. Off I went to buy a suit, business shirts and a bunch of ties, garments I hadn't worn for years.

The familiarisation and interview process were on 8 and 9 June 1993. On the first day, I met academic leaders, administrative staff, and students across UWS Nepean. I shared lunch with the three other shortlisted applicants: my friend Roger Woodward; the respected academic Dr Clive Pascoe; and the composer Dr Richard Hames. I enjoyed swapping notes with the other applicants. Although we were competitors for a highly significant position, it was a friendly and relaxed lunch, and it helped me to focus on the afternoon presentation I was scheduled to give to the faculty and students.

My topic, as advised a week earlier, was to show how my skills and experience would contribute to the development of music within the Faculty of Visual and Performing Arts at the university and out in the community. The university wanted a long-term strategic plan and immediate goals to achieve the relevant pedagogical outcomes. It had to resonate with the cultural matrix of contemporary Australia. I proposed the following principles:

- Pursue excellence in contemporary music performance and music education.
- Develop curricula through a team approach based on music in Australian society today.
- Include teaching and research in music for theatre, dance and film.
- Explore, understand and develop dynamic multicultural and multimedia collaborations.
- Provide hands-on support for developing Indigenous contemporary music, with access to state-of-the-art recording studios and equipment.
- Offer performance, musicological and technological strands emphasising vocational training, conferences and seminars on the performing arts, topics including music and marketing, music therapy, ethnomusicology, film music, improvisation, music for youth and early childhood, and instrument making.

Each applicant attended a formal interview on the second day. It was chaired by the Vice-Chancellor, Brian Smith, and included UWS

Nepean CEO, Professor Jillian Maling; Associate Professor David Hull, Dean of the Faculty; and academics from other institutions, as well as representatives of industry. I had met David once before and he reminded me it was when I was performing in Hyde Park during the Sydney Festival. I was doing an audience interaction with percussion and invited David and his son to join in.

I walked into the interview room at 2 pm and sat at the end of a long table facing ten people. Each person had a question for me that was linked to the essential and desirable criteria. That I didn't have a doctorate didn't arise, because I referred to my continuing engagement in research. I could outline my 'mosaic' education, and my research degrees in English literature, languages, plus qualifications in musicology and ethnomusicology at Sydney University and the University of New England. I asserted that my publication of books, compositions and recordings and film and music theatre scores made up a profile that aligned with the values of the faculty and the mission of the university.

The only question that made me hesitate before answering was 'If successful with your application, how will you adjust to the demands of the position that will restrict your composing, performing and touring work?' I had given little thought to it because I didn't want to get ahead of myself. I answered by reassuring the committee that I would begin in the role by giving full attention to the development of a music department, then augment my professional practice and research profile.

The interview hour went quickly. I left the room satisfied that I had given my best, and walked across the park at Kingswood, heading towards the station for my train ride home. I felt as if I had composed and performed a music score for another scene of my life. It was satisfying, whatever the outcome.

Ros was waiting for me at home, and we had a chat over dinner about the trip. We put Emily and Marc to bed, and I went into my studio under the house to do some editing and mixing. The phone rang; it was Jillian Maling from UWS. It surprised me to receive her call. She apologised for the timing of the call and told me she was calling to say I had impressed the committee with my application. 'We reached a decision and I'm calling to offer you the position of Professor of Music. We believe you will provide the leadership and experience for the job. I hope you will accept?' I was stunned, speechless, and my mind chattered *Who? Me? Surely not. What about the others?* I broke my silence with stuttering, 'Wow, that's great.' Jillian said I should expect a letter of offer in the next mail.

Nirvana! Just as I had matriculated against all odds in 1969, I was about to become a foundation professor, with a tenurable position at a young and dynamic university. I went upstairs to tell Ros, 'Guess what? That call just now … I'm going to be a professor!' It was as if a 250 to 1 rank outsider just landed the Melbourne Cup. Ros beamed and said she knew I was in with a chance due to my broad background and experience. As an academic in the Law School at Sydney University, she knew, from sitting on selection panels, all about applicants who could impress with interesting careers and backgrounds.

Once I had received the offer and accepted it formally, I thought of the transition from freelance employment to a salaried position. The only hurdle to overcome initially was the travel distance. We lived in a substantially mortgaged house in the Eastern Suburbs. I would have to walk to Edgecliff station, catch a train to Town Hall, change for Kingswood on the western line and then walk across a park. This amounted to three hours of travel time per day. Driving would take two hours, but Ros needed the car for dropping Emily and Marc at their schools.

I commenced at UWS Nepean in July 1993, ready to embrace the challenges, with a plan to stay in the role for five years assuming, of course, that I passed the probation period for tenure. We thought about moving closer to the campus, but that would mean Ros having to travel into Sydney CBD and being a bit far from her parents and the children's friends. If the travel became too much, I would look at renting a small unit near the campus to stay there for a couple of nights a week.

Music at UWS

On my first day, I went to see the dean of the faculty to debrief following my interview and to discuss my plans. His secretary, Barbara, greeted me outside his office with 'Oh, you're going to have to work awfully hard.' She wasn't wrong, because I met Jillian later in the day, and she suggested we commence enrolments in December for a 1994 intake. I accepted the challenge, although there were few precedents for such a rapid development of a music department. My enquiries showed that developing a department usually took a year. At least I had the scaffolding of an existing faculty in which to establish a music department, a faculty with an impressive track record in theatre and fine arts.

The university supported my need to fulfil existing commitments, including a tour to Korea, but I knew that everything else required the pause button – composition, film composition, school concerts, Musica Viva – the lot. I needed to commit every waking moment to a 1994 commencement and was about to learn business development on the job at light speed. First I prepared a timetable of meetings with Financial Services, Capital Works, Human Resources and the library. Negotiations for a budget, facilities, staff, books and materials were paramount.

I used to think I was composing and recording a film score on a tight deadline, balancing my freelance musical activities of teaching, playing and serving music government arts funding committees. Now it felt as if I were carrying the baton in every leg of a relay race.

The days and weeks flew by. I wrote the degree document in four weeks. It had to be evaluated by all areas of the university and passed through the faculty before going to the university's Academic Board. I consulted a distinguished panel of music-makers, academics and community leaders in collaboration with colleagues in the faculty. Mark Pollard (now Professor of Contemporary Music at the University of Melbourne), whom I had met at the Australia Council, provided support. He chaired an industry advisory panel to evaluate the content and quality of the course before they could approve it.

For staffing, the word went out that a new department was in development. There were four hundred applicants. I needed a high-performing core group to contribute and help me fast-track the growth of the new department. The budget permitted the equivalent of four full-time academic positions, plus an administrator and a technical officer. Interviews brought a powerful field of musicians to my attention, and I would have appointed twenty if I had the budget. The dean chaired the selection committees, and we appointed two full-time and three half-time staff on three-year contracts. This gave me a stable team to help develop and deliver the first-year curriculum.

Come October, with the staff team due to begin in November, I began a frenzied period of ordering books, serials, scores and CD recordings for the library, plus musical instruments and audio equipment. Soon I was relying on the expertise and unstinting support of composer-performer-academics including Diana Blom, Michael Whiticker and Jim Franklin. Diana, whose friends call her 'Dinty', an affectionate diminutive from her jolly husband, Axel, was a true all-rounder made for our team. She played piano, harpsichord, percussion and double bass. She was an excellent teacher of music craft and theory. Her energy and happy nature made her very popular. As I write, she remains a pillar of the department, mentoring first-year students and supervising doctorates, and somehow managing to maintain a role in international music teaching pedagogy.

Conservatorium-trained Michael Whiticker, a composer who had spent time in Germany, was also part of the foundation team. He was an excellent organiser and ideas person. He was passionate and committed to music composition and performance. I relied on his skills in selecting equipment and building a library collection.

Jim Franklin joined us from Sydney University. He brought deep knowledge of composition and electronic music, as well as his virtuoso skills in traditional Japanese shakuhachi performance. Jim also brought performing experience as a keyboardist in progressive rock. And when we added Julian Knowles, a former ABC music engineer with experience in live electronic performance, we were looking like a formidable team. The other member to join on half-time basis was the musicologist, Sally Macarthur, with a strong interest in Australian women composers.

There was never any linear progression in putting the department together. It became a bit like jumping in and out of dodgem cars, driving in this one, then another, and so on. I was soon like a kid in a lolly shop when I consulted retailers to buy pianos, marimbas, timpani, African drums, strings and much more. I did deals everywhere and spruiked organisations to endow music prizes. Turramurra Music, the Guitar Factory and Sound Devices became stalwarts of the new department. I aimed to establish high-level music technology facilities and equipment and studios. We would eventually fund and build one of the best campus recording studios in Australia because I saw that the rapid development of new technologies had enormous implications for the evolution of the performing arts. The capacity to combine sound and image with live performance surely had to be a priority for equipping graduates for employment.

Meanwhile, the university's publicity department contacted every high school in NSW about the new degree. It generated intense interest and excitement and hundreds of enquiries. In September, we began auditioning 240 applicants. By December, we selected and made offers to our first 50-strong student cohort. The Western Sydney region bristled with multi-talented and highly enthusiastic students. I wanted to provide an Australian alternative to the prevalent Eurocentrism of tertiary music education.

It was a favourable time to reflect the interests of diverse and dynamic communities within Australia, to emphasise cultural contexts and develop new areas of research. We desired to develop graduates capable of originating new music in many musical styles and genres. Western Sydney was a rising population powerhouse, the demographic heartland of the nation's largest city. It deserved a different music qualification that embraced diverse cultures – one in which Western art music was but part of the picture.

A new approach to music education

Music at UWS would not be a celebration of the past, rather, of what was to come. I carried in my heart the words of Gough Whitlam in 1975. He gave us confidence in 'a multicultural nation, in which the linguistic and cultural heritage of the Aboriginal people and all the peoples from all parts of the world can find an honourable place'. Australian musicians have long been attracted to Asian music. The music of Indonesia and Japan has inspired several artists seeking alternatives to Eurocentrism. Our acceptance of destiny within the Asian region has led to an increased sensitivity to the cultural life of our near neighbours.

Contact between Asia and Australia is centuries old. During the fifteenth century, the Chinese were trading with Sumatra, Java, Timor and Macassar in the Celebes. It is feasible that Chinese ships may have visited Australia's north coast as early as two hundred years before the British colonisation. The Macassans became welcome traders with Australia's Indigenous inhabitants. They traded metal, rice and dugout canoes. As a result, there are Macassan words in the languages of northern Australia.

The first Chinese immigrants arrived in the 1850s gold rush period. From these immigrants came one of our famous sayings, 'Fair dinkum': 'Dinkum' comes from '*ding gum*', the Cantonese expression for a piece of gold. The impact of Chinese music during and following the gold rush is undocumented. However, in Bendigo,

Victoria, there is a Chinese museum which holds one of the largest processional dragons in the world. It suggests that, at least, processional music-making accompanied these Chinese immigrants. Today there are groups of Chinese musicians in our largest cities, including the Australian Chinese Orchestra in Melbourne.

The 1960s was a time of eclecticism in Australian composition. The music of Japan and Indonesia, which first influenced our composers, led the university music departments to study ethnomusicology. Composer Peter Sculthorpe introduced students at Sydney University to recordings and transcriptions of Asian music. A fascination for Japanese culture soon transcended the bitterness of the Pacific war.

Asian cultures came to be appreciated on their terms, rather than just engaging with them from a colonialist perspective. The Whitlam government's policy of Australianising in the early 1970s meant both a withdrawal from aspects of British heritage and a reassessment of our identity within the region. This was reflected, for example, in the abandonment of British knighthoods and other titles. The impact on our music-making has been significant and lasting.

From day one, every student was multi-tasking. They were expected to perform on two instruments, compose, study theory and musicology, and embrace music technology with computers and audio engineering. Students were to collaborate on projects. For example, for a student expecting to play the piano, their first concert practice could be assigned to doing live sound, compèring or stage management. We encouraged students to explore their interests. For example, a concert pianist wanted to do an installation with pre-recorded sounds overlayed with live harmonica playing. We said, 'Go for it! Research, plan, document it, and do it well!'

We were keen on students improvising as well as playing existing music. This was tested in their auditions. I might ask drummers to pick up marimba mallets and improvise a one-minute African dance. Similarly, a pianist might improvise a one-minute film score for a storm, starting with the trickle of rain to a deluge and then calming.

A vocalist could adapt on the spot a 4/4 verse to work in 7/8. Guitar players were asked to improvise on the piano using clusters and plucking the strings under the lid. Applicants enjoyed this aspect of the audition. Only a few thought it was 'a bit weird', usually those who wanted a more traditional, conservatorium-styled soloist pathway playing their best two prepared items. We wanted all applicants to have a positive experience in the audition itself, and to appreciate the enthusiasm of the staff team preparing for the new degree.

The first question to each applicant was, 'If we offer you a place to study with us, what attributes will you bring to share with your fellow students?' Their responses were as important as their musical skills. We wanted to select the first cohort to experience a highly collaborative, project-based approach. Teamwork above competition was desirable.

The degree document was fast-tracked and approved in December. We enrolled sixty students in January 1994. Approximately 65 per cent came from Western Sydney, the rest from other parts of Sydney, rural NSW and even interstate. But one obstacle remained, and it was a major one. I needed dedicated performance spaces, labs, offices, and storage to launch a university department. I knew on my first day that I would be assigned temporary space on the Kingswood campus because UWS Nepean was close to completing plans for a performing arts centre at Werrington. The aim was to build it in two stages. The first one, for completion in 1997, was to house Theatre and Dance; the second in 2002, would accommodate Music and Electronic Arts. However, a music department needed spaces, now and fast. I gained some of the Kingswood library building for practice rooms, a percussion space, and a recording performance hall. I could repurpose a lower ground floor area under the library for staff offices and seminar rooms. It involved knocking a wall down and some reconfiguring. Nothing happened. I waited politely for the current occupants, Accounting, to move in response to a memorandum from the vice-chancellor.

Nothing happened over the Christmas-New Year closedown. I waited patiently until mid-January, still sharing an office in the Dean's Unit. The Accounting occupants were stalling. Jillian Maling, the CEO, was away, but the moment she returned, I told her about my predicament. The impasse hindered the commencement of the course at the start of the semester.

She was annoyed and picked up her phone to call the head of 'the squatters'. 'Hello, John? Jillian here. I'm coming to see you in ten minutes and bringing Professor Atherton with me.' She knocked on John's door. He came out into the corridor, and after civilities, she pointed to a wall and said, 'John, Professor Atherton is founding a new department for the university. I informed you in writing two months ago about your relocation. I am giving and you and your staff twenty-four hours to vacate this building before the builder arrives to knock this wall down.' She spoke civilly but with purpose, befitting the remarkable leader that she was. He capitulated. The wall came down, opening the area to what would become a lecture room, small studio, amenities and offices. Three weeks later and one week before students arrived, the area was furnished and fitted out with nameplates on the doors, new 'Macs' on every desk, and sound systems and whiteboards installed in every room. We were ready to roll. I raised the baton. Let the music begin.

Two years later I proudly issued a press release, *A snapshot of a day in the life of the Music Department*. It included this excerpt.

> Two violinists are playing contemporary minimalist music in the Common Room – Steve Reich's 'Violin Phase'. A pianist is playing a Beethoven piano sonata in an adjacent room. A group of students is recording percussion and sound effects in a digital studio. Down the corridor, a Latin jazz band is in rehearsal. A rock trio is performing original songs later today at Kingswood Swamp Bar. Outside the library, there's a calypso specialist from Trinidad rehearsing the steel pan

band. A master of the traditional Japanese Shakuhachi teaches music software programming in the computer lab. A performer-composer enthuses students with a high-energy jazz-rock trumpet in a lecture hall. A solo percussionist improvises electronic music triggered by his drums. Meanwhile, a film crew has arrived from Korea to interview students learning traditional Korean percussion.

A hallmark of our degree was that students completed a common first year, then chose two specialisations from Performance, Composition, or Music Technology. We felt that this approach would encourage students to develop a broader skill set than, say, just enrolling in performance. We hoped our students understood the role of the arts in contemporary society and, in the broadest sense, in shifting cultural conditions (social, political, technological, economic). The course aimed to produce music-makers capable of working in several avenues in professional music, including composition for a variety of media; innovative performance; audio engineering; artistic direction and production; music administration; and new collaborations.

We achieved a lot in a short time, but not everyone supported our new venture. There were one or two broadsides from other providers because they deemed us to be pinching their potential enrolments. However, the industry at large recognised we were adding to opportunities for students. An incident with a philanthropist also brought home to me that my vision for the Australian music of the future was by no means universally welcomed.

Unfortunately, there was no tradition of philanthropy for a new department, no alumni to mentor or support what we set out to do. So when an offer came from a lady in Woollahra to donate $10,000 to the Music Department to support the study of the piano, it delighted me to receive her letter. We met to discuss the piano scholarship. However, a month after handing over the process to the university's fund-raising department, I received an unexpectedly deflating letter from the benefactor:

> Dear Professor Atherton,
>
> I must confess that ever since our first meeting early in April last, at which you expressed undisguised enthusiasm for the study of electronics, acoustics, and other technologies only peripherally connected with music, in my opinion, I have had misgivings about your vision for the future of the Department of Music in your university.
>
> My worst doubts were confirmed on reading the article in Spectrum in the Sydney Morning Herald of 4 June 1994, which referred to your prowess in playing the didgeridoo, the hurdy-gurdy, the Turkish saz, etc., and your hopes of fostering young peoples' interest in what I would regard as non-music, simply noise.
>
> Thus, it has become only too clear that your views on music and mine are widely divergent, and I am now convinced that you would not be interested in furthering the study of the piano, least of all the classical piano, which I wish most earnestly to assist and encourage.
>
> It is therefore with great regret and deep disappointment that I have decided to withdraw my offer to donate $10,000 to the Department of Music within the University of Western Sydney and to look for some other means of advancing the study of the piano.
>
> Yours sincerely,
> ......

The words embodied a jaw-droppingly narrow-minded view of music that smacked of class and privilege. I was merely a 'professor of noise'. However, after the initial impact of the letter, I decided not to dignify its bias with a reply. Instead, I became more determined to develop an eclectic, modern, and multicultural educational pathway for our students. My diametrical opposition to the musical apartheid shown in the letter was unshaken.

∽

We had a responsibility to mentor undergraduates towards employment. The course experience had to be relevant. Our students would leave university with a HECS debt. I worked out quickly that if a student collaborated with the community, they became not only more visible and engaged, but also more likely to be entrepreneurial. In the United States, some universities called it 'academic service-learning' in which we could assess a student in the field as a volunteer. This prompted me to prepare a paper that I called 'A song going down the road', drawing on the words Ghanaian ethnomusicologist J. H. Kwabena Nketia used to describe interlocking drum patterns. I asserted that the visual and performing arts provide ideal opportunities for project-based learning experiences involving the community. The School of Contemporary Arts at UWS had shown that collaborative projects, especially those from music, dance and fine arts, achieved highly successful learning outcomes for students, staff and local communities.

Working outside the comfort zone of the campus encouraged students to think beyond a careerist 'me' generation envelope and look for ways and means to contribute to their community. The students could learn through 'hands-on' participation in meaningful and planned experiences in the community. They should start and coordinate their projects while supervised by academics with community partners.

They would apply knowledge and skills to real-world problem-solving activities; develop interpersonal skills and become more empathic. This encouraged leadership and flexibility through career-related work before graduating. It provided students with instruction in project planning, guidelines and reporting, including discussions of related issues such as professional ethics and self-assessment procedures. I expected students to display a high level of initiative and integrity in undertaking a collaborative project.

Assessment strategies focused on consultation, management, an artistic report and a viva voce exam. The principal lecturer acting as a mentor coordinated the unit, with help from academic colleagues in reviewing student engagement and progress. At least two colleagues took part in the exam. We included testimonials from community partners.

Projects in 1995 and 1996 included:

- volunteer work in correctional centres (performance, instruction)
- church music (researching, composing, and organising)
- music therapy (clinical assistance)
- diversional therapy, children's hospital performances (recreational music)
- suburban bands and orchestras including the Royal Australian Air Force
- community centre (music & spirituality discourse)
- pre-school, high school (a cappella, technology, free improvisation, song writing)
- music grading (playing and assessing performance levels of Australian music)
- Indigenous music involvement in mentoring and recording bands
- music projects to empower Greek and Irish communities in Penrith

One student went back to her old high school in Liverpool to set up and direct a vocal ensemble, because there were no singing groups when she was there. Another student wrote a fanfare for the RAAF band at Richmond air base because most of their repertoire was from the USA or the UK. She has since become a leading orchestral conductor. A student devised and implemented a music program for his local church.

Sometimes, a collaborative project combined ethnomusicology and community engagement. The interest I developed during my trips to Korea became the focus of a project involving the Korean Resource Centre in Sydney. I met a group of approximately twenty-five Korean Australians who met weekly to practise a style of traditional drumming and dancing called *Pung mul*. The group invited me to a rehearsal, which was held in an industrial area, in an underpass beneath Parramatta Road. This outdoor space was perfect, as there were no houses in the area.

The performers began by stretching out, preparing their bodies for the strenuous physical activity that is necessary for performing *samul nori*, a development of traditional Korean percussion based on shamanic and farmers' music. They each helped the other to strap on the drums and rehearsed parts in pairs, while they expectantly waited for their teacher, who had recently arrived from Korea. As the rehearsal progressed, the performers became increasingly animated and exuberant. Afterwards, they went to a house in Strathfield to cook a meal together.

None of these musicians had performed professionally except for their teacher. One was a biologist, another a high school teacher, and several were businesspeople and accountants. They used music to maintain their connections with Korea, and others joined in just for the exercise and relaxation in a comfortable atmosphere.

One drummer told me, 'We are trying to help each other, and our children, to feel what it is like to be proud of our music here in Australia, and to let Australians share our sounds.'

This group of Korean Australians was delighted to assist me in my wish to develop a Korean percussion group at the university. I shared some rehearsals by taking a group of students to the underpass. The students learned drum patterns, filmed the interaction, and interviewed some performers. I invited them to share their discoveries and write up an ethnomusicology report, which I shared with the Korean Resource Centre. It responded by sending us a teacher to develop our ensemble.

By 1995, the Music Department was ready to showcase our development in a uniquely entertaining way, taking an idea from John Cage's 'Musicircus'. Musicircus was an invitation to gather several ensembles of any kind, preferably in a large auditorium, and have them perform simultaneously whatever they wished. This could generate an event that lasted a few hours in one day. In typical Cage style, there was no score, no parts, nothing specified except the concept. He said, 'You won't hear anything: you'll hear everything.' However, the illustrious New Zealand ethnomusicologist-composer, Jack Body, first brought the term 'Sonic Circus' to my attention. He directed such an event in 1974 in Wellington. It lasted six hours and was performed across eight different venues on the Victoria University campus.

I directed a Sonic Circus at UWS Nepean in September 1995. Students handled sound and lighting, stage management and programming. I held the event over two nights. It showcased a synergy of cultures, instruments, and approaches reflecting student creativity. We selected most items from concert practices and ensemble performances, in consultation with the students. Others were specially composed for the event. Each performance was four hours of non-stop entertainment, allowing the audience to experience an aural banquet of individual and group music-making.

We based the Sonic Circus in and around the Playhouse Theatre on the Kingswood campus of the university. The first sounds to greet the unsuspecting audience were the responsibility of a second-year student in the foyer. We wrapped him in bandages and hooked him up to an ECG monitor and MIDI system. His heartbeat, which itself was stimulated by interaction with the audience, controlled the sounds and vice versa. The printed program was rapped by the outstanding Phil Burton playing the drum kit.

Imagine the juxtaposition of seemingly disparate genres and styles reflecting the diversity of music-making in our society, attempting to counter the privileging of one style over another. African song followed by brass and timpani fanfares, heralding the audience from outdoors into a theatre, where elements of improvisation, music technology, mime, dance and new composition are experienced – Javanese gamelan counterpointing keyboard minimalist excursions, followed by an alfresco fugue of actual car horns, accompanied by percussion, on the lawn nearby – frenetic dancing, followed by jazz-funk inside the theatre foyer, morphing into computer music manipulations back in the theatre, including MIDI-triggered electro percussion – and all this followed by a menu of piano solos and duos, including Rachmaninov and Debussy, Gershwin, Messiaen and Stockhausen, as well as student compositions and improvisations. There were comic routines, a wind band, a song cycle by Peggy Glanville-Hicks, and a percussion piece by Ross Edwards. And all the above concluding with a massed choir. That is how it happened! The concept proved so popular that I became the 'ringmaster' for more circuses between 1996 and 1999. The event grew so much that we spread out to a sports field, where I put up a circus tent and powerful sound systems to cater for larger ensembles and audiences.

We celebrated the first graduation of forty-five students in 1997, some with enthusiasm for going on to an honours year. I led the development of the honours degree and guided its passage through the Academic Board ready for enrolment. The department was thriving. We doubled the number of staff. Not only were our students contributing to the cultural life of the campus and the local community, but they also enjoyed the benefits of an engaging concert series on campus, called *The Art of Sound*. I curated and managed the series from 1994 with input from Diana Blom and Michael Whiticker. The concerts were free for all staff and students at UWS. We brought the 'best to the west' – voice and piano, jazz, percussion and electronic music and Indigenous performers. Artists included the Song Company; pianists Daniel Herscovitch and Julia Adams; Alan Dargin (didjeridu); the Dale Barlow trio; Ashok Roy (Indian sarod); B'ttuta percussion; Alpha Centauri (contemporary art music); and Judy Bailey and Sandy Evans (Jazz).

We seamlessly integrated music with the Faculty of Visual and Performing Arts. Students in Theatre and Dance were keen to collaborate with us. I had the pleasure of participating in a ceremony to turn the first sod for the new Centre for Contemporary Performance. This was a $7 million investment for UWS Nepean and a major development for Penrith. It opened in February 1998. We built 5,200 square metres of floor space to house 250 staff and students. There was a key performance area for 300 people plus a black box theatre. There were studios with sprung floors and mirrors, many office spaces, a box office, technical workshops, storage for costumes and props, tutorial rooms, computer lab, physiotherapy room and an outdoor performance space. This was Stage One. The second stage was planned to be ready in 2002, to house music and electronic arts.

Looking back, 1993 to 1999 were the halcyon years for the development of the Music Department. I am pleased to see that many of our students now have high-profile careers: vocalist Phil Burton, who has a brilliant ear for harmony and contemporary music styles, is a founding member of the internationally renowned vocal group Human Nature. Sarah Williams went on to study conducting in Russia and is the artistic director of the Metropolitan Symphony Orchestra. And Amanda Brown, who came to us after a successful career in the Go-Betweens, has become a leading screen composer.

The Golden Stave Music Therapy Centre

My vision for the new School of Communication Arts (SOCA) included the establishment of a music therapy course. I argued a case drawn from my Rivendell experience that a clinical referral and teaching centre would be ideal in Western Sydney. I believed then, and still do, that musicians have much to offer above and beyond concerts in enhancing the wellbeing of the community. Only witness the response musicians made during the onset of the Covid-19 pandemic in 2020.

However, back in the 1990s, it was an arduous process for me to capture my colleagues' interest in music therapy. The university's Academic Board needed to understand and appreciate the significance of music therapy as a means of combining creative music and clinical practices, especially from psychology. I had to demonstrate that the clinical placement of therapists and one-on-one supervision were essential components of effective training. One professor said dismissively that what I proposed was typical of a 'school of singing and dancing'. Undeterred, I pressed on. Suddenly, an opportunity to make a bigger splash fell into my lap.

An organisation called Nordoff-Robbins Music Therapy approached me soon after I was appointed the inaugural head of the newly formed School of Communication Arts. I met music therapist Robin Howat and Nick Hampton, the chair of the Nordoff-Robbins Board. They needed a new home and had money to put on the table. It was a substantial sum generated by the Golden Stave Foundation; a charity funded by several successful rock musicians. Together we would build a teaching centre offering a Master of Clinical Music Therapy. There would be a music therapy clinic and we would take referrals from the local community for group and individual sessions. Following initial elation at the opportunity to increase the university's community engagement, I became frustrated with the delays in securing the partnership. Month after month, I pestered the senior managers close to the vice-chancellor but was met with

'We'll look into it'. This confirmed for me that since the recent university restructures, professors were now readily referred to as Level E appointments rather than the professoriate which helped to guide the direction of the university. 'Bean counters' ruled the show.

Neoliberal control was the new normal. The controlling elite inhabited a bunker-like concrete building on the Werrington campus. I saw it as an impenetrable grey citadel. And I was reminded of an acronym from Geoff Scott, a professor of education. He once described someone as a POPO – someone who is 'pissed on and passed over'! Something that happens in the politics of a fast-growing new university such as mine. Had I become a POPO? Possibly.

Anyway, Nick and Robin were increasingly restless. All I could do was to reassure them that I had got the degree title and its units of study through the Academic Board. The Australian Music Therapy Association had endorsed the quality and values of the course. And SOCA, my faculty, was happy that small enrolments would not impose on its budget.

Knowing that Nick and Nordoff-Robbins were close to withdrawing their offer, I played a wild card. I informed the vice-chancellor and the director of finance that Golden Stave was about to re-direct their funding to the University of Technology, Sydney (UTS) within a week, unless UWS acted. Surprise! I received a phone call from the director of finance to say a memorandum of understanding between the university, Nordoff-Robbins and Golden Stave was ready for signatures and that an architect would be appointed immediately. I called Nick and Robin. They were both ecstatic and relieved. I didn't hold back about my feelings of frustration with my university's intransigence. It was like shifting a grand piano one leg at a time.

In 2001 we realised our dream, the opening of The Golden Stave Music Therapy Centre. I was thrilled that Marie Bashir became its patron and opened the Centre in her capacity as Her Excellency, the Governor of NSW. It was a celebration, one that the university management lapped up. My speech, to an audience of benefactors, academics, arts organisations, and members of the community, reflected upon the initial indifference to what has since become a well-established clinical and teaching facility on the Penrith campus and a catalyst for a research culture and a major service to the community. I went on to supervise four successful PhD students and sought scholarships and philanthropic funding from iconic Sydney organisations, including J. Albert and Sons and the Sydney Mechanics School of the Arts. I encouraged clinical psychologists to join me on panels supervising higher degree candidates and pointed music technologists towards devising interactive electronic tools for creative music therapy.

At a celebration for our ten years of operation, I asserted that the establishment of the partnership was a significant milestone in the university's commitment to community engagement. We joined forces with Nordoff-Robbins in November 2001 to create Australia's first purpose-built music therapy facility. Today, it continues to provide an invaluable service and has an enormous impact on the local community – exemplary music therapy services and the training of music therapists to the highest international standards.

Practice and research

The expectations of a professorial chair in an Australian university are that one is a research expert, a leader who implements the nexus between research and teaching, and a senior manager and entrepreneur competing for and administering funds. For me, this always meant balancing the above with my creative practices. Ernest Boyer's model of scholarship influenced my credo as a professor. Boyer described four overlapping functions for the work of a professor as 'the scholarship of discovery; the scholarship of integration; the scholarship of application; and the scholarship of teaching'. As an artist-scholar, I valued research that grew out of community engagement and research that drove teaching.

A concert at the Opera House

In January 1995, I embraced a role I never contemplated when I was a fifteen-year-old, plinking on a guitar in Bunnerong Migrant Hostel. I was a soloist in a classical music concert at the Sydney Opera House. The carpets had faded in the Green Room, and the furniture creaked from twenty years of use. I walked through the maze of post-Utzon mish-mash corridors leading to the backstage of the concert hall. I found the musicians' mustering station, a narrow room with an old television monitor and a tangle of chairs. It's an in-between place, where the sound of instruments competes with the rumble of the air conditioning spreading the unavoidable aromas of the kitchen and cafeteria.

I looked for space among the random spread of violin, viola and cello cases on fold-up tables. Some were closed; some were open, soft cleaning cloths draped over the instruments. Others were showing spare strings and the odd postcard tucked into the linings. The wall TV monitor showed the orchestra rehearsing on stage, taking advice from the conductor. There was a chair waiting for me next to the conductor.

I sat down and unlocked my case. How would these musicians receive what I was about to share with them – the absurdly wonderful proportions of an eighteenth-century hurdy-gurdy? What mechanical tyranny could challenge the hegemony of a string orchestra made up of a long tradition of crafted and acoustically honed violins, violas, cellos and contrabasses? Would they regard it as effrontery that I take a soloist's role with my lute-backed conglomeration of drones and clattering keys, fretting the gut strings as I turn a crank handle to play a tune? Surely, a heretical inclusion? Nothing more than the sound of a bagpiper crossed with the raw energy of a pub folk fiddler.

I tuned up, ready to walk onto the stage to rehearse with the orchestra. I was now 'Der Leyerer', the hurdy-gurdy player as stated in the music. It was my first solo engagement with an orchestra.

The concert featured *German dance* in C (K 602 No3) and *Menuet* in C (K 601 No2). Mozart composed these light pieces for a carnival ball in 1791 while he held the position of 'Kammermusicus' – the chief composer at the court of Emperor Joseph II. He scored the music for full orchestra. The hurdy-gurdy plays in the 'trio' sections.

Members of the orchestra looked intrigued as I adjusted the strap on the hurdy-gurdy that went around my back. They had neither seen nor heard such a mechanical contraption. I was nervous but trusted the conductor, Maestro Georg Tintner. He was a lovely man. He memorised every piece he conducted and kept a mini-study score at hand. Georg introduced me to the orchestral players and invited me to say a few words about my instrument. I explained it was an eighteenth-century form of the instrument, exquisitely handcrafted by luthier Charles Moller at his workshop in Marrickville, NSW. Beautiful Australian timbers, including Tasmanian blackwood and Huon pine, were used to make my instrument, which also included metalwork for the crankshaft handle and tuning pins. Over five hundred pieces went into making the hurdy-gurdy.

Seated and ready to play, I felt my nervousness diminish as I looked out at the 2,000 empty seats. Now, it was up to me to revel in this opportunity and show the audience that Mozart included the sounds of a hurdy-gurdy to satisfy his curiosity about a rustic instrument that once had a place both in the village and in the court.

Maestro Tintner raised his baton and reminded the orchestra to play softly for my entry. I counted an 8-bar rest in my part and turned the handle. The rosined wheel created friction on the strings. I pressed the keys, and the instrument came alive in melody, as I depressed its keys to fret the *chanterelles* or melody strings. The four sympathetic strings vibrated in response. The balance was perfect, and the conductor smiled and asked me if I wanted to run it again. I accepted his offer, because I wanted to extend the bliss of playing with an orchestra, as well as becoming fully prepared for the concert in the evening.

When I came on stage at 8:30 pm for my item in the concert, there was a full house waiting in anticipation. I could hear the audience murmur as I bowed to them and strapped this unique instrument to my waist before looking at the maestro to show my readiness.

We performed just as we had done in the rehearsal. Both the tempo and balance were perfect. But the two dances were all over too quickly. I wanted more. The audience clapped thunderously. I bowed. Maestro Tintner shook my hand. I strode off the stage, euphoric and probably the first and only person to play music with an orchestra on an Australian-made hurdy-gurdy copied from an eighteenth-century instrument in a European museum. It was a privilege to work with a string orchestra comprising the finest players available.

Writing

Following on from *Australian Made, Australian Played* and ongoing experimentation with different instruments, one major focus in my research and writing has been to explore and publicise the quality and innovation in Australian musical instrument making. I produced a range of publications on musical instruments, along with information on intercultural music and knowledge about performance practices. There were articles for *The Oxford Companion to Australian Music* (1997), The *New Grove Dictionary of Music* (2001), and the Currency Press *Companion to Music and Dance in Australia* (2003).

Take harp building, as an example. Here, advances have also remained hidden. The harp occurs in many guises and musical genres: Hugh Jones used NASA technology to develop a new model concert harp; Ros Bandt created a giant aeolian desert harp for Lake Mungo, and Stuart Favilla perfected an electroacoustic laser harp. As a result, I could see that Australian innovation and ingenuity about instrument making was often unrecognised by the public. In my research, therefore, I sought to open a window on the excellent

Australian products available and thus encourage further scholarship, practice and industry. It is for all these reasons that I approached the Australian Music Centre to devote an issue of the *Sounds Australian* journal to instrument building – *Sounds Unlimited: building the instruments* (2003). I thought it would help foster the development of resources for researching this activity, as well as promote links and networks. I hoped this issue would encourage investment in our instrument builders for the sake of their livelihood and the proliferation of new sounds. The issue focused on hybridity, diversity and future directions, leading to the emergence of virtual software instruments.

One thing that is slow to change is public awareness and acceptance of locally made anything. And music is no exception to the rule. We pit innovation and persistence against a cultural cringe. I can think of lamentable instances of our music institutions spending public money on imported instruments, buying in 'a name' at the expense of supporting internationally renowned local builders. Such is the case in the building of pianos and harpsichords. For example, two piano builders, Stuart & Sons and Ron Overs, are producing superb, technologically advanced instruments, audaciously competing with the Steinway company. Both Stuart and Overs must compete with the cringe and the high costs of small manufacturing.

My residency in 1993 at the Australian Museum had brought me into contact with a copious amount of data on Oceanic musical practices. This included Indigenous Australia (Aboriginal and Torres Strait Islander communities), Southeast Asia, the Pacific Islands and Africa. I submitted a report to the museum that reclassified the collections. There were many anomalies, including incorrectly named and ascribed instruments and objects that were lost.

I found instruments that were never catalogued and noted that some had gone missing. In addition to my report, I wanted to publish a book to benefit scholars and the public. The museum's director at the time was Des Griffin, an excellent leader and spokesperson. And there was Dr Jim Specht, head of the Anthropology Division, an excellent scholar and mentor. Both Des and Jim were unstintingly supportive of my research. However, when Des left, I could not secure any interest in a publishing proposal for a book on the musical instrument collections. Even the museum shop was indifferent to selling copies when my book was released. This was, I heard, symptomatic of a decline in the priorities of science in favour of getting more people through the turnstiles for entertainment activities.

The Swiss company Peter Lang International published the book in 2010. I called it *Musical Instruments and Sound-Producing Objects of Oceania* (2010) and acknowledged the Australian Museum for its collections. A small subvention from my university helped to offset the cost of editing and layout.

I believe my book contributed to an exposition of the Australian Museum's hitherto unknown musical instrument collection. I classified the instruments using principles of organology and added notes on cultural matters. The book included the regions of Oceania: Indigenous Australia, Melanesia, Micronesia, and Polynesia.

The creative reconstruction of lost music

In 1998, during a three-month fellowship in the Anthropology Department at the Australian Museum, I turned my attention to an imagined reconstruction of the ancient music of Egypt and Greece.

I was working on the Pacific music collection. Carolyn MacLulich, the museum's Head of Education, asked for advice on where to buy recordings of ancient Egyptian music. She wanted recordings for 'Life and Death in the Age of the Pharaohs', an exhibition that was coming to the Australian Museum from the National Museum of Antiquities in Leiden, Holland.

Carolyn caught me off guard while I was ensconced in my work, examining Polynesian artefacts in the dark recesses of the museum's stores. I told her there were no authentic recordings because there were no examples of musical notation from ancient Egypt. I urged her not to resort to CDs of Arabic night club music because it was a typical Hollywood anachronism. She left looking perplexed.

Thinking over her question later that night, I asked myself whether I might take up the challenge of composing something for the exhibition. I apologised the following day for not being able to help her. I asked her to tell me more about the exhibition and promised to evaluate a possible creative reconstruction of imagined ancient Egyptian music to play in the exhibition space.

Since there is little known about the music of ancient Egypt and no surviving music notation, or any specific theory about pitch, rhythm, and timbre, I sought answers by examining photos of instruments housed in museums, along with iconography and literary evidence.

The first stage of the project began with a response to the contents of the exhibition, followed by a delving into the ever-increasing output of Egyptological scholarship. A broader musical context had to be established. The big questions loomed large: What did the music sound like? How were the instruments tuned? Was the music polyphonic? The answers were elusive, mainly gleaned from the few instruments housed in museums. There is no surviving music notation or any musical theory which might instruct one about pitch, rhythm, and timbre. It required conjecture and deduction, using the literary and visual record with an examination of surviving instruments.

Combinations of instruments and ensembles appear to be depicted on stelae – stone, wood or plaster tablets with inscriptions, reliefs, or paintings. Many visual representations of music and musicians helped me to distinguish between the role of music in the temple or the fields, between the banquet and the funerary ritual, between the harvest and the public spectacle, between the contemplation and celebration of the Pharaohs and their gods.

I approached the composition and performance of the music by drawing on my experience playing medieval monophony, as well as eastern European and Turkish folk music. This background figured in my realisations, as well as my continuing research into the making and provenance of instruments throughout the world.

Further clues and inspiration came from the outstanding scholarship of Danish Egyptologist Dr Lise Manniche, whose book *Music and Musicians in Ancient Egypt*, (London: 1991) includes many line drawings of players and their instruments. Manniche said:

> The careful examination of all the material by scholars and experts in a variety of fields, evaluating the evidence and considering its implications, offers us the only hope that the music of the ancient Egyptians can sound again, if in our imagination alone. [p. 133]

These words underscored my challenge: to make some interesting sounds. I consulted Mary Demovic, an Egyptologist from Macquarie University. She helped me to translate hieroglyphs and to pronounce the Middle Kingdom Egyptian language in the poetry that I wanted to turn into songs and chants. Following the success of the exhibition, I produced a CD recording, *Ankh: The Sound of Ancient Egypt* (1998).

To get instruments for the project, I went to see my friend Harry Vatiliotis, a leading Australian luthier, who made me some ancient Greek instruments. He is Australia's most prolific violinmaker, having made over 800 violins, violas and cellos.

We had become friends when I was researching Australian instrument makers for my book *Australian Made, Australian Played*. Harry generously offered to lend me the instruments I needed for my project. These included the *sambuca* (boat-shaped harp), the *trigonon* (angle harp), the *kithara* (lyre), and the *auloi* (double-reed pipes).

There are surviving Tutankhamun-period trumpets in the Egyptian Museum, Cairo. To approximate one of these, I adapted a large Thai shawm. I closed off the finger holes and carved a wooden mouthpiece from the body itself. For *sistra*, I used bronze discs and metal rods adapted from Indian rattles. I set them in a light wooden frame, to allow metal shimmering sounds to dominate. For *crotala*, I used pairs of Turkish *zils*, attaching them to handles as seen in instruments in the British Museum.

Recreating the sounds of the ancient Egyptian long lute, came from my looking at the *tidinit* of Mauritania and the Chinese *sanxian* (three-stringed lute). Both have membrane tops. However, I chose the rewap that I brought home from Ürümqi, western China. This instrument has a small bowl-shaped body with a membrane top. I replaced its wire strings with gut and plucked them with a 6×4–centimetre wooden plectrum.

For percussion instruments, I used a *riq*, a modern Egyptian tambourine, as well as the Morrocan *bendir*. But my use of the *udongo*, a clay pot drum from Nigeria, was highly conjectural. I surmised that beating rhythms on clay objects was a likely feature of dance music and a precursor of the modern goblet drum, the darbuka. As a percussionist, I've always been a magpie musician, utilising any available material to make sounds. Therefore, I chose the udongo for timbral variety.

I decided to restrict melodic material to five-, six-, and seven-note scales drawing on the modes of Moroccan *ramal mai* and Persian *afshari*. I looked at numbers of strings and their lengths on ancient harps, lutes, and lyres, relating this information to recent Middle Eastern and North African folk music.

Melodies moved in small steps. I set the 'Hymn to Osiris' and the 'Hymn to Aten' monophonically, including 'call and response' development. Sung items suggested interpolated recitations, to acknowledge a deep connection between language and music.

I invited my friends Mina Kanaridis (vocals) and Philip South (percussion) to record the music with me in the studio at Western

Sydney University. Mina's voice worked perfectly, and Philip played most of the hand percussion, adding a superb improvisational element. Recording on campus, I could add a small group of students to form a chorus for the hymns. I played all the string and wind instruments, including blasts on my Tutankhamun trumpet.

I completed the composition and recording of the music just four weeks before the opening of the exhibition and could negotiate the release of a CD for sale. *Ankh: the Sound of Ancient Egypt* is a favourite creative work because I was on fire racing the clock to complete it in time.

With an ancient Greek trigon (angle harp) by
Harry Vatiliotis, 1998.
Photo: Stuart Humphreys

10

COLLABORATING AND DISCOVERING

Leaving only bubbles in the wake.

There are several pathways open to a musician who internalises another musical culture. You abandon your original viewpoint and attempt to 'lose yourself' in a new place. Or, as in my case, you can develop a personal ecology. I allowed what I discovered to work through osmosis, seeking to interpret cultures without negating the sources, rather than creating a cultural mélange. Of course, this invites questions about the ethics of borrowing and appropriation. As someone curious about playing non-Western instruments, I was always aware of sensitivities about ownership, cultural knowledge, and the importance of respect. As a musical explorer, a process built on equal collaboration and common purpose has underpinned my output, especially in producing and performing recording projects.

Lyrebird

In 1996, Black Sun Records (USA) invited me to produce an album featuring the didjeridu. I suggested we work with Matthew Doyle. Matthew (b.1969) is of Aboriginal and Irish-Australian descent. He is a descendant on his mother's side from the Muruwari people of the Lightning Ridge area of NSW and has been adopted into traditional families in the Northern Territory and Queensland. He grew up in Southern Sydney on Dharawal land.

We agreed to explore a range of didjeridus selected for their varying timbral possibilities and their different pitches. Each instrument had a special space in Matthew's music according to where or from whom he obtained the instrument. They were part of his lived experience of people and place.

Matthew shared with me his knowledge regarding the lyrebird, or wirid-jiribin as it is known in the Dharawal language. This bird is shy and elusive, living most of its life on the ground, having relatively limited flying capabilities. Male and female birds have brownish body feathers. The male has a magnificent tail that averages around a metre in length. Wirid-jiribin is famous for mimicry and for the male bird's courtship dance in which he throws his tail feathers over his head and body to produce a shimmering cascade of enticing silvery hues. In the upright position, the two outer curved tail feathers resemble the shape of a lyre, hence its European name.

Being a totem of the Dharawal people of the Sydney Basin, wirid-jiribin mimics all other birds. It follows, said Matthew, that 'the Dharawal people were permitted by custom to speak languages of other Indigenous people up and down the coast of New South Wales.' There were multiple meanings of wirid-jiribin, and I suggested we include Matthew singing about it. There would be a shared ecology between the avian and the anthropoid in the lyrebird as a living totem of the Dharawal people. I made location recordings of lyrebirds in the Blue Mountains, NSW, and we improvised together on several occasions to explore patterns and combinations of percussion. I composed and performed accompaniments on tuned and non-tuned percussion instruments.

The titles for the CD tracks reveal the ecology of the project: Number 4, *Hand Stencils*, was composed for didjeridu, bass drum, roto toms, temple blocks, and panpipe. It recalls the process of grinding and preparing ochres in liquid form. The artist uses their mouth to spray the liquid ochre onto a rock while using the hands as stencils. Number 5, *Wirid-jiribin: the first lyrebird*, was composed by Matthew and accompanied by clapsticks. It is made from fragments of a language no longer spoken. It describes how the first lyrebird was created. The words 'wirid-djiribin naway illabuka merlay uri ga Dharawal' translate as 'the spirit lives forever with the Dharawal people.'

The *Lyrebird* CD epitomised intercultural collaboration in the pursuit of a different aesthetic from most other didjeridu recordings. Within a broader cultural context, it points towards a 'Koori-wadjila' or 'blackfella-whitefella' shared future. The record company gave us the freedom to collaborate on the recording. While we were grateful for its support, the company let us down with the cover. The simulation of traditional dot painting conjured by a computer graphics program was kitsch. The opportunity for an Indigenous illustrator was ignored. Further, we wanted the Dharawal word, wirid-jiribin, to feature on the cover. But the executive producer stubbornly refused, insisting that 'lyrebird' would be more recognisable in the US marketplace. The full name is a mouthful: *Matthew Doyle – Lyrebird: collages for didjeridu and percussion inspired by the rare Australian bird, produced by and featuring Michael Atherton.*

On the other hand, I was pleased with the recording as the first project in the new studios at Western Sydney University. Here, we could experiment at leisure with microphones, editing and mixing.

Women dreaming

In January 1998, I was at Darwin airport waiting for Tiwi Air Flight 231 to Nguiu on Bathurst Island, having just flown from Sydney. My companions were Mathew Doyle, didjeridu player and dancer, already mentioned, and John Wregg, a librettist who used to work for Opera Australia. We were going to meet Tiwi elders to begin a music theatre collaboration.

The trip was short. We reached the island in thirty minutes and flew over a mangrove-fringed beach with estuaries and dense forest. I saw the windsock hanging limply near the narrow strip at Nguiu. It was oppressively hot on the tarmac as we helped unpack the plane and waited next to the only buildings. Both were toilet blocks on the other side of the fence, for males and females and superbly decorated with Tiwi stories covering the brickwork.

A representative of Tiwi Designs collected us in a ute and drove us past modest, iron-roofed dwellings adorned with little verandas made from timber. After dropping off our gear at a house that was made available to us for a week, we were taken to the main meeting place – a blockhouse in a compound attached to a football oval. There was a sign on the fence saying *No cheques, no credit, no food, no dogs, no spitting*. The club was the only place serving a drink in Nguiu. It opened between 3 pm and 7 pm each day, except Sunday. A glass of beer cost $3 and you had to purchase a ticket at a counter near the bar. The beer was served in plastic cups.

There was a crowd of mostly men inside, talking loudly, laughing, shouting, moving around and sloshing beer here and there. Their bright eyes glinted against their black faces; some were toothless; some were grey, some were young. Outside there was a stage and over the next couple of hours musicians got up to sing. On the field, kids played Aussie Rules. They were so happy and spirited, running free, with limited physical contact. It was a joy to watch their flowing style.

We met Marcus Puruntatemeri, the head of the Tiwi Island Land

Council. He was talking with a man nicknamed 'Foxy', who was non-Indigenous and married to a Tiwi woman. They had three children. Foxy also looked after two people with disabilities and was much admired by his Tiwi mates. They liked to sit on their verandas, or under a shade tree, playing poker and gin rummy. Their games might last all day until the club opened, because very few people had jobs. The women played too but in their own groups, sitting on blue tarpaulins while their children wandered around, and the dogs lay exhausted nearby on the ground. Foxy told me:

> This is it. I have everything. I love these people. And my dog, too. He's a Sheffield Pointer. If someone offered me $5,000, I wouldn't part with him for anything. This is it. It's all I need. I'm happy, what about you?

Before we could answer, we were surrounded by locals coming to check us out. We must have looked like a motley crew – John in his khaki shorts and black hat, looking every bit like a farmer. Matthew, head shaved, with his Irish-Australian and Indigenous looks and complexion, very relaxed and at home here; and me, tall, greying beard, with notebook and camera.

I explained that our reason for coming to the island included learning about Pukumani and the Kurlama ceremony. Then someone called Tim came over to show us his paintings. I bought one for a modest price to give to my in-laws. Foxy loaned me the money because I had nothing in my pocket at the time. I had only met him twenty minutes earlier and he told me not to worry, 'You'll give it back to me.' And I did, the very next day.

We met Clementine Kantilla, Matthew's 'aunty' by cultural adoption. We met her brother Simon Kantilla, whom Matthew called 'uncle'. Simon and Clementine taught Matthew songs and dances when they were hosted at NAISDA, the National Aboriginal and Islander Skills Development Association. Both were very keen to go to Sydney again to perform collaborative work with us. That was part of our plan to have them inform a new work for Music Theatre Sydney, produced by its performing arts manager, Justin MacDonnell.

At 7 pm a siren sounded. It was a shrill, threatening sound to warn the locals to leave the club and go home. This siren was the first warning. It sounded again fifteen minutes later. Time to leave or be pushed out.

We left with Clementine. It was almost dark, and she urged us to sit down by the side of the road rather than walk back to our accommodation. We should wait for the 'patrolling car' to pick us up. This was a community-provided service to ensure inebriated people got home safely. We waited for half an hour for a minibus to arrive. As there were no restaurants or food outlets, we went back to the house and found a few basics to make ourselves pasta to satisfy the hunger brought on by a few beers on an empty stomach. I crashed on the sofa and didn't even make it to my room.

Clementine came to the house the next morning. She wore a blue dress and clutched a handbag by her side. No one knew her age. She was probably in her seventies. But she was fit, feisty and proud. 'You make music. I make a song today,' she said, and produced a crumpled piece of paper from her bag, on which she had written the words of 'Ranku Plantation'. It was a song about her working life on the island, together with other old women. Clementine said, 'I'm a culture-woman.' I offered to notate her song and give her a copy to show her friends.

We met her again at the club later that afternoon. She introduced me to her co-worker, Lindy, a strong, muscle-bound, non-Indigenous woman. She barely spoke. She just looked around and waved now and again. I took out my notebook. I listened to Clementine singing her song and I notated it. Simon came over and invited me to meet other Tiwi people, but Clementine occasionally called me over to hear me recite her words. Each time she took out the paper from her pocket, it became more creased and limp in the 35-degree-Celsius heat.

Clementine wanted to sing her song and approached one of the band to lend me a guitar. But her touching a guitar angered one of the men, who ordered her to put it down immediately. She replied with a barrage of expletives. It seemed okay for men to pick up and play the guitar but not Clementine. I hoped it wasn't my presence that contributed to the situation.

During the confrontation, an old man was wandering around the club with a cattle prod. Simon said he would give a person an electric shock as if to say, 'Look, I don't like what you're doing.' That was enough for us. We left quietly, not wanting to draw any more attention to ourselves and risk undermining our reason for being in Nguiu. We knew that the Land Council could revoke our permits and ask us to catch the next plane back to Darwin.

The following evening it seemed that the level of intoxication was higher than the two days before. The siren sounded three times, and longer. It must have been the football. Four young men in Aussie Rules shirts arrived and were rolling about on each other. It was a scene of absolute unbridled joy as these young men came in to tell the drinking crowd, and their coach, that they were celebrating a football victory on Melville Island. The rivalry between the Tiwi Islands of Bathurst and Melville was as intense as the State of Origin League between Queensland and NSW.

Three days into our tour the mood in Nguiu changed. Clementine couldn't visit us anymore. Her brother was ill. Not far from our house, there was a roughly built shelter made from slender tree trunks and branches and covered with palms and bark. It was next to a small house. An old man was in his bed under the shelter. There were family groups around him, some on the veranda, and some in close attendance with him. He was dying and the process was a community event. I noticed that different groups of people visited the shelter throughout the day.

Clementine came to our house two days later to tell us her brother had passed away. I was unable to ascertain whether this was an immediate brother or, in the traditional Aboriginal sense, a member of her cultural family. She told us there would be a Requiem Mass at 5:30 pm in the Recreation Hall and it would be okay to attend.

A storm had come up just as John and I were about to leave the house. We paused on the veranda and watched the birds gathering nectar in the hibiscus flowers. As the storm settled, we walked into town towards the restaurant, going past the Kurlama site behind some of the houses. We walked past the old man's house. Many people were beginning to gather there. We walked on towards the beach to watch some people fishing.

When we came back, we saw a large gathering, which included Simon, all moving towards the general store. Simon appeared and told us they were here to smoke the restaurant because the 'old fella went in there a lot'. Green leaves, the same type of leaves used in the dance ceremony, were piled outside the restaurant and lit with dry tinder to create smoke. They were transferred into two tins and carried into the restaurant: the closest family moving in first while singing. After a few minutes, people came out and then made their way back to smoke the old man's house and the shelter as well. They went on to smoke the club and I could hear the crying of the grieving women. While all this happened, kids continued to play just outside. Dogs followed them around and people smoked cigarettes. I noticed that different groups of women sat on the roadside near the restaurant, smoking, observing and, just like ourselves, keeping a respectful distance.

The Recreation Hall was a large tin shed. It could have been a large barn on a country farm. There were a hundred people inside. Father Leo and two young men dressed in starched white cassocks were standing near a makeshift altar.

The Catholic service was interspersed with Tiwi singing accompanied by Clementine playing guitar. The old man's body was lying on a wooden table draped in a shroud. A makeshift altar had been bedecked with the paraphernalia for a Requiem Mass. The immediate family sat in a tight circle around the old man, and you could see the impression of his face, and his feet pointing to the ceiling, as he lay under the shroud. Father Leo and the other Catholic participating brother were both relatives, and they sat nearby. One of the altar boys dipped the green leaves in water and anointed the people around the hall. I noticed that people were in groupings of men or women or young men. It suggested family relations, clans and subgroups. During one song, the women all stood to dance near the deceased.

The younger men were, as ever, in their football shorts, whereas the older men wore T-shirts, some with Tiwi designs, others with slogans, and some sporting Bob Marley designs. The women also wore T-shirts, with skirts and some with wrap-arounds. Girls wore shorts and T-shirts, and the toddlers were either naked or in disposable nappies. I noticed the old man's friends were coming and going, bathed in the tropical evening light that was shining through the entrance to the hall. There were openings on all sides to let out the heat. I looked out and saw the trees silhouetted against the sky, which still held a few clouds.

As 'sorry business' continued, the children ran around, playing with abandon. Only when they bounced basketballs and rode their bikes, did some parents intervene and ask them to be calm. Father Leo continued with the service, his words contrasting with hymns sung in Tiwi.

Sometimes mourners clapped in time and cried out in grief. Meanwhile, dogs, which have the same status as cows in India, lay panting heavily on the warm concrete floor. It was oppressively hot, and people drank water from old coke and lemonade bottles. I noticed Simon moving around uneasily. He was a man of the old ways; concerned more with Tiwi traditions, rather than the rituals of the Catholic Church which were taking place. He had a rod in his hand that may have been a subordinate's spear. At the end of the service, Father Leo invited the gathering to comfort each other, and for those on the perimeter, to greet the mourners.

With the Mass over, the immediate family were to stay with the deceased overnight until the burial at the graveyard the next morning, a proceeding that would last a long time. All of his belongings and clothes would be burned after he was finally laid to rest.

Attendance at the actual gravesite the next morning was only for family. But we were able to observe from a distance. I could see Pukamani poles interspersed with gravestones. It was raining as the interment ceremony commenced and the 'sorry business' was conducted in Tiwi.

The following day, Simon introduced us to John Baptist, a storyteller. He told us about bloodlines and family relationships and presented us with anecdotes about the animals. Through Simon, we asked John Baptist and his friends to show us a dancing ceremony at a sacred site in the bush. We borrowed a four-wheel-drive vehicle belonging to the Tiwi Land Council chairman, who was going to Darwin for the day. We dropped him at the airport and went to collect Simon, his son Walter, and friends Iglio and Cisco waiting for us in another vehicle.

We drove off-road to the beach at Tarntipi. Simon collected a few small rocks lying in the sand and ground them in a corned beef tin, adding just the right amount of water. The men chatted and rolled cigarettes. They stripped to paint themselves for the ceremony, Matthew, too, while John and I sheltered under a tree. I watched Iglio take a small bunch of leaves and dip them in white ochre. He applied the paint to his body by dabbing himself with the leaves.

While we waited for the paint to dry, we drove to a burial ground. We had to walk into the spot, which was a small clearing in the dense bush. There was a mound covered in flowers. On top, there was a blue tarpaulin with a cross with the name of the deceased person inscribed on it. Around this stood intricately decorated Pukamani poles celebrating the deceased. Simon and the others, including Matthew, gathered leaves away from the site. They put these leaves on a small area of the ground, placing them between where they would dance and the graves. These were for the smoking ritual as there was a deceased person buried there. One of the men produced a cigarette lighter and lit the leaves, which began to smoke. This was to show respect and appease restless spirits.

This done, Simon led the Pukamani song and dance. The men carried spears and wore armbands. During the dance, they kept calling out the names of ancestral beings. I was encouraged to film them as research for the musical. Despite the sound of insects in the foreground of the recording, I managed to record valuable material. Each dance was a short representation of a buffalo, a dugong, a mullet, a pelican and a crocodile. After this business was done, we packed up and headed to a nearby waterhole for the dancers to wash their ochre off and for all of us to take a cooling dip.

For me, the culmination of our visit to Bathurst Island was when Simon showed us the Kurlama ceremony site in the centre of Nguiu. It takes two days and three nights to enact. He described how he would draw a circle on the ground and clear the area. The ceremony was led by women, and each family group was expected to sit in a designated place. Unfortunately, Simon's animated description of the Kurlama was tempered by his concern that young people were not dancing it anymore. He told us that there were only twenty people who knew how to lead it.

With only a day left, I met Clementine again, to tell her about a song I had learned from Ted Egan, the folk musician and bush poet living in Alice Springs. Ted called it the 'The Dugong Song'. Clementine told me it was a famous song made by Daniel Pautjimi from nearby Melville Island. She taught me the dance movements that go with the song.

I was keen to work on her song, 'Ranku Plantation'. Clementine wanted to sing it for Matthew's son Sean, who had tragically died because of leukaemia a few years earlier. Clementine confided to me that she and Simon had used bush medicine and magic to try and help Sean. They were in Nguiu. Sean was in the hospital in Sydney.

Tragically, Matthew and his wife Vicki lost two sons to this disease. I played in a memorial performance for Sean at the Belvoir Theatre. Happily, their third child was spared.

Our final meeting was to visit a linguist, Jenny Lee, who had lived on Bathurst for seven years. She lived in a demountable near the beach. Jenny was feeding two baby wallabies when we arrived. She had one in a towelling bag hanging from a door and another tucked down her jumper, which she wore on a hot day. The fans whirred incessantly overhead as she sat there feeding one of the wallabies from a small dripper. Her house was awash with papers and all sorts of paraphernalia. She told us that she took the wallabies in to save them because the mothers had been hunted. She tried to raise the babies and release them in the bush. Jenny was compiling a Tiwi dictionary to identify ancient and modern Tiwi language. She said the language was changing very quickly and it was becoming impoverished as a result. She was also translating the Gospel into Tiwi for church services and helping to produce cassette recordings and broadsheets for Tiwi hymns.

We went to the airstrip with our baggage and gifts for family and friends, purchased from Tiwi Design, loaded them into the Cessna and took off for Darwin. At 3,000 feet in our climb, I looked down on Tarntipi Beach where we had gone with the dancers to paint up for the ceremony. It was the end of an unforgettable experience so different from anything else in my life.

At times, I had felt like a foreigner. The Tiwi people seemed so far away and yet so close. I began to appreciate their independence as a nation. They were also different from mainland Aboriginal people that I knew. Sadly, their language, customs and rituals were changing rapidly through contact. It's galling to see how little recognition Tiwi people were given for their effort in World War II. They were the frontline defending Australia against the attempted Japanese invasion.

Kamawarah

The proclamation of the Commonwealth of Australia on 1 January 1901 brought the six Australian colonies together as a nation. It was a democratic process. Australia was the first nation that came into existence by a decision of its people, made freely and peacefully at the ballot box. Much has been achieved since the Federation, for example, votes were extended federally to women in 1903, although South Australia led the world in 1894 by granting women equal political rights with men. The first Australian-born governor-general came to office in 1931, and we recognised Indigenous Australians in the 1967 referendum. In the Mabo decision in 1992, the High Court of Australia decided that *terra nullius* should not have been applied to Australia. It recognised that Aboriginal and Torres Strait Islander peoples have rights to the land – rights that existed before Europeans arrived and can still exist today. We absorbed millions of post-war immigrants into the fabric of Australian life.

A major event to celebrate Federation was planned for Centennial Park in Sydney in January 2001. I was invited to compose the opening music as a 'grounding' to represent Indigenous and non-Indigenous Australians. I visited elders of the Aboriginal Land Council at La Perouse to seek their advice on Indigenous involvement. I met Rhoda Roberts, a Bundjalung woman from northern New South Wales, and asked her for help with finding a suitable text. Rhoda is a writer and actor and was artistic director for the Sydney Dreaming Festival.

I composed the music for orchestra, voice, didjeridu soloist, dancers and clapsticks. I featured the wonderful soprano, Yorta Yorta woman Debra Cheetham. She would sing in the Gadigal language of the Eora people, welcoming everyone to country:

'Talipani jeminga tali yudi tyelkala tali norar kamawarah gomul norar.'

I called the work *Kamawarah* to contextualise the settlement of Australia within the continuing culture of the Indigenous peoples. It also acknowledged that the Centennial Park area, situated as it is between Sydney harbour and the sweeping expanses of Botany Bay, was an important ceremonial site for local Indigenous communities. There would be a large group of dancers, a didjeridu player, Sean Choolburra, and the Australian Youth Orchestra directed by Lyn Williams.

At dusk on 1 January 2001, I sat in the audience on the grass and listened to the pre-recorded sound of thunder that introduced my piece. Rows of lights placed along the top of a ramped stage glowed bright red, their beams shining through the smoke from machines used to simulate the traditional smoking ceremony. My music commenced with sustained unison drones and clapsticks as the dancers appeared through the smoke. The orchestra gradually built up a lush texture until a solo harp accompanied by pizzicato strings introduced the beautiful soprano voice of Deborah Cheetham. She walked up from a tunnel at the back of the stage accompanied by dancers. The woodwinds joined her soaring voice, and the music reached a crescendo on her final note.

From this point, the music became a dance and ended with a repeating anthemic statement. As the music faded, Bob Carr, Premier of NSW, walked from the rear of the stage to give an official Federation speech. I don't think any politician has had a more dramatic entry. I found out when I met him again on a NSW state delegation to Korea, that he loved opera. I had given him a Wagnerian moment!

CD recordings: Abundance and Aurora

A collaboration from 2001 involved Jim Franklin. Jim is a master performer of the shakuhachi, as well as a trained composer and expert in live electronic music. Our collaboration focused mainly on the shakuhachi, guitars and percussion, eventually adding electronics. We recorded two CDs, *Abundance* (2001) and *Aurora* (2003).

In *Aurora*, music is an experiment in cultural interaction. Two of the instruments employed – shakuhachi and *koto* – derive from

Japan's traditional musical culture. These instruments interact with those from Western cultures including a dilapidated piano, some guitars, a marimba and a double bass. The notion of interaction permeates the combination of instruments in another way. In using instruments such as an ancient piece of bamboo alongside an old piano – a modern incarnation of one of the earliest harmonic instruments – the binding element becomes performance. This is so because all the sounds on the album were played rather than programmed and this choice was made to elicit the inner life of the tones through the liveness of their creation. Two of the pieces, 'Blue Globe Saltarello' and 'At the Rising of the Dawn', were recorded as improvisations in single takes and appear on the album with no editing.

In several respects, the music of *Abundance* (2001) and *Aurora* (2003) is sonic research, or an experiment, the outcomes of which are tested in sound. One aspect of the experiment is that of space and spatiality. Apart from the usual technical process whereby instruments are recorded in a relatively lifeless studio – artificially placed in a reverberant space – this work involves the placement of sounds in 'unusual' spaces. For example, in the composition titled 'Again the Stars,' an instrument was played while moving in the space surrounding it. Consequently, the swirling harmonics define a moving space surrounding the melodic shakuhachi that anchors the texture. Both albums offer enrichment of the source traditions on which they have been drawn: Western and Eastern music.

Jim and I also included performer-composer Tony Wheeler in our projects. Tony lived in China for a few years and studied Chinese classical music instruments including the *guqin* (a Chinese 7-stringed board zither) and the *ruan* (a 4-stringed, round Chinese guitar). The three of us composed and produced an intercultural exploration on a CD, *Nine Elemental Songs* (2006), blending our range of styles: from jazz to meditative pieces, sound sculptures, fixed compositions for the instruments, and improvisations. As it turned out, the instruments played on this album contained all eight 'elements' of ancient Chinese musical instrument classification: animal skin, gourd, bamboo, wood, silk, earth/clay, metal, and stone, with the addition, perhaps, of another element of ether, the 'element' of the electronic theremin.

A feature of our exploration was the period bridged by the instruments. At one end of the spectrum, the guqin has remained unchanged for 3,000 years. At the other end, a theremin is an early electronic instrument dating from the 1920s, used in one of its most recent incarnations, a Moog Etherwave Pro, 2004. Very old and new, acoustic and electronic, metaphorically rubbed shoulders with one another and sound worlds which at first would seem contradictory were revealed as closely overlapping and complementary. Again, unity and dialogue were created.

Change at UWS

The UWS music offerings moved from Bachelor with Honours to postgraduate and we began supervising PhD candidates. Music was flying, but in any university system, faculties are subject to the inevitability of change. UWS Nepean faced a political fight in the lead-up to the eventual amalgamation and expansion of the university members. One casualty of the process was Jillian Maling; She resigned in 1995.

Emeritus Professor Jillian Maling AM was at the University of Western Sydney Nepean for ten years. First, she was principal of the Nepean College of Advanced Education until 1988. She became deputy vice-chancellor and chief executive officer of UWS Nepean, one of the three members of the newly established university, in 1989. Hawkesbury Agricultural College and the Macarthur Institute of Higher Education became UWS Hawkesbury, and UWS Macarthur, respectively. Enrolments at UWS Nepean increased by 35 per cent under Jillian's leadership. She was building the profile of the university with industry, business and the community, and the residents of Western Sydney. Jillian counted Gough and Margaret Whitlam among her friends, as well as other Labor Party figures.

Jillian and some of her senior managers wanted to build on the success of UWS Nepean in teaching and research. It was eclipsing the other members. There was a move by UWS Nepean to secede from the federation and become a university. They put the name Chifley University forward. Jillian had crossed her Rubicon and was counting on Federal Labor to endorse her plan, but it wasn't to be. We were in an election year. Western Sydney is a large and volatile electorate. The other members of the federation objected to UWS Nepean's ambitions because they felt undermined by an action that might have turned them back into colleges of advanced education. Jillian had the support of the UWS Nepean Academic Board. But the circulation of this support to media prompted a special meeting of the Board of Trustees. The board and other powerful voices behind the scenes argued that she had breached their trust. They forced her to resign.

They drew me into the skirmish as one of Jillian's supporters. But I didn't get my wrists slapped, although a couple of professors were forced out. With Jillian gone, I worried about the future of the performing arts in UWS Nepean. However, the incumbent, Chris Duke, an advocate for deep engagement with local businesses and the community, was steadfast in his support. Things calmed down, but there was momentum to unite the members, to drop Nepean, Macarthur and Hawkesbury in favour of the University of Western Sydney.

The competition was always there between the members. When the restructure came, it was apparent that there were lots of duplications of courses, staff and infrastructure over the three members. It was a bloody time with many redundancies. Once the single university emerged with its six campuses and four colleges, there was another restructure. This time there was a move to dismantle colleges in favour of a flat structure – sixteen schools. I objected to the loss of being able to refer to the Music Department, to be known henceforth as the 'music area' within the School of Contemporary Arts. We might have become invisible. I responded tactically, arguing successfully to move the degree nomenclature from a Bachelor of Arts (Music) to a Bachelor of Music (BMus), which has more prestige. A BMus is a professional music degree and not an arts degree with a music major.

The year 1999 was another momentous year at the university. It was the culmination of a period of restructuring that began in 1996 and coincided with the election of the Howard Coalition government in Canberra. The Minister for Education, Amanda Vanstone, foreshadowed significant cuts in higher education expenditure and new user-pays and competitive funding arrangements. As we moved forward under the leadership of Janice Reid to become a unified rather than three-member university, older and more established universities asserted themselves as the lead institutions. They called themselves the Group of Eight (Sydney, UNSW, Melbourne, Monash, the Australian National University and the Universities of Queensland, Adelaide and Western Australia). We nicknamed them the 'sandstones'. This group was politically motivated to lobby the government for higher research funding at the expense of new universities such as mine, surely an outcome of the Howard government squeeze. It was widely known that the Group of Eight would have been happy to see new and regional universities be reclassified as teaching-only institutions, thus keeping them out of the research funding pool.

11

THE SCHOOL OF CONTEMPORARY ARTS

And then came the noise.

The late 1990s became an exhausting time for me. I was moving the department into a period of consolidation, and I continued, as I had done for seven years, to travel 130 kilometres a day.

It was also when Ros and I grew apart, finding it difficult to resolve differences. The demands of our academic careers, as well as a decline in my mental health, contributed to the situation. Depression was on the horizon and separation imminent. I might have sought help earlier rather than soldiering on like the high achiever who believes nothing is impossible.

We decided to sell our house and then divorce. So, in 2000, we moved into a rental property for six months while the house was on the market. I purchased a unit in Double Bay, close to the water's edge, and Ros bought a townhouse in Edgecliff. Emily and Marc went with her. Marc was thirteen, Emily almost nineteen. They came first in our arrangements. Marc agreed to board at Cranbrook School. Emily began studying psychology and music at Sydney University.

Moving towards separation and divorce was an emotionally raw time. I kept myself together by paddling a sea kayak in Sydney Harbour. Whenever possible, I tried to get home from UWS well before dusk. I would carry my sunburst-orange fibreglass kayak out of my garage in Wiston Gardens to drop into the water at Double Bay. A life jacket, a paddle and a bottle of water, and I'd take off alone, weaving through the moored yachts and out into the harbour. I have always liked to paddle in rivers and bays, including trips up the Nepean River from Tench Reserve, Jamisontown to Warragamba. The Nepean is a haven for fish and birds, with its unspoilt riverbanks, bends, and gorges. On Sydney Harbour I chose a different course each time, including going around Fort Denison, Clark Island, Shark Island and the destinations Watsons Bay, Chowder Bay and Clifton Gardens. Paddling was excellent therapy and exercise. The paddling rhythm helped me clear my head of the messiness of running a faculty amid a restructure. It eased my troubled mind as Ros and I dealt with separation following twenty-five years of marriage. Paddling, like music, could be transcendent. It inspired poetry.

Watsons Bay to Manly

Blade down,
Catch! Bubbles rise, arm draws the water,
pull to the release.
Blade up,
escaping its grip on the river.

The long glide,
my cadence in the poetry of paddling.
The rhythm of effort countering wind and wave,
exhilarating, cantering,
unaware yet fully aware.

Crossing the heads, contemplating
the unknown open sea,
a blue Pacific calling me siren-like,
and the foaming following seas
carrying me forward, edging,
running, left-right rudder
leaving only a bubbling wake.

Lane Cove River

My blade at sunrise carves a watery mirror,
spawning flecks of light in the bow waves
dancing past the sleek hull.

My thoughts glide in and out,
measured in mindfulness.
What lies ahead soon becomes wake,
bubbling eddies left behind.

Each bend rounded brings a new surprise:
a cormorant, a heron or a mullet jumping.

That said, poetry, therapists, and new surroundings couldn't assuage the feeling that I had failed my children. The months spent touring, the endless hours embroiled in the university responsibilities, and the politics of restructuring, dampened creativity in my life. The music became silent, replaced by the chatter as I tried to fall asleep at night, sometimes waking in a sweat trying to steer a car with no brake down a steep hill. But instead of conceding that I needed a rest, I jumped at a new role at the university, reinventing myself, not in name but in my job description.

Study leave, January 2001

Late in 2000, the position as Head of the School of Contemporary Arts was advertised. I applied reluctantly yet urged on by colleagues, including my friend David Hull, the former dean of the faculty. The restructure was protracted, and the future of Music's new facilities was under threat as someone rumoured that Stage Two of the Werrington Performing Arts building wasn't going ahead. I was desperate for personal academic study leave to research and write some music. Meanwhile, my application was successful, and I became the inaugural head of the new school. The university, however, appointed an acting head to enable me to take leave.

I went overseas in January 2001, stopping first in England to see relatives, before going to Sweden and Finland to meet composers, choral directors and educators. I met up with Catherine Kagan, who was overseas at the same time. Catherine was an educator involved in early childhood music programs at Macquarie University and the Sydney Conservatorium. We had once collaborated on sequences for the ABCs *Playschool* program. Our meeting up again revealed many shared interests. For example, we both worshipped Doreen Bridges, a doyen of music educators, and the peerless and wonderful Richard Gill. Catherine came to hear choirs singing my music and I accompanied her to teaching demonstrations with pre-school children.

In the minus 30 Celsius temperatures of Finland in January, it was inevitable that we decided to keep each other warm. I asked Catherine to meet my German aunt, Christa. We spent a lovely week in Stuttgart before visiting another aunt in Belfast.

It was Tilly, the wife of my long-departed and much-loved Uncle Arthur. Tilly lives in County Down, a quiet region of greater Belfast. We stayed with her for a week and reminisced about her life in Liverpool with Arthur and their visiting me in Cheshire.

From Tilly's, we travelled south to the University of Maynooth, in the Republic of Ireland, where I was heartily welcomed by the cohesive and collegial staff of its Department of Music. The dean secured me an office in Logic House, in the Maths corridor opposite Music. I offered to mentor a few senior students and advise on research supervision and curriculum development. I thrived in the small environment on a beautiful campus in Maynooth, a rural town in Kildare. It was the perfect respite for me after a seven-year unbroken stretch developing music at UWS and the department's integration into a faculty of performance and fine arts.

Catherine and I stayed in newly completed lodgings on the top floor of the seminary that shared the same grounds as the university. We soon discovered the delights of Ireland in Spring – pub sessions in Dublin and the joys of Guinness on warm twilit nights. I was moved to pen some verse:

Night bus to Maynooth

The old bus bucks and rattles.
We huddle into our seats
mellowed with endless Guinness,
celebrating my sabbatical.

Flanking us on the last ride from Dublin,
are comatose youth
lurching forwards in their seats,
numbed by substances and music
above the threshold of pain.

We alight at Maynooth
and shuffle in step,
across the railway bridge.
Chilled by the crisp air,
we crave the comfort of our bed.

Hushed beneath an autumn moon,
St Pat's steeple glows sharply
in contrast with the ghostly ruins
of the Norman keep.

Safely through the gate
and into the seminary grounds,
we drink the perfume of its rose gardens,
daring to tread on the forbidden grass.

We tiptoe through the south wing door,
and tread gingerly down the dark corridors
passing rooms where priests are snoring.

Winter of discontent

I came back to Sydney refreshed from working in a new environment away from UWS, and I moved into Catherine's apartment in Crows Nest. Unfortunately, the afterglow of a northern hemisphere summer led to an approaching winter of discontent as soon as I returned. The executive dean of the college welcomed me with relief in his voice, 'Well, I'm glad you're back,' and burdened me with the details of a leadership crisis in the school while I had been away. The acting head had struggled to keep the peace and had fallen ill. But there was worse: the dean told me bluntly, 'Now you are here, you need to address a $2.5 million deficit, the legacy of the latest restructure.' I was crestfallen because this meant more organisational change. There would soon be blood on the floor! I was no longer simply the Head of Music but a senior manager in the college, with no time at all for creative pursuits. I was imprisoned by insidious managerial duties that included pressuring colleagues to accept funding cuts and redundancies.

Things got even worse. I suffered a ruptured appendix and needed urgent surgery. I came out of recovery on 11 September 2001, heavily drugged and catheter'd, waking up to staff gazing at television sets in my ward, watching planes crashing into New York hi-rise buildings. It was my first time in a hospital. The terrorist attack on New York contributed to my disorientation and trauma. It felt as if my body and the world were under threat. My recovery was slow, with some complications, but I kept thinking that I had to get back to work to sort out the mess.

Returning to UWS meant endless meetings, and encounters with angry staff and students from Theatre and Fine Arts. Factions were forming as the impact of the cuts loomed. The then two Associate Heads of School, part of my managerial support, became adversaries.

My vision for a multi-performing arts school in western Sydney, analogous to the West Australian Academy of the Performing Arts, had all but faded. I wasn't happy to work there now. Theatre Performance students were accustomed to a generous staff–student teaching ratio, more than any other students in the School. They expected acting, singing and fencing lessons, productions and industry showcases for scouting theatrical agents. There was now a 'moat' around their course. Even their teachers went cold on the idea of collaborative work that was engaged with other disciplines in the School. Running an acting course required a disproportionate amount of the budget. Theatre students went on the warpath in the press, vilifying the university and trying to embarrass me because they believed it was I who wanted to close them down. This was a misguided judgement. It committed me to working towards a solution that involved a partnership with the Riverside Theatre to support the acting course while searching for philanthropic money.

Dance had another problem. It lacked direction and saw itself as mainly producing dance teachers rather than performers. The enrolments declined. Ironically, they enjoyed some of the best dance facilities in the country. Dance became an easy target. The course ceased and the staff took redundancies. Meanwhile, the Fine Arts course, which had become top-heavy after absorbing staff from other members during the amalgamation, became unfinancial.

I began to drown in a toxic environment as I was increasingly targeted for a perception that I was supporting the 'death by a thousand cuts' approach by the University. I was like a kangaroo in the headlights and still recovering from my illness. Having to shed staff, cut contact hours, reduce space allocations was not a role I enjoyed. It needed someone a little more ruthless. I felt ill and emotionally drained and went to find the executive dean late on a Friday afternoon to tell him I wanted out. He said, 'Don't back down, we can sort it out on Monday.' But I had made my mind up. On the weekend, I wrote a letter to the vice-chancellor, resigning as Head of School and requesting leave to manage my health.

12

DEAN'S UNIT

Searching for ma – *the silence that shapes the sound.*

I was so troubled that I came within a whisker of giving up my professorial chair and leaving the university for good. There was a festival director's job coming up. I applied half-heartedly and didn't get an interview. Just as well, because there were better times ahead for me at UWS. The dean of the college had formed a team including an Associate Dean (Research), an Associate Dean (Teaching) plus a College Manager and a College Financial Controller. The incumbent Associate Dean (Research) took extended leave to write fiction. The dean invited me to act in the position. So, while the organisational change was rolling on and the staff shedding continued, I became part of the inner sanctum. I moved to the Dean's Unit on the Bankstown campus in 2002. This was an easier M5 drive home to my new accommodation in North Sydney.

My brief as Acting Associate Dean (Research) was to increase postgraduate numbers, improve supervision quality and build completion rates, and assist the dean in the development of research. I felt whole again and relished the opportunity to present occasional lectures for Music colleagues and join in concerts and seminars. I stayed in that role for two years. The incumbent left to join a research centre. The university advertised the position internally. I applied successfully. It empowered me to forge ahead with a team-based, negotiated development of research and research training. I could also supervise a small cohort of PhD students in a range of topics, including performance, composition, ethnomusicology, music and literature, and music therapy.

I had time as a supervisor to shower my doctoral students with attention. It's beyond this book to mention them all, but some of their projects and how they applied themselves made me joyful through their interaction. Composer and violinist Hollis Taylor's research on the pied butcherbird was brilliant. It's taken her around the world. Peter McKenzie, an Aboriginal elder from La Perouse, produced a fabulous portfolio of songs, recordings, poems, photos and a thesis on intergenerational Indigenous music history in New England. Alison Creighton's PhD used communicative musicality to look at the role of songs in the mother–infant relationship. And Paul Koerbin, a multi-instrumentalist and expert in Turkish bağlama, wrote an intellectual tour de force in his account of the music of Pir Sultan Abdal, an important sixteenth-century figurehead of the Alevi, a religious minority in Türkiye.

In 2004 I was over the moon. Catherine and I were married in our rented apartment in Kirribilli. There were no bagpipers in the Great Hall this time, rather a modest but lovely civil celebration in the loungeroom, looking over Fort Denison and the Sydney Opera House. It was a significant occasion for being able to share the ceremony with Emily and Marc and to bring my parents, John and

Gisela, together with Catherine's parents, Anatol and Dawn. Bringing the long-divorced John and Gisela together on the same day was a crucial consideration in choosing the time and place. Catherine and I had talked about a wedding to share with our parents and my children, and when the dates looked good, I pounced. Indeed, I told my colleagues not to expect me at work for a couple of days. I booked a celebrant, ordered champagne and gourmet food, and we tied the knot on a sunny July day.

The Associate Dean (Research) takes two days off to get married. *l-r:* Me; Catherine; her mother Dawn; my mother Gisela; Marc; Anatol, Catherine's father; Emily; and John, my father.

And behold, Jared Bryce Atherton was born in July 2005. I became a father again at 55. Catherine was 41. She had popped the question – should we or shouldn't we? – half expecting me to say no, but I said life isn't a rehearsal. Let's go for it. Our parents were instantly besotted, especially Dawn, who became a first-time grandma at 79. Anatol, 91, had eight grandchildren from two earlier marriages, whereas John, 85, and Gisela, 78, had six grandchildren.

Working in a research leadership position was a halcyon period for me. I assisted the college dean in growing the research centres, Writing and Society; Social Justice and Social Change; Religion and Society; and Critical Psychology. The demons of the last toxic restructure were exorcised, and I felt free again, basking in the afterglow of the research success of the college. Postgraduate numbers were increasing rapidly and completions came rolling in. This bought extra Commonwealth funding to the college, and research-active staff in the centres pulled in substantial grants. The college publication profile increased exponentially. It was a propitious time for me. It overlapped the work on the Aurora Festival and travelling overseas to perform in Paris and New York. I was writing and publishing again.

Improvising percussion in the recording studio, University of Western Sydney, 2007. Foreground: Talempong (Sumatran gongs); water drum, buk (Korean drum); and rototoms. Photo: Peter Mackenzie

Sync: experiments in music technology

In 2005, when I was ensconced in a senior management role as Dean of Research at the Western Sydney University, I chaired the interview panel for Garth Paine, who was applying for a music technology position. Garth was appointed, and we became colleagues and close friends. He was interested in experimental, interactive sound environments, although he had begun his career as a flute player in the Tasmanian Symphony Orchestra before studying for his doctorate.

I was able to improvise with Garth in between the commitments of my academic leadership role. We formed an electroacoustic duo called Sync, to focus on the interface between acoustic and electronic music. Sync was an experimental ensemble for diverse instruments and live electronics, including the processing of live acoustic input, cross-synthesis and synthesis artefacts. It was a composition and performance collaboration seeking to contextualise ancient and modern musical languages within a single form. My oud, hurdy-gurdy, marimba, waterphone and percussion were the sonic foundation for complex live electronic processes developed by Garth. It was about blurring the notions of instrument, composition and performance. We could use a Wacom Drawing Tablet, for graphic designers, as a control surface for live performance. Garth could discard the constraints of the laptop, the usual platform for an electronic musician, and draw on the tablet to produce and modify sounds. Such experiments were developed into a CD album. One of the works was 'Al Anbiq Dialogue' in which the timbres of a Turkish oud were used as the template to bring to life a range of other sounds achieved through cross-synthesis. It was a kind of genetic engineering, drawing on the signifiers of different musical traditions, to create a fresh and invigorating voice.

Another track, 'Encounter', explored the rich sonic potentials of my hurdy-gurdy, from fluttering sympathetic strings to bold and substantial drones. The hurdy-gurdy acts as the catalyst for a wide range of electronic colours derived from the acoustic input and augmented by the synthesis, in a dialogue that explores what it means to bring these widely divergent musical heritages into the same musical space.

Although only a part-time project, Sync was invited to participate in several festivals. Highlights were going to Paris in 2006 and New York in 2007. In Paris we went to IRCAM, short for Institut de Recherche et Coordination Acoustique/Musique (The Institute for Research and Coordination in Acoustics/Music). This is a prestigious research environment founded by modernist composer and conductor Pierre Boulez. It is situated in the Place Igor Stravinsky, next to, and organisationally linked with, the Centre Georges Pompidou in Paris. IRCAM is one of the world's largest public research centres dedicated to both musical expression and scientific research. Much of the institute is located underground, beneath the Stravinsky fountain to the east of the buildings.

NIME is the acronym for New Interfaces for Musical Expression. It is a research entity that assists a different country each year to host a conference. Both IRCAM and NIME included Sync as performers in the 2006 and 2007 programs. It was the perfect forum for Sync. We met developers of new instruments and computer composition.

Sync was invited to New York the following year to catch up with friends at the Electronic Arts Festival. Garth and I enjoyed the support of the legendary Joel Chadabe, an international pioneer of interactive music systems. Not only did he introduce us to a cohort of leading composers, but he took us to the best Jewish delicatessen in the Bronx. It was Matzo ball soup and pastrami heaven. I was able to take Catherine and our two-year-old son Jared to New York. When I wasn't busy with workshops and seminars, we took daily walks through Central Park – everyone's back yard – where we saw fashionably dressed women walking their pooches. We found the John Lennon memorial there. Catherine took us to see the Alice in Wonderland sculpture. She had sat on this as a child visiting her grandparents, who lived in New York, and wanted to take a photo of Jared in the same place.

Unfortunately, Sync fizzled out because Garth and I lived too far apart to develop new programs. However, I was pleased that we made some recordings, and that Garth went on to secure a permanent job in the USA.

In 2016, I teamed up with music technologist and composer Jon Drummond to explore electroacoustic music further. We have performed live on ABC Radio and presented concerts in art galleries and other spaces. Much of what we play involves my hurdy-gurdy, waterphone, hand pan percussion instrument and wind instruments. Like Sync, we must fit in around other activities. Jon, who was a PhD student in my faculty at Western Sydney University, is now a busy associate professor at Newcastle University, NSW.

Melismos

Harry Vatiliotis, while supporting my ancient Egyptian project, urged me to explore ancient Greek music, too. So I formed Melismos, again working with Mina Kanaridis and Philip South, to meet the challenge. This was workable because some songs and instrumentals survive on stone tablets and papyrus, including lines from Euripides' play Orestes, circa 408 BCE.

Harry loaned me an *aulos* (a double-reed instrument with a cylindrical bore), a trigonon (an angle harp with twelve or more strings), a *pandourion* (a small, 3-stringed lute), a kithara (a seven-string lyre plucked and strummed with a plectrum) a *psythyra* (ladder-shaped rattle), and a *tympanon* (a hand-held frame drum).

I contributed a *syrinx* – a raft-shaped set of six cane tubes (panpipe) I made from bamboo. Next, I fashioned a *photinx* – a transverse six-holed flute. I collected primary musical sources from facsimiles of holdings in the British Museum. There are also books with considerable information on literary texts. Some of the manuscripts were missing notes, and I had to interpolate material based on the intervals and rhythms. And for arrangements, I studied poetic imagery and metaphor, tone, and scansion.

I asked Professor Kevin Lee, from Classical Studies at Sydney

University, to advise Mina on the pronunciation of ancient Greek. Meanwhile, Phil adapted frame drum techniques from Turkish music. Melismos played at the Greek Festival of Sydney. We toured the group to festivals and accepted live broadcast opportunities on ABC Radio.

Melismos ancient music trio, 1998. *l-r*: Mina Kanaridis (sistrum made by Michael Atherton); Philip South, tympanon (frame drum); and Michael Atherton (kithara by Harry Vatiliotis). Photo: Tod Clarke

Songs of Stone and Silence

In 2008, I made a field trip to research a new vocal composition. I drove 20 kilometres from the Sydney CBD to visit the Ku-ring-gai Chase National Park and find a path into the bush called the Elvina Track, which runs off West Head Road. Here I found one of the many thousands of art galleries in NSW: not a corporately sponsored brick and mortar building, but a fabulous embodiment of Indigenous culture engraved into the sandstone. The rock pavements lie exposed between hardy and colourful native flora, covered in engravings made by the Ku-ring-gai custodians of the area thousands of years ago when they painstakingly abraded the sandstone to create outlines of totemic animals.

I live just 30 kilometres from this ancient spiritual place and feel privileged to see the imprint of people, just as I was when I visited Neolithic tombs and circles in Cornwall and Brittany. Further, I have found inspiration in the hill forts and stone walls of Ireland, and the cairns of Scotland. These structures proclaim longevity, robustness, and the sharing of history over aeons.

My curiosity about Aboriginal rock art was first aroused by Burnam Burnam (1936–1997), whom I consider a hero. He was a Woiworung-Yorta Yorta activist, storyteller, and writer, and taken from his family as an infant. In 1988, during bicentenary celebrations, Burnam 'landed' at Dover to 'invade' England. He erected an Aboriginal flag and proclaimed he would offer the British a negotiated peace. He promised no harm to England's 'native people', nor would he poison their water, lace their flour with strychnine or introduce them to alcohol and toxic drugs.

In his preface to Stanley and Clegg's *Field Guide to Aboriginal Rock Engravings* (1990), Burnam visualised the Australian continent as a vast art gallery of rock art dating back many thousands of years. This inspired me to discover how important are the special places where engravings are visible, where there are bush flowers, animals, and connections to the people that live and lived in the area. Their art makes a connection between past and present. I realised that I live in a city connected to and surrounded by the richest heritage of prehistoric engraving sites in the world.

I became absorbed in two series of poems by David Campbell (1915–1979), an Australian poet whose superb lyricism deserves more recognition. The titles are *Ku-ring-gai Rock Carvings* and *Sydney Sandstone (Rock Carvings)*. Some of Campbell's poems reflected my experience of the Elvina track. I composed a work for the Sydney group Halcyon, featuring its two sopranos.

Campbell's use of poetry to comprehend the spiritual and aesthetic footprint of the Indigenous Australians was inspiring. I wanted to use music to move the listener, to contemplate the significance of non-written histories and to see through the poet's imagination the beauty of the flora and fauna in places such as Ku-ring-gai Chase. Words in the poem 'Lyrebird' suggested the title, *Songs of Stone and Silence*.

> The lyrebird dancing in a trance
> Of stone and silence makes
> A song in amber sweeter than the pause
> Between the honeyeaters sipping notes.

I chose sixteen four-line poems selected from both series and rearranged them in four groups before I set them to music. Stones and rocks are recurrent words that are thematic. They suggest eternity, like the captured, frozen moments in the rock engravings.

Songs of Stone and Silence was supported by a commission from Ars Musica Australis. The work included piano, bass clarinet, cello and clapsticks. It was first performed at the Aurora Festival in 2008 and broadcast live by ABC Classic FM. I am grateful to Mrs Judith Campbell and family for permission to set her husband David's poems to music, and to his biographer, John Perse, for helping me contact the family.

Community music

Looking back at my humble beginnings in music as a late-starting, self-taught rock-and-roll guitar player, I'm convinced that any opportunity for involvement in music is potentially life-changing. We are innately musical in our capacity for expression. Therefore, I don't subscribe to dichotomies such as classical versus popular. Hard boundaries don't exist. They are just stereotypes.

Community involvement has always been as important to me as music in the academy. I remain open to unusual musical instruments and combinations of the same, folk and vernacular music, and, as described earlier, music in wellbeing and therapy. So, when in discussion with Matthew Hindson, the visionary director of the 2008 Aurora Festival, I pitched an idea for a musical event that would attract first time performers and a new audience. His eyes lit up when I said it involved utes! I explained why.

Utility Horn Groove

In 1933, a Gippsland farmer's wife wrote a letter to the Ford company and asked, 'Can you build me a vehicle that we drive to church in on Sunday without getting wet, and my husband can use it to take the pigs to market on Monday?' So the idea of combining a car and a truck was something that Llew Bandt, a junior designer from Geelong, came up with. He took the 1933 model coupe and built a back on it and strengthened the chassis so that it would carry the load. The design was approved, and it went into production in 1934. From the front, it's just a very nice Ford coupe passenger car. At the back, of course, is the workhorse part of it. But inside, this is exactly what the farmer's wife from Gippsland wanted. She wanted wind-up windows, she wanted comfortable seats, she wanted a roof that didn't let the rain in, and Llew Bandt provided just the car for her.

I composed music for cars, their horns, and their revving engines. Car horns in a musical context were not new, but a 'concerto' featuring a great Aussie icon, the ute, may have been a first. It was a combination of orchestral and jazz-rock instruments, spoken word, hip-hop, rap, Javanese gamelan, contemporary dance, and the audience. It was an experiment in postmodern mayhem conflating harmony and noise. I thought of it as a 'sonic circus', and this is how it worked.

I contacted the Campbelltown Arts Centre to help me find five utes for the project. The president of the NSW Ute Club thought I was a 'whacko' when he received my request, but he found me five curious and enthusiastic ute owners. I asked them to meet me in the car park in the Centre after work. Their impact was stunning. The driver-owners arrived in customised utes, each painted in a different colour of metallic paint with chrome details. The spectacle thrilled me. None of the drivers had ever played a musical instrument or done any acting. I reassured them it wasn't a problem; I wouldn't embarrass them, rather help them enjoy a fun event. They were to be the stars. I wanted them to sound their horns on cue, to rev on cue and to do a little acting. One of them said, 'I didn't think no car could make such nice music!' His ute's bonnet featured spray-painted sharks. 'It's a miracle what you can do with a bit of practice.'

I composed a jazz-funk piece for horns, brass, synthesizer, vibraphone, bass, drums, timpani, and chimes. I added a DJ turntabler whose job it was to entertain the audience as it built up, to inject sound effects when the utes were revving.

I went to see the late Chris Belshaw, a legendary Head of Music at St Andrew's Cathedral School. She loaned me ten tuned 'mag' wheels. I recruited students from a local school. The Arts Centre found me two sixteen-year-old rappers. I wrote a script, gave them cue points and asked them to improvise on my text.

We rehearsed twice before the performance, by which time I had worked out some choreography for the utes and a series of horn-honking, light-flashing and revving manoeuvres. They were shy about my last request. On cue, I wanted them to jump out of their utes and simulate a road rage skirmish, followed by a hug and back into seats for the finale. Occupational Health and Safety was paramount. The Centre set up a no-go zone with ropes and witches' hats for the entrance of the utes. I once was responsible for the public burning of a decrepit piano for a festival event at my university. I hired firefighters to be on standby.

The performance exceeded expectations. The event was free, and many of the audience had never been to the Campbelltown Arts Centre before. High octane utes and fusion music met. The DJ warmed up the crowd; the utes arrived in a line, circled and parked in a horseshoe shape in front of the band. No burnouts were allowed!

I set the scene with a short narrative about the ute as an Aussie icon, and the band cut loose, leading into the rappers, doing a call and response with the audience. The mag wheel players had their short interlocking ostinato. I waved my baton and somehow it all came together. Mission accomplished.

There was a lot of publicity before and during the event. Reuters interviewed me, and they shared it with forty different countries. When asked why a professor was doing something so offbeat, I said, tongue-in-cheek, 'It's all about the traffic jam of life. I hope you enjoyed the humour in *Utility Horn Groove*.' My title was inspired by one of my musical heroes, Frank Zappa, who named his studio the Utility Muffin Research Kitchen.

Utility Horn Groove was a hit with the audience, but the combination of cars and a cast of musicians, dancers and rappers meant the music was unlikely to be repeated unless the conditions were favourable. However, another opportunity did come my way to create a community music event, this time involving motorbikes.

Sonic Boom

The Powerhouse Discovery Centre (PDC) at Castle Hill wanted to celebrate its fifth birthday, in 2012, with an eclectic open day program. It invited me to be a guest artistic director to celebrate music and technology with rare and curious sound-producing objects, motorbikes and mayhem, hands-on heritage pianos and music-making fun!

I planned several musical sequences which I called: 'Rare and Curious', 'Hands on Heritage', and 'Heralding the Past' – culminating in a contemporary and light-hearted spectacle, '*Rev'n*', composed for Harley Davidson motorbikes, three drum kits, two opera singers, a synthesizer player, rap artists and narrator. The day was itself 'composed' in such a way that visitors would become involved.

I began with 'Rare and Curious' musical instruments from my

collection and those of the PDC. It was great to do this in the storehouse, surrounded by rare pianos and a myriad of other objects. Members of the audience stepped forward willingly to join me in playing the instruments. This led nicely into the next session called 'Hands on Heritage', in which they invited visitors to queue and sit alongside pianists seated at pianos chosen from the collection. The pianists played specially composed left-hand ostinato patterns and grounds, while the visitors improvised their melodies on the black keys.

I counterpointed the above sequences with a trio of brass instruments that played composed fanfares at different locations in and around the displays throughout the day. While the aim was festive, I chose brass instruments to reflect on the transport collection and the workers' bands that contributed to the fabric of our social and cultural history.

The finale also had music, transport and technology connected. 'Rev'n', as I called it, was a 30-minute outdoor music spectacle composed for the day, in front of a lawn between two driveways. I'd persuaded members of a Harley Davidson motorbike club to feature, to which I added drum kits, brass instruments and electronic sounds. I remembered how the opera singer, Howard Spicer, dressed all in leather, used to ride up to school concerts on his Harley and wheel his bike into the hall while singing an aria. His sense of fun inspired me and 'Rev'n' began with the audience standing up to sing the national anthem, which was also revved 'melodically' offstage by the motorbike throttles.

The bikes entered, with one of them carrying Motodiva, the soprano, to the stage. The drum kits then tried to overpower each other. Motomacho, the tenor, stood up in the audience to woo Motodiva in a love duet. They were followed by a rapper before another duet. I then asked the beatboxer to introduce a finale that involved the audience playing car wheel rims, vuvuzelas, shakers and rattles made during the day. I gambled on putting 'Rev'n' together in only two rehearsals, as well as on the weather. It was unseasonably wet. But the rain held off, and the show went on. I used the opportunity to have a go at writing a rap lyric:

> Call me Jay Tee, you know I'm cool,
> I belong to the Harley-D school,
> I own a knucklehead bobber
> and a shovelhead chopper.
> I'm the masta, I buzz past ya,
> I'm the kinda rider
> who can rhyme when he hasta
>
> Gas up and go, I'm lean and slam
> See me rev'n baby, I am your HD man.
> I'm the masta, I buzz past ya,
> I'm the kinda rider
> Who rhymes when I hasta.
> See the motadiva
> and a moto-machoman
> Riding their Harleys
> And getting it on
> Two love birds
> Who love the leather
> And riding with the gang
> And going wherever
>
> Ride a hardtail chopper,
> A supercharged horse.
> Hammer down and crack it,
> Going for G force.
>
> Ride a hardtail chopper,
> With a front-end rake.
> And a V-twin cookin,
> And a highway to take.
>
> Ride a hardtail chopper,
> A carving machine,

With twin foxy pipes.
Keep the shiny side clean.

Ride a hardtail chopper,
Look at the slam,
Check out my leather
It's fully glam.

Ride a hardtail chopper,
Stitching the line.
Chasing the twisties,
The road is mine.

[Chopper = modified bike; Knucklehead and shovelhead = types of Harley; Slam = low to the ground; Hardtail = no suspension; Hammer or crack = to open the throttle; Twisties = bends; Carving = tight steering control; Stitching the line = riding on the broken line in the centre of the road.]

Big Drum Up

Quirky titles were important to me as a way of challenging expectation. I'm proud of my community music creations, *Utility Horn Groove*; *Sonic Boom*; and *Rev'n*. I called my last one *BigDrumUp*.

This was for RiverBeats, a festival in Parramatta. I worked with three community drumming groups, each one maintaining their strong cultural connections: Reef Thunder comprising Tongan, Samoan & Cook Islander drummers; Uruguayan Candombe; and C'darz, a Lebanese wedding music group. There were 100 musicians.

I wanted to discover and share similarities and differences in a multicultural perspective of percussion. We explored each other's rhythmic patterns, textures, and dynamics. I think of composing as a form of sculpting to represent something of our experience of the world, and if it elicits an interactive response from the audience, whether singing, clapping or joining in on stage, it becomes a work of art that one can touch.

Dean's Unit

I ran a public workshop for the RiverBeats performance in the square next to St Patrick's Cathedral and used it to shape the piece. Each group played for the others. Reef Thunder began playing log drums and double-headed side drums. Entire families responded to their director, who asked them to play a series of Cook Islander, Samoan and Tongan beats. It was a high-energy display of Polynesian pride.

The group C'darz was next. Twenty young men of Lebanese, Syrian and Iraqi background played large *debke* drums. It was driving and powerful, the kind of music heard in a traditional wedding ceremony. The energy that passed from Reef Thunder to C'darz flowed on to Uruguay Candombe who pounded their red-painted barrel drums with sticks and bare hands. After each group played, they cheered each other. It was electrifying.

Later, after the exhilaration of trading beats and learning a shared sequence, we drummed northwards along Church Street and down to the riverbank to take part in an evening spectacle.

My world was rosy again. I composed choral music, engaged in community music projects, and enjoyed raising Jared with Catherine. We bought a good-sized house in Lane Cove with a generous lawn for Jared to run around. It was next to a park with swings. The local primary school was a short walk away, and I had fun being a school dad again, though I was often mistaken for Jared's grandpa because of my now-white hair. Workwise, I had lingering doubts about staying on at Western Sydney, where I might have put my hat in the ring for a pro-vice-chancellor (research) position that was coming up. I certainly enjoyed a lot of success as a senior manager, playing a role in developing research centres and institutes. But did I want more of the same, more restructuring, more administration and distance from music and the books that I wanted to write?

By the end of 2012, when the neo-liberalisation of the university was becoming diabolical, when the spreadsheet and bottom line ruled everything, and when staff were only valued regarding how much research funding they could bring in, I was ready to say no. I didn't want to return to the Department of Music or head a research centre. I looked at my options, including a post at another university. Indeed, there was an opportunity to apply for the Director of the NSW Conservatorium of Music position. I could run such an entity with my eyes closed, save for one thing: the bitterly divided staff and the legacy of a revolving door of leaders. I had no stamina to fix the mess the place was in. Family life and time to write ruled my decision. I engaged a financial advisor, looked at my superannuation, and negotiated my retirement. Assuming I was selected to lead the Conservatorium, it might have been a fitting bookend for someone whose music career began as a three-chord guitar strummer. But Australian universities and cultural life, in general, were rapidly being eroded by a neo-liberal outlook that looked askance at the creative output as inferior when seeking the holy grail – research grants. In practice, innovative work as research is recognised both economically and socially. I recall vividly the dismissive comments about staff who couldn't manage to hit high-impact journals or score money from the Australian Research Council. Good teaching became undervalued and, simultaneously, face-to-face teaching hours were diminishing rapidly under the rubric of blended learning, with the move to online delivery of lectures and seminars. Students were being short-changed. At least I ensured that the research professors committed to undergraduate teaching.

 At the government level, arm's length funding began to disappear. Ministers intervened to overrule peer-reviewed ARC decisions, and the Australia Council was nobbled.

 On reflection, I had enjoyed good years helping students go on to big things in a more generous and supportive environment. Joining UWS was an honour and a privilege. I enjoyed contributing to the dynamic intellectual environment of a place I nicknamed the

'University of Western Paddocks' because of its six campuses, some of which are on the fringes of the metropolitan area. I was a foundation professor of music, head of a new school of contemporary arts and a dean of research. I also served as acting executive dean and a member of the Academic Senate. In 2018, I would be appointed a Member of the Order of Australia for 'significant service to the performing arts, particularly through music composition, performance and education'.

The time was right. UWS and I had shared nineteen years, longer than my intention to stay for five. As an emeritus professor I could claim an office and visit from time to time to mentor students, so I did not have to sever all connections with university life, but I wanted to look at my daily activities through another lens.

Family selfie, 2023. Front: Ava-Mae, Cristian, Noah. Middle: Jared, Emily, Ciro, Cara, Alessandro, Hidie, Aurora, and Catherine. Rear: Michael and Marc.

CODA

It's a perfect day when I can listen to new music, read words that challenge me, and play for family and friends.

Some people buy a Winnebago and become grey nomads when they retire. In my case, I became a full-time student at the University of Technology. I found myself, once again, looking for new ideas and direction through the lens of education, and enrolled in a Doctor of Creative Arts (DCA) as a post-retirement activity. I planned to write a novel and an exegesis. It became the most intense writing project I have done.

I went back to the myriad references I had gathered on Octavius Beale, who founded the successful Beale Piano company. Beale's life was just as intriguing as his contribution to piano manufacturing. He would be the main character in a novel about happenings in a piano factory.

While developing a plan, the sheer weight of historical material I was discovering on the piano in Australian life overwhelmed me. Indeed, it took over, and I felt impelled to write a cultural study. I jumped ship and completed a PhD, which I morphed into a book called *A Coveted Possession: The Rise and Fall of the Piano in Australia*, published in 2018. It describes the many roles of the piano in Australia as a coveted, necessary and ubiquitous possession, showing how it was woven tightly and intimately into the cultural, social, political and economic life of the nation, particularly during the period of transition from a collection of colonies into a nation-state.

The other book I completed was *In Exile from St Petersburg*, fulfilling a promise to my late in-laws, Anatol and Dawn, and my wife Catherine, to publish the remarkable memoir of her grandfather, a famous publisher and academic, Abram Saulovitch Kagan, a refugee from Lenin and Stalin's Russia and Hitler's Germany.

Had I stayed on in the academy as a research leader or senior manager, I wouldn't have done things that had been on hold for a long time. Since leaving UWS, I have completed a PhD, published three books, and, more importantly, have made time to be around to watch grandchildren arrive and grow. And this memoir in print is much more for them than anything else. I have shared how creativity brings hope and how a career is not necessarily linear. In my case, a belief in celebrating diversity, collaboration and unbridled curiosity was the cornerstone of my self-realisation. When opportunities came along, I moved quickly. Indeed, I used to say to my students and Jared, take the fork when you come to a fork in the road! And what am I doing now? I'm indulging myself in writing and self-publishing poetry, tinkering with landscape and street photography, and learning Welsh. I might have changed my name in 1975, but the Jones remains there. I've traced my 40 per cent Welsh ancestry following a trip to Wales on a spiritual journey to learn this ancient language. Now I understand the connections between my north Welsh and Irish ancestors and the Viking blood from my north German mother. They are the multicultural heritage underpinning my music, and they drive a need to share the same with the world, especially as a proud Australian citizen.

ACKNOWLEDGEMENTS

'No man is an island, entire of itself; every man is a piece of the continent, a part of the main.' (John Donne). I am deeply grateful to people in the web of interconnectedness who have shaped my career. Many names have already appeared in this book. Still, I must thank family, friends, colleagues, mentors, musicians, instrument makers, sound engineers, producers, writers, directors, concert promoters, public servants, politicians, and more. Apologies to those names I can't recall in my seniordom.

Family – Catherine Atherton, Jared Atherton, Rosalind Croucher (Atherton), Emily Atherton, Marc Atherton, Tony and Karen Jones, Jenny and Leon Le Cerf; *Family friends* – Brian Little, Jan Matthews, Don Godden, Alexandra Yuille, Michael and Wendy Feher, Ted Hall, Sandra Ridgewell, Lynn Jackson, Irina Atkins, Barra Boydell, Joanna Anderson, Jan King, Peter & Lorraine Moffitt, Sylvia Enfield, Karen Aspden; *Academic colleagues* – Jillian Maling, Jim Franklin, Diana Blom, Bruce Crossman, John Encarnacao, Michael Whiticker, Ian Stevenson, Andrée Greenwell, Clare Maclean, Leone Palermo, Sue Bell, David Hull, Julian Knowles, Sally Macarthur, Tanya Meade, Andrew Cheetham, Rhonda Craven, Wayne McKenna; *Mentors* – Harry Heseltine, Mary Chan, Ross Steele, David Goldsworthy, Stephanie Wade, Paul Ashton, Gabrielle Carey, Patricia Rovik, Peter Platt, Jim Specht; *Composers* – Nerida Tyson-Chew, Mark Pollard, Ruth McCall, Ross Edwards, Garth Paine, Vincent Plush, Edward Primrose, Matthew Hindson, Christopher Gordon, Stephen Leek, Jon Drummond, Nigel Butterley, Peter Sculthorpe; *Instrument makers* – Peter Biffin, Linsey Pollak, Gerard Gilet, Arnold Black, Justin White, Rodney Berry, Martin and Catherine Healy, Kevin Johnson, Moya Henderson, Mark Binns, Ian Mackenzie, Mark Eliott, Andy Rigby, Peter Hyde, Peter Kempster, Mark Binns; *Music educators* – Richard Gill, Doreen Bridges, Deanna Hoermann, Felicia Chadwick, Karen Carey; *Musicians* – Roger Woodward, Winsome Evans, Jonathan Rubin, Michael Askill, John Napier, Jess Ciampa, Paul Koerbin, Bill O'Toole, Andrew de Teliga, Guy Madigan, Mina Kanaridis, Philip South, Margot McLaughlin, Alan Lem, Margaret RoadKnight, Cathy Summerhayes, Yanawirri Yiparrka, Ros Bandt, Dale Barlow, Rigel Best, Mark Elliot, Hester Wright, Wayne Richmond, Colin Offord, Tony Lewis, Guy Strazzullo, Mara Kiek, Llew Kiek, David Miller, Helena Rathbone, Ted Egan, Paul Brown, Jenny Tebbutt, Andrew Allen, Ingrid Walker; *Health professionals* – Charles Enfield, Belinda Church, Jon Plapp, John Parkinson; *Film makers* – David O'Brien, Gary Steer, Alec Morgan, Curtis Levy, Christine Olsen, Mike Balson, Pip Karmel, Richard Brennan, Richard Frankland, Ursula Kolbe; *Radio and television* – Phillip Adams, Clive Robertson, Jos Davies, Penny Lomax, Maureen Cooney, Andi Ross, Cathy Peters, Jane Ulman, Wendy Mcleod, Craig Preston, Ivan Lloyd, Philippa Horn, Felix Hayman, Andrew Ford, Malcolm Batty, Sylvia Rosenblum, Christopher Lawrence; *Music business* – Shane Simpson, Carillo Gantner, Anne Keats, Jack Carmody, Max Bourke, John Davies, Mary-Jo Capps, Lyndall McNally, Philip Henry, Virginia Braden, Justin Macdonnell, Warren Fahey; *Publishers and writers* – Vincent Plush, Tim Bowden, Peter Skrzynecki, Andras Berkes-Brandl, Veronica Sumegi, Ivor Indyk, Di Quick, Dion Kagan; *Producers and sound engineers* – Mike Gissing, Grahame Rule, Di Manson, Christo Curtis, Dave Connors, Max Harding, Yossi Gabbay, Mitchell Hart, Russell Stapleton; *Theatre* – John Bell, Michael Creighton, Maddie Slabacu, Eckart Rahn, Guy Sherbourne.

GLOSSARY OF MUSICAL INSTRUMENTS

auloi – a pair of double-reed pipes from ancient Greece.

aulos – a single double-reed pipe instrument from ancient Greece.

bağlama – a long lute played in Türkiye, Azerbaijan and Armenia.

banjar – a West African forerunner of the modern banjo.

bendir – a frame drum played through North Africa, originating in the Middle East.

bilbil – a split bamboo instrument played by the Kalinga people.

bilma – clapsticks.

bodhran – a frame drum played with a stick or *tipper* in Irish music.

bombarde – a double-reed wind instrument from Brittany.

bouzouki – a popular Greek long lute.

cittern – a small, flat-backed, wire-strung plucked instrument that emerged in the Renaissance.

cor anglais – a double-reed aerophone in the oboe family.

crotala – a pair of ancient Greek percussive instruments similar to castanets.

crumhorn – a sixteenth-century wind-capped double-reed instrument.

dap (or daf) – a frame drum originating in Persia.

darbuka – an hourglass-shaped drum prevalent in the Middle East.

debke – a folk dance performed throughout the Middle East.

dhol – a double-headed drum played throughout India.

djembe – a West African rope-tensioned goblet drum.

dutar – a two-stringed long lute played in Iran and Central Asia.

ejik – a short-necked spike fiddle in the Uyghur music of western China.

faglong – a fretted bowed lute from the Philippines.

frolong – a long lute from Mindanao.

Gaita Gallega – a bagpipe from northern Spain.

gamelan – an Indonesian ensemble of mainly hand-forged bronze gongs and chimes.

gemshorn – recorder made from a closed, conical animal horn.

guqin – a Chinese seven-stringed board zither.

hourglass drum – a term to describe a drum's shape.

hurdy-gurdy – a lute- or flat-backed fiddle with a keyboard. Its strings are sounded by the rim of a wheel turned by a crank.

kaval – an end-blown flute played throughout the Balkans.

kithara (lyre) – a seven-stringed lyre from ancient Greece.

kubing – a lamellophone (jew's harp) from the Philippines.

koto – a thirteen-stringed zither from Japan.

lagerphone – an Australian percussion instrument made from beer bottle tops attached to a pole.

nagasawaram – an Indian double-reed instrument.

pakkung – a split bamboo buzzer from the Igorot people of the northern Philippines.

pandourion – a small, 3-stringed lute from ancient Greece.

pejogedan – a Balinese ensemble of xylophones for accompanying the Joged dance.

photinx – a transverse six-holed flute from ancient Greece.

psaltery – a small, plucked or bowed, trapezoidal or triangular zither popular in the Middle Ages.

psythyra – a ladder-shaped rattle or xylophone from ancient Greece.

oud – a pear-shaped, fretless lute played throughout the Middle East.

rauschpfeife – a wind-capped, double-reed instrument from sixteenth-century Europe.

rebec – a small, three-stringed, bowed lute.

rewap – a Central Asian long lute of the Uyghur people in western China.

riq – a frame drum with metal jingles, popular throughout the Middle East.

ruan– a four-stringed, circular-shaped plucked instrument from China.

sambuca – an ancient Greek angle-harp with a skin soundboard over a tortoise shell or wooden resonator.

sanxian – a three-stringed, fretless lute from China.

saz – *see* bağlama.

shakuhachi – the traditional end-blown bamboo flute from Japan.

shawm – the Medieval and Renaissance double-reed ancestor of the oboe.

sistra – the plural of *sistrum*, an ancient Egyptian rattle asscociated with the worship of Isis.

sitar – an Indian long lute with a calabash or gourd resonator.

syrinx – the Greek name for a pan flute or pan pipe.

tabor – a double-headed portable side drum in varying sizes, appearing in the Middle Ages.

theremin – an electronic musical instrument invented by Leon Theremin.

tidinit – a plucked lute from Mauritania.

tongali – a four-holed bamboo nose flute from the northern Philippines.

trigonon – a triangular harp from ancient Egypt and Greece.

tympanon – a frame drum from ancient Greece and Rome.

udongo – a clay percussion instrument from Nigeria made from a pot.

uilleann pipes – a bellows-blown bagpipe from Ireland.

vibraphone – a percussion instrument with graduated metal bars laid out like a xylophone.

yangqin – a trapezoidal Chinese struck zither, derived from a Persian antecedent.

zils – small metallic finger cymbals from Türkiye.

www.ingramcontent.com/pod-product-compliance
Lightning Source LLC
Chambersburg PA
CBHW030543080526
44585CB00012B/236